P9-DTJ-057

DATE DUE

DE 4 '97
NO 28 '00
DE 18 '00
NO 7 '03
DE 3 '03
DE 18 '03
JE 4 '05

DEMCO 38-296

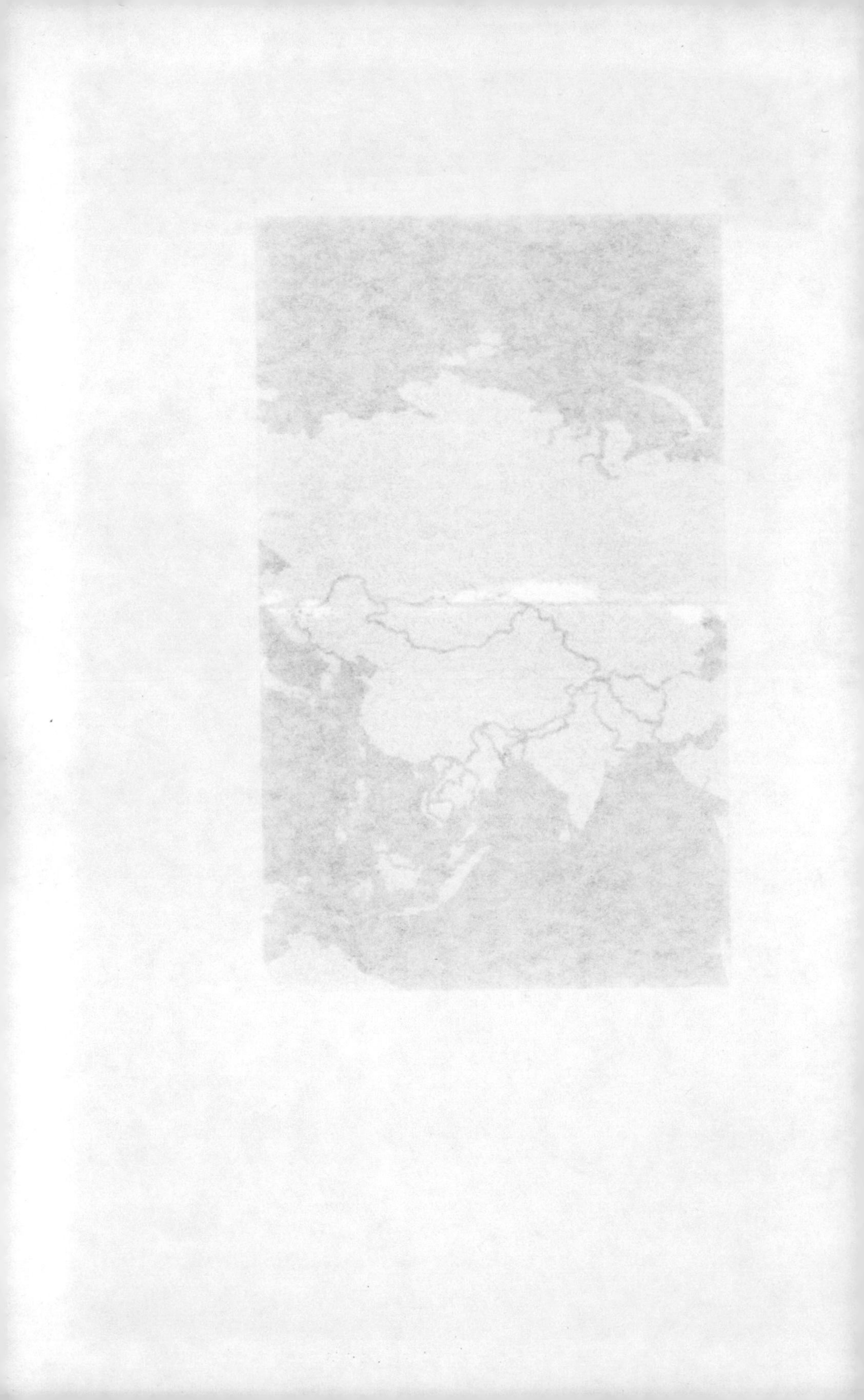

Venezuela
a country study

Federal Research Division
Library of Congress
Edited by
Richard A. Haggerty
Research Completed
December 1990

Riverside Community College
Library
NOV '94 4800 Magnolia Avenue
Riverside, California 92506

On the cover: Oil rigs, Lago de Maracaibo

Fourth Edition, First Printing, 1993.

Library of Congress Cataloging-in-Publication Data

Venezuela : a country study / Federal Research Division, Library of Congress ; edited by Richard A. Haggerty. — 4th ed.
p. cm. — (Area handbook series, ISSN 1057-5294) (DA pam ; 550-71)
"Supersedes the 1976 edition of Area handbook for Venezuela written by Howard I. Blutstein, et al."—T.p. verso.
"Research completed December 1990."
Includes bibliographical references (pp. 229-250) and index.
ISBN 0-8444-0747-X
———Copy 3 Z663.275 .V46 1993
1. Venezuela. I. Haggerty, Richard A., 1954- . II. Blutstein, Howard I., Area handbook for Venezuela. III. Library of Congress. Federal Research Division. IV. Series. V. Series: DA pam ; 550-71.
F2308.W4 1993 92-10376
987—dc20 CIP

Headquarters, Department of the Army
DA Pam 550-71

For sale by the Superintendent of Documents, U.S. Government Printing Office
Washington, D.C. 20402

Foreword

This volume is one in a continuing series of books prepared by the Federal Research Division of the Library of Congress under the Country Studies/Area Handbook Program sponsored by the Department of the Army. The last page of this book lists the other published studies.

Most books in the series deal with a particular foreign country, describing and analyzing its political, economic, social, and national security systems and institutions, and examining the interrelationships of those systems and the ways they are shaped by cultural factors. Each study is written by a multidisciplinary team of social scientists. The authors seek to provide a basic understanding of the observed society, striving for a dynamic rather than a static portrayal. Particular attention is devoted to the people who make up the society, their origins, dominant beliefs and values, their common interests and the issues on which they are divided, the nature and extent of their involvement with national institutions, and their attitudes toward each other and toward their social system and political order.

The books represent the analysis of the authors and should not be construed as an expression of an official United States government position, policy, or decision. The authors have sought to adhere to accepted standards of scholarly objectivity. Corrections, additions, and suggestions for changes from readers will be welcomed for use in future editions.

Louis R. Mortimer
Chief
Federal Research Division
Library of Congress
Washington, D.C. 20540

Foreword

Acknowledgments

The authors wish to acknowledge the contributions of Howard I. Blutstein, J. David Edwards, Kathryn Therese Johnston, David S. McMorris, and James D. Rudolph, who wrote the 1976 edition of *Area Handbook for Venezuela.* The authors also are grateful to individuals in various agencies of the United States government and private institutions who gave their time, research materials, and special knowledge to provide information and perspective. These individuals include Ralph K. Benesch, who oversees the Country Studies/Area Handbook Program for the Department of the Army.

The authors also wish to thank those who contributed directly to the preparation of the manuscript. These include Sandra W. Meditz, who reviewed all textual and graphic materials, served as liaison with the sponsoring agency, and provided numerous substantive and technical contributions; Mimi Cantwell, who edited the chapters; Marilyn Majeska, who managed editing and production; and Barbara Edgerton, Janie L. Gilchrist, and Izella Watson, who did the word processing. Cissie Coy performed the final prepublication editorial review, and Joan C. Cook compiled the index. Linda Peterson of the Library of Congress Printing and Processing Section performed phototypesetting, under the supervision of Peggy Pixley.

Graphics support was provided by David P. Cabitto, who prepared the maps and charts. He was assisted by Harriett R. Blood and Greenhorne and O'Mara. The illustrations for the cover and the title page of each chapter were designed by Kimberly Lord.

In addition, several individuals who provided research support are gratefully acknowledged. Tim L. Merrill wrote the geography section in Chapter 2, prepared several map drafts, and provided sources for several tables included in the Appendix. Janie L. Gilchrist filled gaps in the Bibliography. Special thanks are also due to Karen Sturges-Vera, who provided both photographs and helpful commentary regarding the text.

Finally, the authors acknowledge the generosity of individuals and the public and private agencies who allowed their photographs to be used in this study. They are indebted especially to those who contributed original work not previously published.

Contents

Page

Foreword iii

Acknowledgments v

Preface xi

Country Profile xiii

Introduction xxi

Chapter 1. Historical Setting 1
James D. Rudolph

DISCOVERY AND CONQUEST 4
SPANISH COLONIAL LIFE 6
THE EPIC OF INDEPENDENCE 8
A CENTURY OF CAUDILLISMO 12
THE TRANSITION TO DEMOCRATIC RULE 17
THE TRIUMPH OF DEMOCRACY 24

Chapter 2. The Society and Its Environment 39
Iêda Siqueira Wiarda

GEOGRAPHY 42
Topography 42
Climate 45
Hydrography 46
POPULATION DYNAMICS 48
Population Profile 51
Migration 53
Settlement Patterns 55
SOCIAL STRUCTURE 58
The Elite 58
The Middle Class 59
The Peasants 61
The Workers and the Urban Lower Class 62
ETHNIC GROUPS 63
MODERNIZATION, SOCIAL VALUES, AND RELIGION .. 66
SOCIAL WELFARE 70
Education 70
Health and Social Security 74

Chapter 3. The Economy 79
Daniel J. Seyler
GROWTH AND STRUCTURE OF THE ECONOMY 81
ECONOMIC POLICY 84
Fiscal Policy 84
Monetary and Exchange-Rate Policies 85
LABOR 86
Formal Sector 86
Informal Sector 89
AGRICULTURE 89
Land Policies 90
Land Use 91
Crops 92
Livestock 95
Farming Technology 95
Fishing and Forestry 96
ENERGY AND INDUSTRY 97
Petroleum 97
Natural Gas and Petrochemicals 101
Electricity 103
Mining 104
Manufacturing 111
Construction 114
SERVICES 115
Banking and Financial Services 115
Transportation 118
Telecommunications 122
Tourism 123
FOREIGN ECONOMIC RELATIONS 124
Foreign Trade 124
Balance of Payments 127
Foreign Debt 128
Foreign Assistance 130

Chapter 4. Government and Politics 133
Howard J. Wiarda and Iêda Siqueira Wiarda
THE GOVERNMENTAL SYSTEM 137
Constitutional Development 138
The Executive 140
The Legislature 143
The Judiciary 145
Public Administration 147

Local Government 149
The Electoral System 151
POLITICAL DYNAMICS 153
Political Developments since 1958 153
Interest Groups and Major Political Actors 155
Political Parties 162
Formal and Informal Dynamics of Public
Policy 164
The Mass Media 165
FOREIGN RELATIONS 167

Chapter 5. National Security 175
Richard A. Haggerty

HISTORY OF THE ARMED FORCES 177
STRATEGIC SETTING 182
Venezuela and the United States 186
Venezuela and Colombia 187
Venezuela and Guyana 189
Venezuela and Brazil 191
ROLE OF THE MILITARY IN NATIONAL LIFE 192
Missions 192
Manpower 194
Defense Spending 195
ARMED FORCES ORGANIZATION, TRAINING,
AND EQUIPMENT 196
The Army 198
The Navy 199
The Air Force 200
The Armed Forces of Cooperation
(National Guard) 201
Uniforms, Ranks, and Insignia 202
INTERNAL SECURITY AND PUBLIC ORDER 203
Threats to Internal Security 203
Law Enforcement Agencies 208
The Criminal Justice System 209
The Prison System 210

Appendix. Tables 213

Bibliography 229

Glossary 251

Index 255

List of Figures

1 Administrative Divisions of Venezuela, 1990 xx
2 Topography and Drainage 44
3 Estimated Population by Age and Sex, mid-1985 54
4 Employment by Sector, 1989 88
5 Estimated Gross Domestic Product (GDP) by Sector, 1988 90
6 Petroleum and Mining, 1990 102
7 Transportation System, 1990 120
8 Organization of the National Government, 1990 146
9 Boundary Disputes, 1990 168
10 Structure of the Armed Forces, 1990 198
11 Officer Ranks and Insignia, 1990 204
12 Enlisted Ranks and Insignia, 1990 205

Preface

Like its predecessor, this study represents an attempt to treat in a compact and objective manner the dominant contemporary social, political, economic, and military aspects of Venezuela. Sources of information included scholarly books, journals, and monographs; official reports of governments and international organizations; numerous periodicals; the authors' earlier research and observations; and interviews with individuals who have special competence in Venezuelan and Latin American affairs. Chapter bibliographies appear at the end of the book; brief comments on sources recommended for further reading appear at the end of each chapter. To the extent possible, place-names conform with the system used by the United States Board on Geographic Names (BGN). Measurements are given in the metric system; a conversion table is provided to assist readers unfamiliar with metric measurements (see table 1, Appendix). A glossary is also included.

Although there are numerous variations, Spanish surnames generally consist of two parts: the patrilineal name followed by the matrilineal one. In the instance of Eleazar López Contreras, for example, López is his father's name and Contreras his mother's maiden name. In nonformal use, the matrilineal name is often dropped. Thus, after the first mention, just López is used. A minority of individuals use only the patrilineal name.

Preface

Country Profile

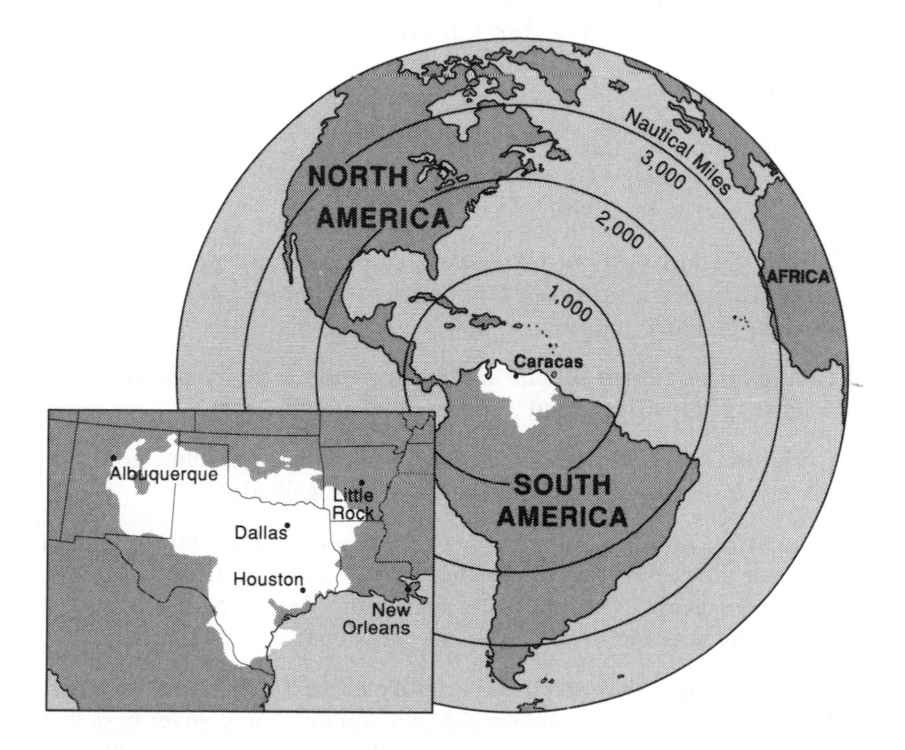

Country

Formal Name: Republic of Venezuela.

Short Form: Venezuela.

Term for Citizens: Venezuelan(s).

Capital: Caracas.

Geography

Size: Approximately 912,050 square kilometers.

Topography: Four well-defined regions—Maracaibo lowlands in the northwest, northern mountains stretching from Colombian border along the Caribbean Sea, central Orinoco plains (llanos), and Guiana highlands in southeast.

Climate: Varies from tropical humid to alpine depending on elevation, topography, and prevailing winds. Rainy season for most regions runs from May through November.

Society

Population: Estimated 19.7 million in 1990. Extremely high average annual growth rate of 3.4 percent from 1950–86; had declined to 2.5 percent by 1990.

Ethnic Groups: About 68 percent of population mestizo (mixed race), 21 percent unmixed Caucasian, 10 percent African, and 1 percent Indian.

Language: Spanish official language. Indian dialects spoken by isolated groups (less than 1 percent of population).

Religion: Over 90 percent nominally Roman Catholic; approximately 5 percent Protestant (mainly evangelical).

Education and Literacy: Over 88 percent of population fifteen years or older considered literate in 1985. Basic education consisted of nine years of compulsory schooling. Best known and oldest university was Central University of Venezuela in Caracas.

Health: Generally good indicators by Latin American standards. In 1990 life expectancy seventy-one years for males, seventy-seven for females. Death rate only 4 per 1,000 population, birth rate 28 per 1,000 population. Average caloric intake 107 percent of minimum established by Food and Agriculture Organization of the United Nations.

Economy

Gross Domestic Product (GDP): Approximately US$58 billion in 1988; per capita income roughly US$3,100. Growth has been tied to status of world oil market. Strong growth during 1970s was followed by rapid decline in early 1980s. Limited economic reforms carried out by administration of President Jaime Lusinchi (1984–89) restored modest growth in 1985–88. Broader reforms instituted by President Carlos Andrés Pérez (1989–) likely to hamper growth in short term in favor of establishing steady growth pattern in long term.

Services: Government and other services (including utilities) accounted for 39.7 percent of GDP in 1988. Commerce accounted for additional 19.6 percent.

Industry: Accounted for a combined 34.8 percent of GDP in 1988.

Subsectors included manufacturing (17.1 percent of GDP), petroleum (12.8 percent), and construction (4.9 percent). Output mostly for domestic market except for processed petroleum and minerals.

Agriculture: Accounted for 5.9 percent of GDP in 1988. Output focused almost entirely on domestic market.

Exchange Rate: Venezuelan bolívar (B) placed on a floating exchange rate in 1989, following a number of official devaluations of currency from 1983 to 1989. In late-1990, exchange rate declined to B43 = US$1.

Exports: Approximately US$10.8 billion in 1989, down severely from 1981 peak of US$20.1 billion. Petroleum and petrochemicals normally accounted for at least 80 percent of export value.

Imports: Approximately US$10.9 billion in 1988, down from peak of US$11.7 billion in 1982. Raw materials represented 44 percent of 1988 imports, followed by machinery (26 percent), transportation equipment (16 percent), and consumer goods (15 percent).

Balance of Payments: Deficit of US$4.7 billion in 1988 mainly result of falling oil prices. Capital outflows and foreign debt payments also contributed to negative balance of payments trend in late 1980s.

Fiscal Year: Calendar year.

Transportation and Telecommunications

Roads: In 1988 approximately 76,600 kilometers—34 percent paved (highest percentage in Latin America), 32 percent gravel. Roads primary means of transportation for both passengers and cargo.

Railroads: In 1988 only 400 kilometers carried 240,000 passengers and freight over two major routes. Main passenger route from Barquisimeto to Puerto Cabello.

Ports: La Guaira, in metropolitan Caracas, leading port. Other major ports included Puerto Cabello and Maracaibo. Other seaports generally served particular industries.

Airports: Eleven international airports and some thirty-six domestic airports. Major airport Maiquetía international outside Caracas.

Telecommunications: About 180 radio stations and over 60 television stations in 1988. Approximately 2.8 million television sets. About 1.8 million telephone lines served 1.4 million subscribers in 1988. Because of inadequate telephone service, some utilities, oil companies, and the military maintained their own systems.

Government and Politics

Government: Functioning representative democratic system established in 1958 after ouster of military dictator Marcos Pérez Jiménez. Constitution of 1961 establishes federal republic of twenty states, two federal territories (Amazonas and Delta Amacuro), a Federal District (Caracas), and a federal dependency consisting of seventy-two islands. Central government divided into executive, legislative, and judicial branches. President, who dominates governmental affairs, elected every five years. Presidents cannot run for reelection until two intervening terms (ten years) have passed. Carlos Andrés Pérez (1974–79, 1989–) first president reelected in post-1958 democratic era. Bicameral Congress made up of Senate and Chamber of Deputies. Members of Congress serve five-year terms, elected from party lists under proportional-representation system. Judicial branch headed by Supreme Court of Justice. No state or municipal court systems; all courts federal courts.

Politics: Mainly two-party system. Democratic Action (Acción Democrática—AD), which adheres to social democratic line, opposed by Social Christian Party (Comité de Organización Política Electoral Independiente—COPEI). AD and COPEI tended to alternate in presidential elections until 1989, when AD's Pérez succeeded fellow AD member Lusinchi. Differences in ideology between AD and COPEI slight; both supported generous social programs and state-directed industrialization efforts until Pérez instituted significant reforms in 1989. COPEI's foreign policy approach somewhat more conservative than AD's. Political campaigns characterized by significant levels of expenditure, particularly on mass media.

International Relations: International outreach and leadership in forums such as United Nations and Organization of American States during 1970s diminished in 1980s as result of economic problems. Foreign policies sought to promote oil exports, to encourage democracy in other countries, and to maintain political stability in the Caribbean and South America. Unsettled border disputes with Colombia (in the Golfo de Venezuela) and Guyana. Other concerns with regard to Colombia included illegal immigration, drug trafficking, and spillover of Colombian insurgent/terrorist groups. Generally close ties with United States.

International Agreements and Membership: Party to Inter-American Treaty of Reciprocal Assistance (Rio Treaty) and Treaty for the Prohibition of Nuclear Weapons in Latin America (Tlatelolco Treaty). Also member of numerous international organizations, including Organization of American States, United Nations and its specialized agencies, Andean Common Market, Organization of the Petroleum Exporting Countries, World Bank, Inter-American Development Bank, Latin American Integration Association, and Nonaligned Movement.

National Security

Armed Forces: In 1990 total strength of the National Armed Forces (Fuerzas Armadas Nacionales—FAN) estimated at 69,000, broken down into 34,000 army personnel, 10,000 navy, 5,000 air force, and 20,000 Armed Forces of Cooperation (Fuerzas Armadas de Cooperación—FAC)—also known as the National Guard.

Military Units: Army organized into five divisions, one for each military region, several independent units in capital area. Navy included main squadron at Puerto Cabello, marine infantry corps, naval aviation command, River Forces Command, and Coast Guard. Air Force organized into three commands: Air Combat Command, Air Logistics Command, and Air Training Command.

Equipment: Armor and artillery assets somewhat antiquated. Major naval vessels—including British-built Constitution-class fast attack craft, Italian Lupo missile frigates, and German Type 209 submarines—purchased during 1970s. Air Force equipped with most modern weaponry, including United States F-16 and French Mirage fighters.

Police: FAC functioned as paramilitary internal security force at national level. Other federal police organizations included Directorate of Intelligence and Prevention Services (Dirección de Seguridad e Inteligencia Policial—Disip) under Ministry of Interior, Technical and Judicial Police (Policía Técnica y Judicial—PTJ) under Ministry of Justice, and Traffic Police under Ministry of Transport and Communications. These three organizations totaled some 8,000 personnel in 1990. Some 18,000 personnel in state, metropolitan, and municipal police forces exercised local jurisdiction. Largest such force was Metropolitan Police Force of Caracas, with about 9,000 members.

Introduction

VENEZUELA IS A COUNTRY that has glimpsed the prosperity that tantalizes so many developing nations. Unfortunately, however, global economic trends and domestic problems combined to nullify the economic gains of the mid-1970s and to push the country into the economic crisis of the 1980s. Although blessed with an abundance of petroleum and other natural resources, Venezuela has been hampered by corruption, mismanagement, and complacency on the part of government officials.

Historically, Venezuela has been in many ways a leader among Latin American nations. The liberation of colonial South America from Spanish rule owed much to the vision of Venezuelans such as Francisco de Miranda and Simón Bolívar Palacios. The nation's postindependence domination by a succession of caudillos was typical of the pattern followed in most of the former colonies. Indeed, until the discovery of oil reserves during the regime of caudillo Juan Vicente Gómez (1908–35), Venezuela was a prototypical, almost stereotypical, Latin American society, with an agrarian economy, an elitist social and economic structure, and a tradition of military rule. The transformation of society that followed in the wake of expanding oil production, however, produced a more educated and politically aware middle class. Representatives of this class, members of the Generation of 1928, led the protest movements that eventually brought democracy to Venezuela in 1945. The reactionary regime of Marcos Pérez Jiménez (1948–58) appeared to represent the last gasp of the old system.

Socially, Venezuelans benefited to a significant degree from the oil boom years of the 1970s. Per capita income became the highest in Latin America, literacy rates climbed, and the standard of living rose for many Venezuelans. Beneath the bright veneer, however, nagging problems festered. Poverty persisted for many. Even for many in the middle class, the prevailing system provided an artificial and impermanent brand of prosperity. The bloated government bureaucracy and heavily protected domestic industries provided employment, but they also strained the resources of a nation heavily dependent on the export of a single volatile commodity. When the bill for years of wasteful spending came due in the 1980s and 1990s, many Venezuelans began to experience a kind of personal privation from which they had previously considered themselves immune.

Economically, Venezuela was a beacon for other Latin American states, a beacon that both attracted emulation and warned of potential danger. The national petroleum company, Venezuelan Petroleum Corporation (Petróleos de Venezuela, S.A.—PDVSA), was a world-class multinational corporation. The country was also a leading producer of natural gas and petrochemicals. By 1990 Venezuela met half of its electricity needs from hydroelectric production, and significant potential power generation remained to be tapped from this source alone. The production of other industries, such as bauxite, iron, aluminum, steel, and gold, appeared poised for expansion during the 1990s if sufficient capital and infrastructure support could be secured. Yet by the 1990s, it had become clear that the public sector, saddled with an oppressive external debt and still reliant on income from the stagnant oil market, could not stimulate the economic growth required in the next century.

By the 1990s, Venezuelan politics had changed considerably since the reestablishment of democracy in 1958. A two-party system, pitting the social democratic Democratic Action party (Acción Democrática—AD) against the Social Christian Party (Comité de Organización Política Electoral Independiente—COPEI), gradually took hold, offering an alternative to direct military interference in the nation's governance. Eventually, the influence of the political parties on many different spheres of life—labor unions, public-sector employment, and the military, among others—came to shape and define Venezuelan life to a significant degree. Beyond its borders, Venezuela also became a leader and an example in both regional and global forums. Oil-rich and politically stable, the nation sought to shape global policy under such activist presidents as Rafael Caldera Rodríguez (1969-74) and Carlos Andrés Pérez (1974-79; 1989-). Economic crisis, however, curtailed such activism in the 1980s and dimmed Venezuela's star somewhat in the international firmament.

The Venezuelan military, the National Armed Forces (Fuerzas Armadas Nacionales—FAN), had also developed since 1958. By the early 1990s, the FAN had become a more professional, better-trained, better-equipped, and better-disciplined force than it was under the regime of Pérez Jiménez. Nevertheless, although the FAN was technically removed from politics, it was not an apolitical institution. Members of the officer corps were known by their party inclinations, and the fortunes of careers rose and fell with the tides of the national balloting. By the 1990s, however, the role of the military no longer appeared to be that of political arbiter, even though participants in the surprising and unsuccessful military coup against President Pérez in February 1992 appeared to be at least partially motivated by a desire to return to such a role. Therefore, the true role of the military was subject to debate. Most signs indicated that the majority of Venezuelans respected military personnel for their professionalism and their traditional image as guarantors of stability and national sovereignty. At the same time, however, the absence of a viable external threat (Venezuela has never fought a war outside its own borders) undercut the FAN's most vital raison d'être. Although internal security was in fact a mission of the FAN, it was not one about which the institution was particularly proud or enthusiastic. With the waning of the global communist threat and the slow disintegration of the regime of Fidel Castro Ruz in Cuba, the FAN will be forced to reassess both its strategic assumptions (e.g., the need to maintain a capability to project power in the Caribbean Basin region; see Glossary) and its order of battle during the 1990s and beyond.

Venezuelan society faced a similar reassessment. By 1992 the old assumptions about the nation's future appeared to be no longer valid. Despite impressive reserves, oil-based growth had proved to be as erratic as that based on any other commodity. The social welfare system, adequate under normal economic conditions, proved insufficient to provide for the basic needs of many Venezuelans under the extraordinary circumstances that prevailed under the second Pérez administration.

President Pérez returned to the country's leadership vowing to restructure an economic system that had appeared quite prosperous and successful during his first term. True to his word, Pérez proceeded to implement policies aimed at opening the Venezuelan economy and reducing state intervention, control, and subsidies that distorted that economy's performance. As was true elsewhere in Latin America and in Eastern Europe, however, these major policy adjustments, among them elimination of subsidies and devaluation of the currency, inflicted suffering on the majority of the population, especially the poor. Privatization of state-owned industry also entailed hardship for both lower- and middle-class workers whose jobs were lost in the transition to private ownership.

The irony of the domestic economic program lay in the fact that, macroeconomically, Pérez's policies produced positive results rather rapidly. During the first half of 1991, the gross domestic product (GDP—see Glossary) grew at a very healthy 10-percent annual rate. The administration actually needed to slow the economy down somewhat by cutting back on public spending in order to avoid boosting inflation. Accordingly, the monthly rate of increase in prices slowed from 3.1 percent in July to 1.9 percent in September. Overall, projections held that the country's oil-related GDP would increase by an impressive 8.7 percent and that non-oil GDP would follow close behind at 7.7 percent. Unemployment figures also showed a positive trend, with overall unemployment dropping from 10.9 percent in 1990 to 10.3 percent during the first half of 1991. One worrisome element in the positive trends was that some portion of the increased growth rate was attributable to a rise in world oil prices.

If many Venezuelans complained privately about economic conditions and the performance of the government, groups such as labor unions and university students took their grievances to the street. Some of the worst of these disturbances took place in November 1991. On November 7, the main labor confederations called for a twelve-hour general strike to press their demands for a repeal of gasoline price increases, approval of a wage increase equal to 30 percent of inflation, a reorganization of the social security system, and a halt to the planned dismissal of 300,000 government employees. The actions were effective, slowing transportation and economic activity in Caracas, Aragua, Bolívar, and Carabobo. Rioting reportedly broke out in the state of Bolívar. Confrontations between police and student protesters in Caracas on November 20 left three dead.

Another assumption about Venezuelan society—that drugs were strictly a Colombian problem—also fell victim to the events of the 1990s. It remained true that the major drug organizations operated out of Colombia. By the early 1990s, however, their encroachment into Venezuela, an encroachment that Caracas once viewed as no more than a minor irritant, had become significant. Colombian drug traffickers, under increasing pressure at home, began to expand their operations into Venezuela. The porous frontier region between the two countries had always facilitated some level of smuggling, illegal immigration, and guerrilla movement. The intensity of transshipment and money laundering activity, however, rose dramatically as the Cali Cartel, allegedly with the assistance of Sicilian organized crime families, began to exploit the infrastructure of Venezuela's export-minded economy. The drug dealers also reportedly benefited from contacts with corrupt Venezuelan politicians. As a result, estimated annual cocaine exports to the United States through Venezuela rose from 88 tons in 1990 to perhaps 220 tons in 1991. In addition to the possibility of increased domestic drug consumption, the rapid expansion of this illicit commerce threatened to eat away at the foundations of a society already suffering from the effects of the government's economic shock program.

Despite domestic criticism, Pérez continued, during his second term in office, the foreign activism that had marked his first. The president was a prominent voice in the debate over what policy approach Western Hemisphere nations should take with regard to Fidel Castro's Cuba in light of the collapse of communism in Eastern Europe and the Soviet Union. Pérez argued in favor of expanded ties with Cuba in order to promote democracy in the island nation. Pérez also sought to expand economic cooperation with Colombia and moved to allow tariff-free imports into the Venezuelan market from the islands of the Caribbean. The president's most visible gesture took place in late September 1991, when he accepted as an exile the ousted president of Haiti, Jean-Bertrand Aristide. The administration strongly supported Aristide, a Roman Catholic priest and a devotee of liberation theology (see Glossary), and helped push for the embargo of Haiti eventually adopted by the Organization of American States (OAS).

In the immediate aftermath, it was not clear what factors exercised the most influence over the participants in the attempted military coup of February 4, 1992. The first news of the uprising came as a shock to observers outside of Venezuela. Coup rumors apparently had been circulating for some time in Caracas; most Venezuelans had heard such talk before, however. Shortly after midnight, troops from at least five army units attacked key sites in the capital and three other cities. One objective of the attacks was to assassinate the president. Reportedly, some small arms rounds did strike the president's office, even leaving bullet holes in his desk. The high command and the overwhelming majority of FAN units remained loyal to Pérez, however, and quelled the uprising within twenty-four hours.

In many ways, the aftermath of the coup attempt proved more interesting than the insurrection itself. Although not supported by the majority, the conspiracy apparently had attracted a significant number of mid-level officers (captains through lieutenant colonels), including many young officers considered to be the "best and brightest" in the FAN. The conspiracy's leader, Lieutenant Colonel Hugo Chávez Frías, seemingly struck some resonant national chords with his postcapitulation statements condemning the corruption and indifference of the government. Some of the residents of Caracas's *ranchos* (see Glossary), or slums, expressed sympathy with the rebellious soldiers. Some members of the middle class echoed those sentiments. Just as the population at large resented perceived corruption among the government leadership and the bureaucracy, so too did military personnel harbor bitterness toward those at the top. The tightening of the defense budget, combined with the general economic woes, also had had an impact on the military. Lower-ranking officers and enlisted personnel, who once had believed that their comparatively comfortable standard of living was secure, increasingly objected to the prosperity of their general officers, a prosperity allegedly based on corruption. If nothing else, the coup attempt almost certainly will prompt heightened attention from the government to military pay and perquisites.

Pérez publicly vowed to maintain his economic policies despite the coup attempt and marked absence of popular support for his government. It appeared likely, however, that government spending on social programs would increase in an effort to respond to popular discontent. The return to prosperity, if it can be achieved, will have to be accomplished equitably. As of the early 1990s, however, that appeared to be a difficult and demanding task.

March 30, 1992

* * *

Venezuela continued to suffer from unusual manifestations of political instability as 1993 approached. Public demonstrations against the Pérez government became regular events. Discussion of Pérez's stepping down before the end of his five-year term in February 1994 was commonplace, not only in the media and among the population, but also among members of Congress. Lieutenant Colonel Chávez, the leader of the February 4, 1992, military coup attempt, assumed the status of a cult figure among Venezuelans who identified with his public statements condemning government corruption. Although coup rumors have long been a staple of Venezuelan political life, such speculations now carried more weight than they had hitherto. This climate reflected a regression of sorts in what had been considered one of Latin America's most stable and progressive democracies. Where once the military had publicly supported civilian rule while privately reserving the prerogative of political action to preserve its own interests, the post-February 4 military openly stood as the arbiter of power, the last and loudest voice in the debate over the country's political future. This state of affairs showed clearly in a May 1992 opinion poll, in which 86 percent of respondents believed a new coup attempt was likely or possible; 84 percent thought that the Pérez administration had failed to bring about significant changes in economic and social policy; and 44 percent expressed the opinion that the military actually ran the country, as apposed to the 9 percent who felt that Pérez did so. In another disturbing statistic, a remarkably high 17 percent of respondents said that Lieutenant Colonel Chávez should replace

Pérez. Chávez came in second in this category, trailing only former president Rafael Caldera.

The continuation of popular discontent seemed to reflect the public's skepticism toward Pérez's efforts to shore up his rule in the wake of the coup attempt. Some of the measures initiated or announced by the president included a temporary halt to monthly increases in gasoline prices; a freeze on electricity rates; price controls on food staples; a surtax on luxury goods; increased government priority to public services, crime prevention, education, and agriculture; and the creation of a special fund to promote the construction of middle-class housing. Pérez even floated the idea of a constituent assembly election, with the goal of drafting a new constitution. In an effort to broaden his government's support, Pérez also brought two members of the opposition COPEI party into the cabinet; he also replaced five of nine Supreme Court justices in response to widespread public perceptions of the corruption and ineffectiveness of the Venezuelan justice system. In addition, Pérez promised to crack down on government corruption. These pronouncements appeared to be widely regarded as lip service, however. One statement in particular prompted derisive comments from the media and the public. "Since the beginning of my term," stated Pérez, "there have been no important or significant cases of corruption."

Public demonstrations, mainly keyed to government economic policy or the issue of corruption in general, began in early March but continued on a regular basis. Although student groups and other radical factions organized the majority of the demonstrations, they drew significant participation from the middle class, often in the form of banging pots and pans, either in the streets or from open apartment windows. The government's reaction to the demonstrations was troubling. Spokesmen routinely dismissed or condemned them as the work of "subversives." Police sometimes employed tear gas and truncheons to break up the larger assemblies. Although officials displayed concern over the implications of public protest, an even more worrisome phenomenon soon appeared, that of terrorism.

On September 23, 1992, two gunmen opened fire on AD congressional deputy Antonio Ríos near the headquarters of the Confederation of Venezuelan Workers (Confederación de Trabajadores de Venezuela—CTV) in Caracas. Although badly wounded, Ríos survived. Police captured his assailants, who claimed to be members of a group calling itself the Bolivarian Movement. The movement reportedly had a "hit list" of corrupt political figures whom it intended to eliminate. On September 27, assailants hurled a small explosive device at the home of former president Jaime Lusinchi. The Bolivarian Movement subsequently claimed responsibility. These isolated incidents served as a backdrop for what may have been an attempt on Pérez's life on October 12 in the town of Paraguaipoa near the Colombian border. Accounts of the incident differed, and the government vehemently denied that there had been an assassination attempt. Apparently, two local residents drove their truck through heavy security and struck the president's bus. The occupants of the truck died in a hail of automatic weapons fire from presidential security personnel. Bystanders also suffered gunshot wounds. Although the incident may have been only the work of "two drunks," as the president maintained, it heightened political tensions nonetheless. The following day, the bolívar (B; for value of the bolívar—see Glossary) fell sharply against the United States dollar, and the Venezuelan stock market also fell.

Despite the fluctuations of the currency and the stock exchange, Venezuela's economic news was not entirely negative. Real growth in the GDP was 10.4 percent in 1991, one of the best economic growth figures for any significant economy in the world. The prospect of free-trade agreements with the Caribbean Community and Common Market (Caricom) and with Chile promised to increase non-oil exports. At the same time, however, the oil industry continued to suffer from stagnant prices and excessive debt. Ever more voices began to call for PDVSA to convert from its state-owned status to that of a publicly traded corporation, with foreign investment allowed, at least to some extent. Like the country as a whole, PDVSA appeared to be suffering from stagnation and corruption, and was badly in need of innovative thinking in order to maintain its place in a rapidly changing world.

October 26, 1992

* * *

The president's position continued to deteriorate during late 1992. Recalcitrant military elements staged another coup attempt on November 27, and COPEI handily defeated AD in gubernatorial elections held on December 6. The coup attempt, which left an estimated fifty dead and hundreds wounded, appeared to have been instigated by the same movement of young officers who had launched the previous *golpe* in February. The fighting, marked by crude bombing attempts against the presidential palace from light aircraft manned by rebel pilots, began early on the morning of November 27. Simultaneously a captured state-run television station broadcast a videotaped appeal for public support by February coup leader Chávez. The uprising was short-lived. Pérez announced some ten hours after the coup attempt began that the capital was secure and that he had dispatched an armored unit to Maracay to help put down resistance there. The motivations for the uprising appeared to be similar to those cited in February. The leadership of the November coup, however, apparently included at least two flag-rank officers, an indication of growing discontent within the FAN. The violence of the second coup attempt served as a graphic reflection of the population's rejection of Pérez's presidency and its disillusionment with the democratic system as a whole. The December 6 elections further illustrated this sentiment: early returns indicated that AD had lost between four and seven of its previous eleven state governorships. As usual in Venezuelan politics, the major opposition party proved the primary beneficiary of the ruling party's troubles: COPEI appeared to have picked up the governorships that AD lost. Although much in Venezuela was in crisis, the two-party system, at least, remained intact.

December 9, 1992 — Richard A. Haggerty

Chapter 1. Historical Setting

Statue of Simón Bolívar Palacios in Caracas

THE TERRITORY THAT BECAME Venezuela lay outside the geographical boundaries of the great pre-Hispanic civilizations of Central and South America. And although it was the first locale in which Christopher Columbus set foot on the mainland of the New World, Venezuela was of only marginal consequence within the Spanish American empire during most of the next three centuries. It was not until the late eighteenth century that the colonial region that encompassed present-day Venezuela provoked, thanks to growing agricultural and trading activity under the auspices of the Caracas Company, more than minor interest from the Spanish crown.

Venezuela's historical significance perhaps reached its peak during Spanish America's struggle for independence during the early nineteenth century. In 1810 it became the first colony formally to declare its independence. Venezuela also provided Latin America with its greatest hero of that era, and perhaps of all time, in Simón Bolívar Palacios. Bolívar, known as "The Liberator," played the leading role in expelling the Spanish colonial authorities not only from Venezuela, but also from Colombia, Ecuador, Peru, and Bolivia. He died in 1830, tragically broken after having seen his dream of Latin American unity shattered by the realities of regional caudillismo (rule by local strongmen, or caudillos).

Venezuela remained marginal primarily because it lacked deposits of gold, silver, or the precious stones that constituted Spain's fundamental interest in the New World. No useful purpose existed during colonial times for the petroleum—dubbed "the devil's excrement" by early Spanish explorers—that oozed out of the ground near Lago de Maracaibo. Venezuela's growing prosperity toward the end of the colonial era was based instead on its flourishing production and trade of cocoa. When the ravages of Venezuela's independence struggle combined with a collapse in the international market to put an end to Venezuela's cocoa "boom," coffee became the nation's principal export. This second phase in Venezuela's agricultural export economy lasted nearly a century, until petroleum became king with the popularization of the internal combustion engine in the early twentieth century.

The petroleum industry in Venezuela began under the control of foreign firms. Beginning in the 1930s, it gradually came under the government's authority. The nationalization of the remaining assets of the foreign oil firms in 1976 represented the culmination of full government control. Nonetheless, the government had little effect on the international price of crude oil, despite the efforts of the Organization of the Petroleum Exporting Countries (OPEC), of which Venezuela was a founding member. Fluctuations in the price of oil during the 1970s and 1980s exercised a commanding impact on the political as well as the economic life of the nation.

In strictly political terms, Venezuela's republican history exhibits a seeming incongruity between the instability and dictatorial rule of the period prior to 1935 and the stability of its post-1958 democracy. Scholars have posited a variety of explanations for this fortuitous transformation, most of which cite the usefulness of vastly increased petroleum revenues that allowed the state to address the demands of virtually every politically active sector of society. The marked decline in petroleum revenues during the 1980s therefore placed significant strains on this political system, which for over two decades had been the envy of the other nations of Latin America.

Discovery and Conquest

Christopher Columbus first sighted Venezuela during his third voyage to the New World, when he saw the Península de Paria from his ship at anchor off the coast of the island of Trinidad (see fig. 2). Three days later, on August 1, 1498, Columbus became the first European to set foot on the South American mainland. Unaware of the significance of his discovery and of the vastness of the continent, he christened the territory Isla de García. He spent the next two weeks exploring the Orinoco Delta. Fascinated with the vast source of fresh water and the pearl ornaments of the native population, Columbus believed that he had discovered the Garden of Eden.

A second Spanish expedition, just one year later, was led by Alfonso de Ojeda and the Florentine Amerigo Vespucci. They sailed westward along the coast of Tierra Firme (as South America was then known) as far as Lago de Maracaibo. There, native huts built on piles above the lake reminded Vespucci of Venice, thus leading him to name the discovery Venezuela, or Little Venice. Subsequent expeditions along the north coast of South America were driven largely by a lust for adventure, power, and, especially, wealth.

Pearls and rumors of precious metals were the initial attraction of Venezuela. By the 1520s, however, the oyster beds between Cumaná and the Isla de Margarita—at the western end of the Península de Paria—had been played out. The next of Venezuela's native riches to be extracted by the Spanish was its people. Slave raiding, which began in the Península de Paria and gradually moved inland, helped supply the vast labor needs in Panama and the Caribbean islands, where gold and silver bullion from Mexico and Peru were transshipped. These slave raids engendered intense hatred and resentment among Venezuela's native population, emotions that fueled more than a century of continual low-intensity warfare. Partly as a result of this warfare, the conquest of Venezuela took far longer than the rapid subjugations of Mexico and Peru.

The prolonged nature of the conquest of Venezuela was also attributable to the area's lack of precious metals and the absence of a unified native population. Venezuela had low priority compared with regions of Spanish America containing vast ore deposits. Moreover, the territory that comprises present-day Venezuela contained no major political force, such as the Inca or Aztec leadership, whose conquest would bring vast resources and populations under Spanish domain. Rather, the conquerors found a large number of relatively small and unrelated tribes of widely varying degrees of cultural sophistication. Some were nomadic hunters and gatherers; others built cities and practiced advanced agricultural techniques, including irrigation and terracing. A number of coastal communities were reputed to be cannibalistic. One of the more advanced tribes, the Timoto-Cuica, was from the Andean region. The Timoto-Cuica (who apparently were not united, but rather comprised a series of "chiefdoms") built roads and traded with the populations of the llanos (see Glossary), or plains, to the southeast, and the Maracaibo Basin, to the northwest.

Spanish slavers established bases at Coro and El Tocuyo, south of Barquisimeto, in the western part of present-day Venezuela. In 1528, however, they were dislodged by a most unlikely competitor; a consortium of German bankers led by the House of Welser, a German banking firm, had been granted a concession by the deeply indebted Spanish crown to exploit the area's resources. For the next twenty-eight years, a series of German governors administered western Venezuela and engaged in a futile search for the fabled riches of El Dorado. The Germans showed no interest in settling the territory. Rather, they tried to extract from it the maximum amount of human and material wealth as rapidly as possible. In 1556 the House of Welser's contract was terminated. The group had grown tired of its vain search for a mountain of gold to match what the Spanish had discovered in Peru and Mexico, and the Spanish had become equally weary of the behavior of their German concessionaires, which was ruthless even by the ignoble standards of the conquerors.

Spanish explorers, in the meantime, pushed eastward from El Tocuyo, founding Valencia in 1555. After more than a decade of fierce fighting with the recalcitrant native population, forces under Diego de Losada established the settlement of Santiago de León de Caracas in 1567. The value of Caracas lay not only in the fertile agricultural lands in its vicinity, but also in its accessibility, through the coastal range, to the seaport that would later become La Guaira.

The vast majority of what is today the territory of Venezuela was left untouched by the Spanish conquistadors. Instead, tireless Franciscan and Capuchin missionaries explored and Hispanicized the Río Unare Basin to the east of Caracas, the Río Orinoco, and much of the Maracaibo Basin during the seventeenth and eighteenth centuries. Much of the western llanos and the south bank of the Orinoco remained unknown territory to the Spanish even at the close of the colonial period.

Spanish Colonial Life

Colonial Venezuela's primary value to Spain was geographic: its long Caribbean coastline provided security from foreign enemies and pirates for the Spanish bullion fleet during its annual journey between Portobelo, in present-day Panama, and Cuba. Venezuela's own form of mineral wealth, petroleum, was noticed as early as 1500, but after being hastily scrutinized, the country's vast deposits were ignored for nearly four centuries.

Venezuela lacked political unity for the first two and a half centuries of colonial rule, in part because it was of no economic importance to the Spanish officials. Before 1777, what we today label Venezuela consisted of a varying number of provinces that were governed quite independently of one another. These provinces were administered from neighboring colonies that the Spanish considered more important. Beginning in 1526, the provinces came under the jurisdiction of the Audiencia de Santo Domingo. Then in 1550 their colonial administrative seat moved to the Audiencia de Santa Fe de Bogotá, which in 1718 was upgraded to become the Viceroyalty of New Granada. During most of the remainder of the eighteenth century, what is today Venezuela consisted of five provinces: Caracas, Cumaná, Mérida de Maracaibo, Barinas, and Guayana. Because these provinces were far from each other and from the centers of Spanish colonial rule, their municipal officials enjoyed a degree of local autonomy unknown in most of Spanish America.

By the late sixteenth century, agriculture had become Venezuela's chief economic activity. The rich farmlands of the Andean region, the western llanos, and especially the fertile valleys surrounding

Caracas made Venezuela agriculturally self-sufficient, and also provided a surplus of a number of products for exportation. Wheat, tobacco, and leather were among the early products exported from colonial Venezuela. The Spanish crown, however, showed little interest in Venezuela's agriculture. Spain was obsessed with extracting precious metals from its other territories to finance a seemingly endless series of foreign wars. As a result, as late as the early eighteenth century, Venezuela sold the bulk of its considerable surplus of agricultural goods to British, French, or Dutch traders, who, under the Spanish crown's medieval notions of commerce based on bureaucratic control and mercantilism, were labeled as smugglers.

Starting in the 1620s, cocoa became Venezuela's principal export for the next two centuries. Cocoa, a powder containing a mild stimulant used in the processing of chocolate, was a native product of Venezuela's coastal valleys. Its impact on colonial Venezuelan society was immense. Its sizable profits attracted, for the first time, significant immigration of Spaniards, including relatively poor Canary Islanders, and its plantation culture created a great demand for African slaves during the seventeenth and early eighteenth centuries. These two population groups would complete a social hierarchy that became virtually a caste system. On top was a small elite of white *peninsulares* (those born in Spain) and criollos (those born in America of Spanish parentage); they were followed by the white Canary Islanders, who typically worked as wage laborers. Next came a large group of racially mixed *pardos* (see Glossary), who by the late eighteenth century made up more than half the total; they were followed by African slaves, who constituted about 20 percent of the population; and, lastly, by the Indians. The native population, decimated by slavery and disease throughout the colonial period, constituted less than 10 percent of the total population at independence.

Enormous profits obtained from the triangular trade of African slaves for Venezuelan cocoa, which was then shipped across the Caribbean and sold in Veracruz for consumption in New Spain (Mexico), made the Venezuelan coast a regular port of call for Dutch and British merchants. In an effort to eliminate this illegal intercolonial trade and capture these profits for itself, the Spanish crown in 1728 granted exclusive trading rights in Venezuela to a Basque corporation called the Real Compañía Guipuzcoana de Caracas, or simply the Caracas Company.

The Caracas Company proved quite successful, initially at least, in achieving the crown's goal of ending the contraband trade. Venezuela's cocoa growers, however, became increasingly dissatisfied. The Basque monopoly not only paid them significantly lower prices but also received favored treatment from the province's Basque governors. This discontent was evidenced in the growing number of disputes between the company and the growers and other Venezuelans of more humble status. In 1749 the discontent erupted into a first insurrectionary effort, a rebellion led by a poor immigrant cocoa grower from the Canary Islands named Juan Francisco de León. The rebellion was openly joined by the Venezuelan lower classes and quietly encouraged by the elite in Caracas. Troops from Santo Domingo and from Spain quickly crushed the revolt, and its leadership was severely repressed by forces headed by Brigadier General Felipe Ricardos, who was named governor of Caracas in 1751.

The growth of the cocoa trade, the success of the Caracas Company, and the assertion of the royal will manifested by the suppression of the 1749 revolt all helped to centralize the Venezuelan economy around the city of Caracas. In recognition of this growth, Caracas was given political-military authority as the seat of the Captaincy General of Venezuela in 1777, marking the first instance of recognition of Venezuela as a political entity. Nine years later, its designation was changed to the Audiencia de Venezuela, thus granting Venezuela judicial-administrative authority as well.

Barely three decades later, however, Venezuela would suddenly—after almost three centuries on the periphery of the Spanish American empire—find itself at the hub of the independence movement sweeping Latin America. Present-day Venezuelans continue to take pride in having produced not only Francisco de Miranda, the best known of the precursors of the Spanish American revolution, but also the first successful revolt against Spanish rule in America and, of course, the leading hero of the entire epic of Latin America's struggle for independence, Simón Bolívar Palacios.

The Epic of Independence

Miranda was born in Caracas of wealthy criollo parents in 1750. Following a checkered career in the Spanish Army, Miranda spent virtually the rest of his life living in nations that were at odds with Spain, seeking support for the cause of the independence of his native Spanish America. Although he was a professed admirer of the newly independent United States, Miranda's political vision of Latin America, beyond independence, remained equivocal. In 1806 he led an expedition that sailed from New York and landed at Coro, in western Venezuela. Expecting a popular uprising, he encountered instead hostility and resistance. Miranda returned to Britain, where in 1810 Bolívar persuaded him to return to Venezuela at the head of a second insurrectionary effort.

Events in Europe were perhaps even more crucial to the movement for Latin American independence than Miranda's efforts. In 1808 French emperor Napoléon Bonaparte's troops invaded Spain amidst a family dispute in which the Spanish king Charles IV had been forced to abdicate the throne in favor of his son, Ferdinand VII. The fearful Bourbon royal family soon became Napoleon's captives, and in 1810 the conquering French emperor granted his brother, Joseph, the Spanish throne, precipitating a four-year-long guerrilla war in Spain.

These events had important repercussions in the Caracas *cabildo* (city council). Composed of a criollo elite whose allegiance to the crown had already been stretched thin by the gross incompetence of Charles and his feud with his son, the *cabildo* refused to recognize the French usurper. Meeting as a *cabildo abierto* (town meeting) on April 19, 1810, the Caracas *cabildo* ousted Governor Vicente Emparán and, shortly thereafter, declared itself to be a junta governing in the name of the deposed Ferdinand VII. On July 5, 1811, a congress convoked by the junta declared Venezuelan independence from Spain. Miranda assumed command of the army and leadership of the junta.

A constitution, dated December 21, 1811, marked the official beginning of Venezuela's First Republic. Known commonly by Venezuelan historians as La Patria Boba, the Silly Republic, Venezuela's first experiment at independence suffered from myriad difficulties from the outset. The *cabildos* of three major cities—Coro, Maracaibo, and Guayana—preferring to be governed by Joseph Bonaparte rather than by the Caracas *cabildo* never accepted independence from Spain. The First Republic's leadership, furthermore, distrusted Miranda and deprived him of the powers necessary to govern effectively until it was too late. Most damaging, however, was the initial failure of the Caracas criollo elite insurgents to recognize the need for popular support for the cause of independence. Venezuela's popular masses, particularly the *pardos,* did not relish being governed by the white elite of Caracas and therefore remained loyal to the crown. Thus, a racially defined civil war underlay the early years of the long independence struggle in Venezuela.

When a major earthquake in March 1812 devastated pro-independence strongholds while sparing virtually every locale commanded by royalist forces, it seemed that the very forces of nature were conspiring against La Patria Boba. Despite the gravity of the circumstances, Miranda's July 25, 1812, surrender of his troops to the Spanish commander, General Domingo Monteverde, provoked a great deal of resentment among Bolívar and his other subordinates. Miranda died in a Spanish prison in 1816; Bolívar managed to escape to New Granada (present-day Colombia), where he assumed the leadership of Venezuela's independence struggle.

Bolívar was born in 1783 into one of Caracas's most aristocratic criollo families. Orphaned at age nine, he was educated in Europe, where he became intrigued by the intellectual revolution called the Enlightenment and the political revolution in France. As a young man, Bolívar pledged himself to see a united Latin America, not simply his native Venezuela, liberated from Spanish rule. His brilliant career as a field general began in 1813 with the famous cry of "war to the death" against Venezuela's Spanish rulers. The cry was followed by a lightning campaign through the Andes to capture Caracas. There he was proclaimed "The Liberator" and, following the establishment of the Second Republic, was given dictatorial powers. Once again, however, Bolívar overlooked the aspirations of common, nonwhite Venezuelans. The *llaneros* (plainsmen), who were excellent horsemen, fought under the leadership of the royalist caudillo, José Tomás Boves, for what they saw as social equality against a revolutionary army that represented the white, criollo elite. By September 1814, having won a series of victories, Boves's troops forced Bolívar and his army out of Caracas, bringing an end to the Second Republic.

After Ferdinand VII regained the Spanish throne in late 1814, he sent reinforcements to the American colonies that crushed most remaining pockets of resistance to royal control. Bolívar was forced to flee to Jamaica, where he issued an eloquent letter that established his intellectual leadership of the Spanish American independence movement. A number of local caudillos kept the movement alive in Venezuela. One, José Antonio Páez, a mestizo, was able to convince his fellow *llaneros* along the Río Apure that Boves (who had been killed in battle in late 1814) had been mistaken: that the Spanish, not the criollo patriots, were the true enemies of social equality. The alliance of his fierce cavalrymen with Bolívar proved indispensable during the critical 1816–20 stage of the independence struggle. Another caudillo chief named Manuel Piar, after outspokenly encouraging his black and *pardo* troops to assert their claims for social change, however, was promptly captured, tried, and executed under Bolívar's direction. This ruthless disposition of Piar as an enemy of the cause of independence enhanced Bolívar's stature and military leadership as the "maximum caudillo."

Based near the mouth of the Río Orinoco, Bolívar defeated the royalist forces in the east with the help of several thousand volunteer European recruits, veterans of the Napoleonic Wars. Although Caracas remained in royalist hands, the 1819 Congress at Angostura (present-day Ciudad Bolívar) established the Third Republic and

Simón Bolívar Palacios
Courtesy Prints and Photographs Division, Library of Congress

named Bolívar as its first president. Bolívar then quickly marched his troops across the llanos and into the Andes, where a surprise attack on the Spanish garrison at Boyacá, near Bogotá, routed the royalist forces and liberated New Granada. Nearly two years later, in June 1821, Bolívar's troops fought the decisive Battle of Carabobo that liberated Caracas from Spanish rule. In August delegates from Venezuela and Colombia met at the border town of Cúcuta to formally sign the Constitution of the Republic of Gran Colombia (see Glossary), with its capital in Bogotá. Bolívar was named president, and Francisco de Paula Santander, a Colombian, was named vice president.

Bolívar, however, continued the fight for the liberation of Spanish America, leading his forces against the royalist troops remaining in Ecuador, Bolivia, and Peru. In the meantime, the Bolivarian dream of Gran Colombia was proving to be politically unworkable. Bolívar's fellow Venezuelans became his enemies. King Ferdinand, after an 1820 revolt by liberals in Spain, had lost the political will to recover the rebellious American colonies. But the Venezuelans themselves expressed resentment at being governed once again from far-off Bogotá.

Venezuelan nationalism, politically and economically centered in Caracas, had been an ever-increasing force for over a century. During the 1820s, Venezuelan nationalism was embodied in the figure of General Páez. Even the tremendous prestige of Bolívar could not overcome the historical reality of nationalism, and in 1829 Páez led Venezuela in its separation from Gran Colombia. Páez ordered the ailing and friendless Bolívar into exile. Shortly before his death in December 1830, the liberator of northern South America likened his efforts at Latin American unity to having "plowed the sea."

A Century of Caudillismo

Two decades of warfare had cost the lives of between one-fourth and one-third of Venezuela's population, which by 1830 was estimated at about 800,000. Furthermore, the cocoa-based export economy lay in ruins, a victim of physical destruction, neglect, and the disruption of trade. As a result, it was relatively simple for the young nation to shift its agricultural export activity to the production of coffee, a commodity whose price was booming in the North Atlantic nations with which Venezuela was now free to trade. The production of coffee for export would, along with subsistence agriculture, dominate Venezuela's economic life until the initiation of the petroleum boom well into the twentieth century. Venezuela's century-long postindependence era of caudillismo is perhaps best understood as a competition among various social and regional factions for the control of the Caracas-based bureaucracy that served the trade with the North Atlantic nations.

The century of the caudillo started auspiciously, with sixteen relatively peaceful and prosperous years under the authority of General Páez. Twice elected president under the 1830 constitution, Páez, on the one hand, consolidated the young republic by putting down a number of armed challenges by regional chieftains. On the other hand, Páez usually respected the civil rights of his legitimate political opponents. Using funds earned during the coffee-induced economic boom, he oversaw the building of fledgling social and economic infrastructures. Generally considered second only to Bolívar as a national hero, Páez ruled in conjunction with the criollo elite, which maintained its unity around the mestizo caudillo as long as coffee prices remained high.

In the 1840s, however, coffee prices plunged, and the elite divided into two factions: those who remained with Páez called themselves Conservatives, while his rivals called themselves Liberals. The Liberals first came to prominence in 1846 with Páez's surprising selection of General José Tadeo Monagas as his successor. Two years later, Monagas ousted all the Conservatives from his government and sent Páez into exile, precipitating a decade of dictatorial rule shared with his brother, José Gregorio. The abolition of slavery in 1854 was the only noteworthy act by the Monagas brothers.

In 1857 they introduced a new constitution in an obvious attempt to install a Monagas family dynasty. The regime was ousted the following year in a revolt that included elite members of both parties.

The elite factions failed to agree on a replacement for Monagas, however, precipitating twelve years of intermittent civil war so chaotic that few history texts bother to chronicle the details. Between 1858 and 1863, local caudillos engaged in a chaotic power struggle known as the Federal War because the Liberals favored federalism. In the end, the Liberals triumphed, and General Juan C. Falcón was named president. In practice, federalism was a disaster. Falcón's general lack of interest in ruling and his failure to exert strong leadership allowed local caudillos to exert oppressive authoritarian control over their fiefdoms even while they continued to pay lip service to the concept of federalism. Central government authority was finally restored in 1870 by Falcón's chief aide, Antonio Guzmán Blanco, who established a dictatorship that endured for eighteen years.

Unlike his former boss, Guzmán understood the politics of federalism. After removing disloyal Conservative regional caudillos by force, he installed a loyal group of Liberal caudillos in their place. Thanks to a rapid expansion of both coffee production and foreign loans, Guzmán had access to considerable resources to maintain his supporters with generous subventions, backed up, if necessary, by federal troops. This formula brought nearly two decades of much-welcomed peace to the Venezuelan countryside.

Guzmán used the increased revenue for additional activities that contributed to Venezuela's national development. Education advanced notably, while the development of a modern governmental bureaucracy and infrastructures for communications and transportation—roads, railroads, port facilities, and telegraph lines—provided vital support for expanding export agriculture. Caracas especially benefited from public works and grew into one of South America's premier cities. The vainglorious Guzmán, who liked to be referred to as the "Illustrious American," dedicated as many of these projects to himself as possible.

Although Guzmán demanded honesty from his subordinates, he amassed a personal fortune that allowed him to live in the kingly luxury he felt he deserved, both in Caracas and in Paris during the intervals when he deemed it prudent to leave the presidency in the hands of a puppet. During one such period in 1888, civil unrest marked by anti-Guzmán rioting by university students in Caracas convinced the "Illustrious American" to remain in Paris on a permanent basis.

The four chaotic years that followed Guzmán's rule were marked by several failed attempts to consolidate a civilian government. A colorless military regime, led by General Joaquín Crespo, spent most of its energies between 1892 and 1898 fighting to remain in power. Crespo was killed in 1898; in 1899 General Cipriano Castro, the first of four military rulers from the Andean state of Táchira, marched on Caracas with a private army that became a strong national army and assumed the vacant presidency. Castro was characterized as "a crazy brute" by United States secretary of state Elihu Root and as "probably the worst of [Venezuela's] many dictators" by historian Edwin Lieuwen. His nine years of despotic and dissolute rule are best known for having provoked numerous foreign interventions, including blockades and bombardments by British, German, and Italian naval units seeking to enforce the claims of their citizens against Castro's government. The subsequent appearance of United States warships in 1902 convinced Castro to acquiesce to a financial settlement. Five years later, however, he again incited foreign naval intervention, this time by the Dutch, who seized a port and destroyed part of Venezuela's tiny navy. In 1908 Castro traveled to Europe for medical treatment; his chief military aide and fellow *tachirense* (native of the state of Táchira), Juan Vicente Gómez, took this opportunity to overthrow the dictator and assume power.

Gómez was the consummate Venezuelan caudillo. He retained absolute power from 1908 to 1935, alternating between the posts of president and minister of war. A series of puppet legislatures drafted and promulgated six new constitutions at the bidding of the dictator, while the judiciary enforced the will of the "Tyrant of the Andes" within the courts.

The dictator's principal power base was the army. Disproportionately staffed with *tachirense* personnel, the army was used to destroy all of Gómez's regional foes. This "national" army was prudently provided with high salaries and generous benefits, the most modern weapons, and instruction from the Prussian-trained Chilean military. But Gómez's most important means of eliminating political foes was his ubiquitous secret police force. Although some opponents escaped with a simple reprimand, many thousands of others, those who did not manage to escape into exile, were locked up—rarely with the benefit of a trial—in prisons where death by starvation or at the hands of torturers was commonplace.

Gómez justified his harsh dictatorship as the form of government preferred by the primitive, mixed-race Venezuelans. He based his theories in part on the racist notions of the book *Democratic Caesarism* by Gómez supporter Laureano Vallenilla Lanz that became

Juan Vicente Gómez
Courtesy Prints and Photographs Division, Library of Congress

official regime doctrine. In accord with these theories, Gómez believed that national development could be undertaken successfully only by foreigners who enjoyed technological superiority to Venezuelans. Moreover, the climate of stability required for this externally directed development process could only be provided—according to Gómez's doctrine—by strong authoritarian rule.

The Gómez regime coincided with a protracted period favorable to Venezuelan exports. Coffee exports boomed, both in volume and price, during the early years of his rule. Most important, however, the foreign exploitation of Venezuela's petroleum reserves began in 1918, augmenting government revenues to a degree previously unknown and allowing Gómez to pay off the nation's entire foreign debt and to institute a public works program. The beginnings of an urban middle class were also evident in the bureaucracy that grew up around the nascent Venezuelan oil industry. The provision of required local services to the oil industry further expanded this new middle class.

The true beneficiaries of the petroleum boom, however, were Gómez, the army, and the dictator's associates from Táchira. For the vast majority of Venezuelans, the petroleum era brought reduced employment (oil being a capital-intensive industry) and high food prices stemming from a decline in domestic agricultural activity and an increase in imports. Inflation increased, and real wages declined. Little improvement took place in public education and health care, and although the capital-intensive petroleum industry grew impressively, oil-derived revenue was not applied to labor-intensive efforts such as agricultural diversification or the promotion of small-scale industry.

Subsequent events recast the students at the Central University of Venezuela, in Caracas, into the most significant opposition to the Gómez regime. Having closely observed the Mexican Revolution of 1910 and the Russian Revolution of 1917, the students launched a struggle in 1928 to liberate Venezuela from Gómez's grip. The revolt began in February, when Jóvito Villalba and two other students were arrested for making antigovernment speeches. In protest, other students then challenged the dictator to jail them as well, and Gómez complied by arresting 200 student activists. A popular demonstration followed. Police dispersed the demonstrators with firearms, killing and wounding many participants. With the assistance of a few young military officers, the rebels then stormed the presidential palace, which they managed to occupy briefly before being overwhelmed by Gómez's troops. Gómez then closed the university and rounded up the students, many of whom ended up laboring on road gangs. Some of the movement's leadership languished or died in prison; those of the Generation of 1928 who managed to escape into exile, like Rómulo Betancourt, Rafael Caldera Rodríguez, and Raúl Leoni, were later to become the nation's principal political leaders.

Two subsequent efforts to overthrow Gómez—executed by long-exiled caudillo rivals who believed that their landings on the Venezuelan coast would trigger popular insurrections—ended in failure. The "Tyrant of the Andes" ruled until his death, by natural causes, in December 1935 at age seventy-nine. The event precipitated widespread looting, property destruction, and the slaughter of Gómez family members and collaborators by angry mobs in Caracas and Maracaibo. Gómez's twenty-seven years in power brought to a close Venezuela's century of caudillismo; and, according to many historical accounts, his demise marked the beginning of Venezuela's modern period.

Although he was not the last of Venezuela's dictators, analysts of contemporary Venezuelan society commonly cite Gómez's lengthy rule as the true line of demarcation between Venezuela's democratic present and its authoritarian past. Although the nation's post-1958 democratic leaders received their political baptism of fire in Venezuela in 1928, their principal political, social, and economic perceptions were formed in exile in Europe, Mexico, or the United States. During the transition years from 1935 to 1958, the outlines of a national democratic political culture, including the configuration of Venezuela's modern political party system, at last began to take shape.

The Transition to Democratic Rule

During the twenty-three years of transition to democratic rule, institutions developed as the military transferred political power to civilians. However, the military was still very dominant, and the death of Gómez left a leadership vacuum that could be filled only by the old dictator's *tachirense* minister of war, General Eleazar López Contreras. After he finished Gómez's term of office in 1936, the Congress, all the members of which had been appointed by Gómez, selected López to serve his own five-year term in office.

When the riots following Gómez's death precipitated demands for liberalizing the dictatorship, López quickly realized that his survival depended on his allowing some civilian political expression. Accordingly, he freed long-time political prisoners and dismantled the worst part of Gómez's repressive apparatus. Exiles returned to establish the first mass political organizations in the nation's history, the most important of which was the Venezuelan Organization (Organización Venezolana—Orve) led by the populist Betancourt. Another surviving leader of the Generation of 1928, Jóvito Villalba, revived the Marxist-oriented Venezuelan Student Federation (Federación Estudiantil de Venezuela—FEV); the Venezuelan Communist Party (Partido Comunista Venezolano—PCV) was also reorganized, although it remained banned from political activities in the revised constitution of 1936. In a related area, liberalized labor legislation encouraged the organization of the nation's first modern labor syndicates.

A highly effective general strike in June 1936, however, led the López regime to the conclusion that the proper boundaries of reform had been crossed. Accordingly, the López government rejected a November application by Orve and other leftist opposition elements for legal recognition of a united National Democratic Party (Partido Democrático Nacional—PDN) and brutally suppressed a strike by oil workers the following month. The regime justified the outlawing of the nascent labor unions in 1937 by claiming that they had engaged in illegal political activities. Soon thereafter, the regime proscribed virtually all organized political opposition.

López decided instead to concentrate his reform efforts in the relatively noncontroversial sphere of economic modernization. The government established a central bank, along with state-controlled industrial and agricultural development banks, opened new oil fields to exploitation, and, employing the slogan of *sembrar el petróleo* ("sowing the oil"), launched a program for developing the national economic and social infrastructure, although at a lackluster pace that led critics to question the program's efficacy.

In 1941 López's Congress selected yet another *tachirense,* Minister of War Isaías Medina Angarita, to replace López. In this respect, it appeared to be politics as usual. A more ambitious economic development plan, announced by Medina in 1942, was interrupted during World War II when German submarines played havoc with tankers transporting Venezuela's oil. New laws governing the state's relationship with foreign oil companies in 1943 resulted in substantially increased revenues, spurring renewed development efforts in 1944. Construction activity boomed during the waning years of the war, a period that also saw the passage of Venezuela's first income tax and social security laws.

Perhaps more consequential, however, was Medina's expansion of the political opening begun by López. The PDN was legalized and promptly changed its name to Democratic Action (Acción Democrática—AD). Its members soon constituted a vociferous minority in local governments and, after the January 1943 elections, in the lower house of Congress known as the Chamber of Deputies (the upper house was the Senate). The president responded by organizing his own political party, the Venezuelan Democratic Party (Partido Democrático Venezolano—PDV), which waged a vigorous campaign and gained a legitimate victory in the crucial 1944 congressional elections. With his party thus assured of control of the 1945 Congress, which would hold indirect elections for president, Medina appeared poised to designate his successor.

To the surprise of many, he chose Diógenes Escalante, a liberal civilian serving as ambassador in Washington. A delighted AD agreed to support Escalante's candidacy. Medina's opposition on the right, however, which had expected former President López to receive the nomination, was incensed by the choice. Fear was in the air during the summer of 1945, as rumors circulated that the forty-six-year-long rule by *tachirenses* was about to be ruptured by a civil war between the *lopecistas* and *medinistas* (followers of López and Medina). Escalante soon became too ill to pursue the presidency, however, and his announced replacement was a colorless figure widely regarded as a puppet of Medina. Ironically, it was not the *lopecista* right that brought the era of *tachirense* rule to a close. Instead, on October 18, 1945, the AD, in conjunction with junior military officers, suddenly overthrew Medina.

The conspiracy to overthrow Medina had been hatched inside the Patriotic Military Union (Unión Patriótica Militar—UPM), a secret lodge of junior officers who were disgruntled over the persistence of cronyism and the lack of professionalism within the

Venezuelan oil worker, ca. 1942
Courtesy Prints and Photographs Division, Library of Congress

tachirense senior ranks. These officers had invited AD to join their plot in June and asked Betancourt to serve as the president of the new government. AD did not agree to cooperate with the UPM, however, until after the October 1 announcement of Medina's replacement for Escalante.

After the coup, Betancourt named a seven-man governing junta consisting of four *adecos* (members of AD), two military officers, and one independent. AD thus controlled the government, and the UPM controlled the military. All officers who had attained ranks above major before the 1945 rebellions—Carlos Delgado Chalbaud, Julio Vargas, and Marcos Pérez Jiménez—were hence promptly sent into retirement. Political reform was the first item on the junta's agenda, and in March 1946, it decreed a sweeping new electoral law. Universal suffrage for all citizens over eighteen, including women, at last became law. All political parties were legalized, and the number of congressional seats was to be apportioned according to each party's percentage of the total vote.

AD's principal competitor in the October 1946 Constituent Assembly elections, held to elect a body that would draft a new constitution, was the Social Christian Party (Comité de Organización Política Electoral Independiente—COPEI), recently founded by Rafael Caldera Rodríguez. COPEI appealed mainly to conservative Roman Catholics. Other parties of less conservative leanings but narrower electoral appeal included the Democratic Republican Union (Unión Republicana Democrática—URD), a personal vehicle for Villalba, and the communists, whose various factions united in 1947 under the banner of the PCV, which had been legalized in 1942. Although competition among the parties was intense, AD won overwhelming majorities in the Constituent Assembly elections as well as in the presidential and congressional elections of December 1947 and the municipal elections of May 1948.

AD's wide margin of victory (in 1946 it drew 79 percent of the vote; in 1947, 73 percent) led its leaders to believe that they could push through a highly progressive program without considering the conservative political opposition. A new constitution was promulgated in 1947. The party's vigorous pursuit of "social justice and better conditions for the workers" (as stated in a decree by the 1945 junta that established a separate Ministry of Labor) engendered widespread hostility within the business community, both foreign and local. The overhaul of the 1943 petroleum law to assure the government a 50 percent tax on the oil industry's profits intensified the foreign oil companies' antagonism. The junta's aggressive campaign to expand public education and its regulation of both public and private education incensed the Roman Catholic Church. The church, whose dominant role in education had heretofore gone unchallenged, now enlisted COPEI in a strident antigovernment campaign.

The political polarization intensified following the inauguration of Rómulo Gallegos as president on February 15, 1948. At that time, Venezuela's most renowned author, Gallegos proved less than adroit as a politician. His signing of AD's wide-ranging land reform bill in October pitted the nation's powerful landowners against him, and his reduction of the military personnel in his cabinet and advocacy of a reduced military budget alienated the armed forces. In mid-November, the UPM issued an ultimatum to the president demanding that COPEI share political authority with AD and that Betancourt, still AD leader, be sent into exile. Gallegos refused, and on November 24, after barely ten months in office, the military overthrew him in a nearly bloodless coup and exiled him along with Betancourt and the rest of the AD leadership.

The three-man provisional military junta that assumed control of the government was headed by Colonel Delgado. Delgado had joined the anti-AD conspiracy only after Gallegos had rejected the UPM ultimatum and it was clear that his fall was inevitable. Delgado had been a UPM coconspirator in 1945, and had served as a member of the AD junta and as minister of defense under Gallegos.

The military junta's other two members, UPM conspirator Pérez Jiménez and Luis Felipe Llovera Páez, were *tachirenses* who also held the rank of colonel. The junta quickly set about undoing the reforms of the AD *trienio* (see Glossary). It voided the 1947 constitution and restored the traditionalist 1936 constitution. The new military government outlawed AD and persecuted its militants.

Delgado took a more moderate position than his fellow junta members on such issues as the persecution of AD and the potential transition from a military to a civilian government. His disagreements with Pérez and Llovera, who advocated overt military rule in the Venezuelan tradition, became increasingly public. In November 1950, Delgado was assassinated. Germán Suárez Flanerich served as a figurehead for Pérez, who assumed leadership of the junta. Under pressure from non-AD political parties, the junta reluctantly convoked long-deferred presidential elections for November 1952.

AD continued to be proscribed but was extremely active underground. Pérez organized a progovernment party, the Independent Electoral Front (Frente Electoral Independiente—FEI), which he mistakenly believed would be victorious and thus legitimize his rule. Caldera ran a conservative campaign as the presidential candidate of COPEI, and the URD's Villalba ran a fiery antigovernment campaign. When the early election results made it clear that the URD (supported clandestinely by AD) was far ahead of the government party, Pérez ordered the count halted and declared himself president. The other junta members were sent abroad "on vacation," and the leaders of the URD and COPEI joined their AD colleagues in exile.

The next five years saw a brutal dictatorship in a country that by now was notorious as the almost archetypical home of Latin American dictators. A regressive new constitution reverted to indirect elections for president by a puppet legislature. Pedro Estrada, described by historian Hubert Herring as "as vicious a man hunter as Hitler ever employed," headed the vast National Security Police (Seguridad Nacional—SN) network that rounded up any opposition, including military officers, unable to escape. Hundreds, if not thousands, were brutally tortured or simply murdered at the notorious Guasina Island concentration camp in the Orinoco jungle region. Labor unions were harassed, and the Venezuelan Confederation of Labor was abolished and replaced by a confederation under the control of the FEI. When the Central University of Venezuela became a center of opposition to the regime, it was simply shut down. Strict controls over the press recalled the worst days of the Gómez regime. Political power concentrated around Pérez and an inner circle of six *tachirense* colonels who held key cabinet positions. Pérez revived Gómez's old "Democratic Caesarism" doctrine and gave it a new name, the "New National Ideal," under which politics would be deemphasized in favor of material progress (dubbed the "conquest of the physical environment" by apologists for the dictatorship).

Under Pérez, much of the nation's ever-increasing petroleum revenues were used for ostentatious construction projects. These included a replica of New York's Rockefeller Center, a luxurious mountaintop hotel, and the world's most expensive officers' club, all of which served more as monuments to the dictator than as contributions to national development. An even larger share of the state treasury, fully 50 percent according to one estimate, was squandered or simply stolen. By the time Pérez was forced to flee to Miami, he alone had accumulated a fortune estimated at US$250 million. Meanwhile, government expenditures on such human resources as health and education stagnated.

Pérez's staunch anticommunism and his more liberal policies toward the foreign oil companies—compared with the nationalistic stance of AD—won him the open support of the United States government; President Dwight D. Eisenhower awarded him the Legion of Merit in 1954. His seemingly insatiable greed for wealth and power, however, as well as the widespread reports of his debauchery, made him a growing object of scorn among his countrymen. In mid-1957 the united civilian opposition organized an underground movement called the Patriotic Junta dedicated to overthrowing the dictatorship. Opposition to Pérez also flourished within the military, especially among junior officers tired of the corruption and monopoly on power of the ruling generals. Pérez's favoritism to the army alienated air force and naval officers.

A shameless electoral farce in 1957, obvious to all as a bald maneuver designed to perpetuate Pérez in power, proved decisive in the downfall of the dictator. Fearful of an embarrassment similar to that of 1952, Pérez cancelled planned elections and then scheduled a plebescite. Only two hours after the polls had closed on December 15, the government announced an incredible 85 percent vote in favor of Pérez continuing in office. Outrage at this obviously fraudulent result was universal among both the civilian and military opposition.

Air force planes dropped bombs on the capital on January 1, 1958, to signal the start of a military insurrection. The anticipated coup d'état failed to materialize, however, because of the lack of coordination among the conspirators. Nonetheless, the bombing did give heart to the civilian opposition to Pérez by signaling that they were not without allies within the military. On January 10, the Patriotic Junta convoked a massive demonstration of civilian opposition in downtown Caracas; on the twenty-first, it called for a general strike that proved immediately effective. Street demonstrations as well as fighting erupted and quickly spread outside Caracas. When the navy revolted on January 22, a group of army officers, fearful for their own lives, forced Pérez to resign. The following day, Venezuela's last dictator fled the country, carrying most of what remained of the national treasury. In addition, his ouster cost the nation some 300 dead and more than 1,000 wounded.

The five-man provisional military junta at first tried to rule without civilian participation. The Patriotic Junta, however, called for the rebellion to continue until civilians were included. Two businessmen were promptly added to the junta, which ruled during the year that was required to dismantle the institutions associated with the dictatorship and transfer power to a popularly elected civilian government. The junta contained personnel from all three military services; it was led by Admiral Wolfgang Larrazábal, who headed the crucial January 22 naval rebellion.

The junta also began a valiant effort to deal with the grim realities of an empty treasury and some US$500 million in foreign debt. It immediately stopped work on most of the dictator's public works projects and later decreed a sharp increase in income taxes. Most important, the junta increased the government's share of the profits on petroleum extraction from 50 percent to 60 percent.

Under a new electoral law decreed in May, the junta convoked elections for December 1958. The political parties that had participated in the Patriotic Junta found themselves unable to reach a consensus on a single candidate. In the Pact of Punto Fijo, drawn up in October, the top party leaders did agree to resume their cooperation after the elections. They drew up a common policy agenda and agreed to divide cabinet posts and other governmental positions among the three major parties, regardless of whose candidate proved victorious in December. AD then nominated Betancourt, the URD tapped the popular Larrazábal as its candidate, and COPEI again ran Caldera as its candidate. After a hard-fought campaign, Betancourt came out the victor with 49 percent of the total; Larrazábal, who also had the support of the communists, received 35 percent; Caldera garnered 16 percent. AD also gained a majority in both congressional bodies. Although few anticipated it at the time, Betancourt's inauguration as president on February 13, 1959, initiated a period of democratic, civilian rule of unprecedented length in the nation's history.

The Triumph of Democracy

Historians invariably point to Betancourt's inauguration as the pivotal point in four centuries of Venezuelan history. Not since its discovery by Spanish explorers in the late fifteenth century had an event so clearly marked a new era for the country. After nearly a century and a half as perhaps the most extreme example of Latin America's postindependence affliction of caudillismo and military rule, Venezuela's political life after 1959 was defined by uninterrupted civilian constitutional rule.

This stark break with the past has been attributed most often to the government's petroleum-based wealth, which gave it the material resources to win a vast portion of the population over to the democratic consensus, and to the spirit of cooperation among the nation's various political entities (commonly known as the "Spirit of the 23rd of January," after the date of Pérez's fall from power) as embodied in the Pact of Punto Fijo. Betancourt and his AD colleagues had apparently learned from the disastrous consequences of their strident posture during their previous stint at governing. They now reversed themselves by granting concessions to a broad range of political forces that included many of their most bitter enemies during the *trienio*. They guaranteed, for example, the continuation of obligatory military service; improved salaries, housing, and equipment for the military; and, most important, granted amnesty from prosecution for crimes committed during the dictatorship. The Roman Catholic Church, whose active opposition to Pérez had impressed many doctrinally anticlerical AD militants, somewhat enhanced its political image and expanded its influence within the government.

In another pact, the "Declaration of Principles and Governing Program," which was written up during the weeks before the 1958 elections, AD, COPEI, and the URD agreed on a broad range of matters with respect to the economy. In what amounted to guarantees to the foreign and local business communities, the parties agreed to respect the principles of capital accumulation and the sanctity of private property. Local industry, furthermore, was guaranteed government measures to protect it from foreign competition as well as subsidies through the state-run Venezuelan Development Corporation (Corporación Venezolana de Fomento—CVF). With respect to agrarian properties, any expropriation or transfer of title would provide for compensation to the original owner.

Betancourt made other conciliatory moves as well. A new labor code granted unprecedented government guarantees of the right to association and collective bargaining. Vastly enlarged state subsidies

Former president Rómulo Betancourt
Courtesy Prints and Photographs Division, Library of Congress

benefited the poor in such areas as food, housing, and health care. The objective was to institutionalize a "prolonged political truce" by including as many citizens as possible within a popular consensus in favor of the civilian, democratic project. The "Spirit of the 23rd of January" informed the 1961 constitution, which guaranteed a wide range of civil liberties and created a weak bicameral legislature where partisan political conflict could be aired but would cause a minimum of damage. The president was given considerable power, although he was allowed to run for reelection only after sitting out two five-year terms.

The major group excluded from the political pacts of 1958 was the extreme left. This exclusion was the result, initially, of the doctrinal anticommunism of AD—and of Betancourt in particular. The exclusion was subsequently perpetuated by the triumph of the Cuban Revolution in 1959 and the revolution's precipitous radicalization during the early 1960s. The Cuban Revolution had a profound impact on the Venezuelan left, particularly among student groups, who saw it as a model for a successful revolutionary effort in Venezuela. In November 1960, the URD dropped out of the governing coalition with AD in protest over Betancourt's firm stance against Cuban leader Fidel Castro Ruz. AD also suffered the loss of most of its student wing, which in April of that year split from the party to form the Movement of the Revolutionary Left (Movimiento de la Izquierda Revolucionaria—MIR), supposedly to protest delays in the implementation of the government's agrarian reform program.

In 1961 these groups, together with the PCV, consolidated their advocacy of antigovernment guerrilla warfare. The Betancourt government supported Cuba's expulsion from the Organization of American States (OAS), then broke diplomatic relations with the Castro government in December. In May and June of the following year, military officers sympathetic to the left instigated two bloody uprisings, first at Carúpano on the Península de Paria, then at Puerto Cabello. The uprisings provoked Betancourt into legally proscribing the PCV and the MIR, which promptly went underground and formed the Armed Forces of National Liberation (Fuerzas Armadas de Liberación Nacional—FALN). The FALN engaged in rural and urban guerrilla activities throughout the remainder of the 1960s. The activity reached its height in 1962 and 1963, when the FALN sabotaged oil pipelines and bombed a Sears Roebuck warehouse and the United States Embassy in Caracas.

The FALN failed, however, to attract adherents among the poor, whether rural campesinos or the residents of the makeshift shacks, known as *ranchos* (see Glossary), that made up Caracas's mushrooming slum areas. The guerrillas also proved unable to achieve their secondary goal of provoking a coup d'état that would lead to a repressive military regime and, hence, increase popular support for the insurgents. As political scientist Daniel H. Levine points out, the FALN's effect proved to be quite the contrary of what it intended: it actually consolidated the democratic regime by making AD look—to its many former enemies on the right—like the better of two alternatives. At the same time, the insurgency provided a vital military mission to the armed forces, one that removed them still further from direct participation in politics. Ultimately, the FALN's efforts to disrupt the December 1963 elections also proved futile. In the midst of this guerrilla campaign, the government arrested all PCV and MIR congressmen in September, and in November military forces discovered a three-ton cache of small arms—with clear links back to the Castro regime—on a deserted stretch of beach.

Castro was not Betancourt's only enemy in the Caribbean, however. Rafael Leónidas Trujillo Molina, the dictatorial ruler of the Dominican Republic, was implicated in a number of antigovernment conspiracies uncovered within the Venezuelan military, as well as in the bombing of Betancourt's car in June 1960, in which a military aide was killed and the president badly burned. The

Venezuelan president's strong-willed antipathy for nondemocratic rule was reflected in the so-called Betancourt Doctrine, which denied Venezuelan diplomatic recognition to any regime, right or left, that came to power by military force.

Highly unfavorable circumstances in the external sector of the economy handicapped the Betancourt administration. Having inherited an empty treasury and enormous unpaid foreign debts from the spendthrift Pérez, Betancourt nevertheless managed to return the state to fiscal solvency despite the persistence of rock-bottom petroleum prices throughout his presidency. He also managed to continue the effort, begun during the 1930s by President López, of "sowing the oil" by initiating a variety of reform programs, the most important of which was agrarian reform. Aimed not at addressing social grievances but rather at reversing Venezuela's protracted decline in agricultural production, AD's land reform distributed only unproductive private properties and public lands. Landowners who had their properties confiscated received generous compensation. By the end of the 1960s, an estimated 166,000 heads of household had received provisional titles to their new properties.

During 1960 two institutions were founded that made important contributions toward the development of a national petroleum policy: the Venezuelan Petroleum Corporation (Corporación Venezolana de Petróleos—CVP), conceived to oversee the national petroleum industry, and the Organization of the Petroleum Exporting Countries (OPEC), the international oil cartel that Venezuela established in partnership with Kuwait, Saudi Arabia, Iraq, and Iran. Both organizations were the creations of Juan Pablo Pérez Alfonso, who, for the second time, served as Betancourt's minister of energy. During the *trienio,* Pérez Alfonso had earned the wrath of the foreign oil firms with his proposition that the state should gradually assume control of the petroleum industry; this idea now once again became government policy.

Perhaps the greatest of all Betancourt's accomplishments, however, was the successful 1963 election. Despite myriad threats to disrupt the process, nearly 90 percent of the electorate participated on December 1 in what was probably the most honest election in Venezuela to that date. AD standard-bearer Raúl Leoni proved victorious, gaining 33 percent of the total vote in a field of seven presidential candidates. On March 11, 1964, for the first time in the nation's history, the presidential sash passed from one constitutionally elected chief executive to another. It was a day of immense pride for the people of Venezuela.

Leoni, a hard-working but less colorful figure than Betancourt, differed little from his reformist predecessor from an ideological standpoint. Nevertheless, unlike Betancourt, Leoni proved unable to agree to COPEI's conditions for forming a governing coalition and instead made an alliance with the URD and the National Democratic Front (Frente Nacional Democrática—FND), a probusiness party created around Arturo Uslar Pietri, a noted writer and public affairs activist.

Subversive activities quieted considerably during the Leoni administration. By no means were they ended, however. Rumors of military plots were rife throughout the five-year term; the most dangerous military rebellion, an attempted coup d'état in October 1966, was swiftly put down and its leaders court-martialed. The threat from the revolutionary left also persisted, leading Leoni in December 1966 to order an army search of Caracas's Central University for revolutionaries. By 1965, however, the PCV had begun to harbor doubts about violence as a road to power, and over the course of the following two years, it gradually abandoned the revolutionary path. Splinter groups with Cuban ties persisted in their violent activities, however, and in May 1967, a small landing party headed by a Cuban army officer was captured at Machurucuto in the state of Miranda. This incursion would prove to be the pinnacle of Castro's crusade to export his revolution to Venezuela. Insurgent activity subsequently subsided, and bilateral relations with Cuba eventually improved.

Economic growth averaged a healthy 5.5 percent annually during the Leoni years, aided by a recovery in petroleum prices and the relative political tranquility as the AD program attained legitimacy. Leoni kept the Betancourt reform programs on course and also introduced a number of impressive infrastructure projects designed to open up the nation's interior to agricultural and industrial development. Regional integration efforts advanced, albeit slowly, although Venezuela remained outside the newly created Andean Common Market (Ancom; see Glossary) in response to objections from the local business community, which feared competition from lower-priced goods manufactured in neighboring countries.

The governing party split in 1967 over the choice of the party's presidential candidate for the 1968 elections. Stemming in part from a long-simmering rivalry between former president Betancourt and AD secretary general Jesús Angel Paz Galarraga, a highly damaging split led Paz to launch the People's Electoral Movement (Movimiento Electoral del Pueblo—MEP). The MEP tendered Luis B. Prieto as its candidate, and Gonzalo Barrios headed the AD ticket.

The URD joined forces with the FND and the party of former presidential candidate Larrazábal to promote the candidacy of Miguel Angel Burelli Rivas under the banner of a coalition dubbed the Victorious Front. COPEI once again ran Caldera, who proved victorious in this fourth attempt to capture the presidency. His victory resulted both from the split in AD and from COPEI's liberalization of its image away from that of a strictly conservative Roman Catholic party. All four candidates finished strongly at the end of a hard-fought campaign, however, and Caldera eked out a victory over Barrios by a margin of merely 31,000 votes. The passing of the presidential sash from Leoni to AD's principal opposition leader in March 1969 marked yet another first in Venezuela's rapidly maturing democracy.

President Caldera never made an earnest effort to form a governing coalition. Throughout his five-year term, his cabinet consisted exclusively of *copeyanos* (COPEI party members) and independents. In Congress, however, the governing party was forced to form a working alliance with AD in 1970 because mounting student demonstrations and growing partisan intransigence made unilateral rule impossible.

The major concerns of Caldera's government were not unlike those of his two predecessors: agrarian reform and increased farm production, the improvement of educational and social welfare benefits, the expansion and diversification of industrial development, and progress toward local control of the petroleum industry. With respect to the latter, the government's tax rate on the petroleum companies rose to 70 percent by 1971. In the same year, the Hydrocarbons Reversion Law—stipulating that all of the oil companies' Venezuelan assets would revert to the state when their concessions expired—went into effect.

The key policy distinction between Caldera's government and those of his AD predecessors lay in the area of foreign policy. President Caldera rejected the Betancourt Doctrine, which he considered restrictive and divisive, and which he thought had served to isolate Venezuela in the world. Bilateral relations were soon restored with the Soviet Union and the socialist nations of Eastern Europe, as well as with a number of South American nations that had fallen under military rule. By dividing Latin American nations from one another, the Betancourt Doctrine, Caldera believed, had served to promote United States hegemony in the region. Seeking points of unity instead, Caldera established "pluralistic solidarity" as the guiding principle of Venezuelan foreign policy. Among its positive results was Venezuela's entrance into Ancom upon signing the 1973 Consensus of Lima; Ancom had assuaged the fears of the business community by allowing Venezuela to attach a number of special conditions to its membership.

On the one hand, by joining Ancom, Venezuela emphasized its Andean identity. On the other hand, the striking expansion of its investment in the Caribbean Development Bank emphasized the nation's Caribbean character. Caldera thus began to provide oil-based financial aid to the nations of Central America and the Caribbean, an effort that would be greatly expanded in subsequent years.

Although the internal security situation had improved, Caldera adopted a policy of "pacification" toward the remaining armed opposition. The pacification program legalized the PCV and other leftist parties and granted amnesty to revolutionary activists. The government credited the program for the dramatic decline in guerrilla activity. Its opponents, however, pointed out that the most conspicuous decrease in Venezuela's revolutionary violence came under Leoni, when Cuba and the Soviet Union changed their policies in the wake of the 1967 death of Ernesto "Che" Guevara in Bolivia and the 1968 Soviet invasion of Czechoslovakia.

The December 1973 election was a truly pluralistic affair. The twelve presidential candidates ranged from three aspirants of the parties on the left to an even larger number of self-declared representatives of former president Pérez on the right. The MEP, which had moved steadily leftward since 1968, allied itself with the PCV and nominated Paz under the banner of Popular Unity (Unidad Popular), modeled after the Chilean left-wing coalition of the same name that had elected Salvador Allende Gossens in 1970. The URD initially joined the coalition, but the aging Jóvito Villalba later withdrew his party to launch his own candidacy. The other candidate on the left was José Vicente Rangel of the Movement Toward Socialism (Movimiento al Socialismo—MAS), a party that had been founded in 1971 by a group of PCV dissidents with liberal, "Eurocommunist" notions of a modern, election-oriented party. Unlike the Moscow-line PCV, the MAS had little bond to the Soviet Union.

Although the 1973 election was notable for the ideological pluralism represented in the competing political parties, its most important distinction was the primacy achieved by the two principal parties, AD and COPEI. In contrast to 1968, AD converged around the figure of Betancourt's long-time protégé and minister of interior, Carlos Andrés Pérez, thus passing party leadership to its second generation. Campaigning deep into the rural Venezuelan heartland as well as in the *ranchos* of all major cities, Pérez managed to recapture much of the populist appeal acquired by Betancourt thirty years previously. The campaign of his opponent, Lorenzo

Fernández (also a former minister of interior) was, by comparison, a low-key affair.

On election day, an astounding 97 percent of the registered voters went to the polls. Pérez, with 48.8 percent of the valid vote, prevailed against Fernández's 36.7 percent. Between them, then, AD and COPEI captured nearly 86 percent of the valid presidential vote; the two parties also garnered 43 of the 49 Senate seats and 166 of 200 seats in the Chamber of Deputies. AD attained absolute majorities in both congressional houses as well as in 157 of the nation's 181 municipal councils. The showing of leftist parties, in contrast, was unimpressive: the Popular Unity coalition gained 5.1 percent; MAS, 4.2 percent; and the URD, a mere 3.1 percent. "Polarization" was the term used locally to describe the apparent transition of Venezuela's electoral contests into two-party affairs. It was yet another promising sign in the evolution of a stable system of democracy.

Venezuela had still another reason to be euphoric at the dawn of 1974. The October 1973 Arab-Israeli War had triggered a quadrupling of crude oil prices in a period of only two months. When Pérez assumed the presidency in February 1974, he was immediately faced with the seemingly enviable task of managing a windfall of unprecedented proportions. To combat the inflationary pressures that would result from the sudden addition of some US$6 billion in annual government revenues, Pérez set up the Venezuelan Investment Fund (Fondo de Inversiones de Venezuela—FIV), with the objective of exporting 35 percent of this unexpected income as loans to Caribbean, Central American, and Andean neighbors. The greatest portion of this aid money went to the oil-importing nations of Central America in the form of long-term loans to pay for half of their oil-import bills. Venezuela also loaned out its "excess capital" through various multilateral lending institutions, including the Inter-American Development Bank (IDB).

The FIV loan program engendered considerable international goodwill on behalf of Venezuela, particularly among the recipient countries. Building on that prestige, Pérez and Mexican president Luis Echeverría Alvarez (1970–76) founded the Latin American Economic System (Sistema Económico Latinoamericano—SELA). SELA, with headquarters in Caracas, had twenty-three Latin American nations as its initial members in 1975. It was formed to promote Latin American cooperation in international economic matters such as commodity prices, scientific and technological exchange, and multinational enterprises and development projects. SELA, it was hoped, would help create the building blocks of a "new international economic order," in which the developing nations of the southern hemisphere would challenge the economic hegemony of the developed nations of the north.

Pérez's aggressive stance on behalf of the Third World helped to cool Venezuela's traditionally warm relations with the United States. Other contributing factors to this change included Venezuela's displeasure with both the revelations of extensive covert intervention by the United States against the Allende government in Chile and the reluctance of the United States to begin negotiations with Panama over future control of the Panama Canal. The major irritant, however, was OPEC's petroleum policy, marked by OPEC's 1973 price increases, and the embargo on oil shipments to the United States instigated by the Arab members of OPEC during the October War. Despite the fact that Venezuela had increased its oil shipments at that time in order to meet United States needs, the United States retaliated against the embargo by excluding Venezuela, along with the other OPEC-member nations, from the 1974 Trade Act, which created the Generalized System of Trade Preferences to lower tariffs on designated imports from developing nations. Proud of never having denied the nation's oil to the United States, even during periods of war and political tensions, Venezuelans took offense at what they saw as unwarranted punitive action by the United States.

At home, President Pérez put aside his promised intention to "manage abundance with the mentality of scarcity," and embarked on a spending spree designed to distribute Venezuela's oil wealth among the citizenry. Price controls that subsidized the public consumption of food and other commodities were introduced. Government-authorized wage increases, combined with foreign exchange controls that subsidized imports, led to periodic buying binges of Japanese stereos and televisions, German automobiles and cameras, and clothing and processed foods from the United States. Per capita consumption of Scotch whiskey soared to a level among the world's highest. Government subsidies assumed a variety of other forms as well: in 1974, US$350 million in debts owed to state agencies by the Venezuelan farming community were simply cancelled.

The Pérez administration initiated various other programs to spur employment. The 1974 Law of Unjustified Dismissals made it very difficult for employers to fire workers and mandated ample severance payments to those who did lose their jobs. Public employment doubled in five years, reaching 750,000 by 1978. Although unemployment levels thus dropped precipitously, Venezuelans' traditional disdain for hard work increased, leaving many necessary jobs either unfilled or filled by a growing number of *indocumentados* (undocumented or illegal aliens) from Colombia and Brazil.

Although these subsidy and employment programs theoretically sought to improve the lot of the poor, in fact, the actual outcome was that a significant portion of the population continued to live in a state of misery. Income distribution was less equitable in 1976 than it had been in 1960, and one study found that fully 40 percent of the population nationwide were ill fed and undernourished. This contrast of widespread poverty amidst urban development and the conspicuous consumption of the middle and upper classes was particularly damaging to Pérez, who had been elected with a public image as a "friend of the people." AD's failure to address adequately the needs of the poor would plague the party during the 1978 electoral contest.

The government continued, as it had been doing for nearly four decades, to put a large portion of its petroleum revenues into building an industrial base, with the objective of generating future income after the nation's oil reserves had been depleted. With massive amounts of money to spend, emphasis was now placed on large-scale, high-technology infrastructure and industrial development projects. The Pérez administration's Fifth National Plan, conceived during the mid-1970s and scheduled to become operative in 1977, accordingly called for some US$52.5 billion in investments over a five-year period.

In an effort to minimize the bureaucratic entanglements entailed by such a major increase in the fiscal responsibilities of the central government, funding was instead vested in autonomous and semi-autonomous entities. The four years following the 1973–74 oil boom saw the creation of no fewer than 163 such entities, including textile and lumber companies, a hydroelectric consortium, shipbuilding firms, and a national steamship company and airline. By 1978 the budget outlay for state-owned enterprises and decentralized agencies was 50 percent higher than the federal budget.

The centerpiece of this state-directed program of industrial development was the massive industrial complex at Ciudad Guayana. Located near major deposits of iron and other raw materials in the vast Guiana highlands, the complex was placed under the supervision of the Venezuelan Corporation of Guayana (Corporación Venezolana de Guayana—CVG). Ciudad Guayana was developed during the early 1960s as an effort to decentralize industrial development away from Caracas. It attracted considerable private as well as public investment—most notably the Orinoco Steelworks (Siderúrgica del Orinoco—Sidor), a CVG subsidiary—and grew quickly; by 1979 its population reached 300,000. During the Pérez administration, Sidor benefited from massive new investments, including a US$4 billion project designed to increase its refining capacity fivefold. The government erected modern, large-scale aluminum and bauxite refineries and massive hydroelectric projects with a vision of converting the Orinoco Basin into a Venezuelan Rhineland.

In January 1975, the government cancelled the iron ore concessions of subsidiaries of two United States-owned firms (United States Steel Corporation and Bethlehem Steel) operating in the Guiana highlands. It was not an unexpected move, as local ownership of raw-material extraction had been frequently addressed during the 1973 presidential campaign. The nationalization process took place smoothly: the two companies accepted US$101 million in compensation and agreed to sign one-year management contracts to provide continuity in the operation of the mines during the transition.

Congressional approval, the following August, of a bill nationalizing the petroleum industry had also been anticipated. The fourteen foreign oil companies involved did not object vigorously to the move; the Venezuelan government had granted them no new concessions since 1960, and their share of the profits from the petroleum they extracted had dropped to 30 percent. The US$1 billion they received, although only a fraction of the replacement cost of the assets they surrendered (including 12 oil refineries with an aggregate capacity of 1.5 million barrels of oil per day, along with some 12,500 oil wells), was generally believed to be as fair and generous a compensation as possible under the circumstances. The fourteen foreign firms were consolidated into four autonomous entities, modeled after the four largest of the foreign enterprises, and placed under the administrative supervision of the Venezuelan Petroleum Corporation (Petróleos de Venezuela, S.A.—PDVSA), a holding company fashioned out of the CVP. General Rafael Alfonso Ravard, who had managed the CVG in a highly efficient, technocratic manner quite atypical of most government ventures, was chosen to head PDVSA.

The Pérez administration had devised its grandiose Fifth National Plan under the assumption that rising oil prices would boost government revenue throughout the 1970s. Instead, Venezuela's oil income leveled off in 1976, then began to decline in 1978. Foreign commercial banks, awash with petrodollars deposited by other OPEC nations, provided loans to make up the shortfall so that Venezuela's development program could proceed on schedule. On the one hand, the banks saw oil-rich Venezuela as an excellent credit risk, while, on the other hand, the autonomy of Venezuela's state firms allowed them to borrow excessively, independent of central government accounting. To expedite their receipt of this external financing, the autonomous entities opted for mainly short-term loans, which carried higher rates of interest. As a result, by 1978 the public-sector foreign debt had grown to nearly US$12 billion, a fivefold increase in only four years. An estimated 70 to 80 percent of this new debt had been contracted by the decentralized public administration.

Between the vast increase in oil revenues before 1976 and the immense foreign debt incurred by the government, the Pérez administration spent more money (in absolute terms) in 5 years than had all other governments during the previous 143 years combined. Perhaps inevitably, a great deal of money was squandered in mismanagement and corruption. Despite expansive overseas programs to train managers of the new public entities, the lack of competent personnel to execute the government's many sophisticated endeavors became painfully evident. The delays and myriad cost overruns that ensued formed the backdrop of frequent malfeasance by public officials. Overpayment of contractors, with kickbacks to the contracting officers, was perhaps the most rampant form of graft. Featherbedding and the padding of payrolls with nonworking or nonexistent employees also became common practices.

By the time of the December 1978 elections, these issues had brought serious doubts to the voters as to the competence and the probity of the AD government. AD's candidate, Luis Piñerua Ordaz, lost to COPEI's Luis Herrera Campíns by a little over 3 percentage points. The loss had less to do with the program presented by either candidate than with the public's rejection of the free-spending, populist style of President Pérez. Otherwise, the 1978 campaign was most notable for the vast sums spent by the two major candidates on North American media consultants. More than any previous electoral contest, this campaign was conducted on television, increasing the relative importance of image over substance. The two major parties captured almost 90 percent of the total vote; a divided left shared 8.5 percent of the total among four candidates. In the subsequent June 1979 municipal council elections, however, the MAS, MEP, PCV, and MIR presented a united slate that captured a more impressive 18.5 percent of the vote.

Announcing during his March 1979 inaugural address that Venezuela could not continue as a "nation that consumes rivers of whiskey and oil," President Herrera promised to assume an austere posture toward government fiscal concerns. Public spending, including consumer subsidies, was ordered cut, and interest rates were increased to encourage savings. When the Iranian Revolution and the outbreak of the Iran-Iraq War caused oil prices to jump from US$17 per barrel in 1979 to US$28 in 1980, however, Herrera abandoned his austerity measures before they had had a chance to yield results.

Early on in his term of office, President Herrera also pledged to pursue policies aimed at reviving the moribund private sector. However, the first of these measures, the elimination of price controls, only contributed further to rising inflation. As with his commitment to austerity, the president failed to persist in his pledge to business; yielding to political pressures from the AD-dominated Confederation of Venezuelan Workers (Confederación de Trabajadores de Venezuela—CTV), in October 1979 the administration approved sizable wage increases. Meanwhile, the number of those employed by state-owned enterprises and autonomous agencies, which Herrera had promised to streamline and make more efficient, proliferated instead. The administration initiated, among other projects, a huge coal and steel complex in the state of Zulia, a new natural gas plant with 1,000 kilometers of pipeline, a new railroad from Caracas to the coast, and a bridge linking the Caribbean Isla de Margarita with the mainland, running in the process a deficit of some US$8 billion between 1979 and 1982. A retired Venezuelan diplomat, writing in *The Miami Herald* in 1983, noted that, "There must be examples of worse fiscal management than that of Venezuela in the last eight or nine years, but I am not aware of them."

The lack of confidence in President Herrera's economic management by the local business community contributed significantly to a precipitous decline in the growth of real gross domestic product (GDP—see Glossary) from an annual average of 6.1 percent between 1974 and 1978 to a sickly −1.2 percent between 1979 and 1983. Unemployment hovered around 20 percent throughout the early 1980s.

An unexpected softening of oil prices during late 1981 triggered further fiscal problems. World demand for oil—on which the Venezuelan government depended for some two-thirds of its revenues—continued to decline as the market became glutted with oil from newly exploited deposits in Mexico and the North Sea. The resumption of large-scale independent borrowing by the decentralized public administration came amidst publicly aired disagreements among various officials as to the magnitude of the foreign debt. Not until 1983 did outside analysts agree on an approximate figure of US$32 billion.

Compounding growing balance of payments difficulties, rumors of an impending monetary devaluation precipitated a wave of private capital flight overseas in early 1983. While the Central Bank of Venezuela (Banco Central de Venezuela—BCV) president argued with the finance and planning ministers over what measures to adopt to meet the growing crisis, some US$2 billion left the country during January and February alone. At the end of February, the government at last announced a system of foreign exchange controls and a complicated three-tier exchange system. Under this system, the public sector retained the existing rate of US$1 = B4.3, selling bolívars (B; for value of the bolívar—see Glossary) to the private sector at a higher rate of US$1 = B6.0 or more, while a free-floating rate was established for tourism, "nonessential" imports (luxury items), and other purposes. At the same time, price controls were reinstated to control inflation. The annual increase in consumer prices, which had hit a peak of 21.6 percent in 1980, fell to 6.3 percent for 1983.

Seeking a way out of the dismal economic situation, the Herrera administration decided to transfer a greater share of ever-growing government expenses to PDVSA. The Central Bank of Venezuela appropriated some US$4.5 billion of PDVSA's reserves to pay the foreign debt, thereby throwing the petroleum corporation's autonomy to the wind. Partisan politics began to play a larger role in the selection of members of PDVSA's board of directors. In September 1983, Ravard was forced out as head of PDVSA and replaced by Humberto Calderón Berti, who as minister of energy had spearheaded the effort to bind the oil giant closer to the central government. The rapid politicization of PDVSA drew criticism both at home and abroad and cost the government credibility as well as its good credit rating with foreign banks. The unceremonious firing of the highly respected Ravard was condemned by both candidates for the December presidential election and was reversed by the new administration the following February.

By historical standards, the 1983 electoral campaign was a dull affair. Enjoying a substantial lead in opinion polls from the start, AD's Jaime Lusinchi coasted to an easy victory over former president Caldera, who was burdened with both the miserable record of the outgoing COPEI administration and the undisguised hostility of his fellow *copeyano,* President Herrera. Lusinchi, a physician with no previous administrative experience, ran a campaign that focused on the failings of the Herrera administration, and won the contest on December 4 with 56.8 percent of the valid vote, the highest percentage gained by a candidate since the dawn of the democratic era in 1958. Caldera gained 34.9 percent; the combined vote of the two candidates on the left totaled 7.4 percent.

Although the 1983 elections again demonstrated the predominance of the two major parties, the record of ineffective government (known locally as *desgobierno*), corruption, an increasing foreign debt, and a growing list of unaddressed socioeconomic problems all contributed to a widespread disillusionment with the political process among the electorate. After twenty-five years of gradual consolidation of democracy in Venezuela, doubts had emerged as to the future stability of the much-cherished democratic political process that had proven so elusive before 1958.

* * *

There is a wealth of first-rate literature in English on the history of Venezuela. Perhaps the most useful general histories are Judith Ewell's *Venezuela: A Century of Change* and John V. Lombardi's *Venezuela: The Search for Order, the Dream of Progress.* On the all-important oil industry, volumes by Rómulo Betancourt (*Venezuela's Oil* and *Venezuela: Oil and Politics*) and Franklin Tugwell's *The Politics of Oil in Venezuela* are standards, while Jorge Salazar-Carrillo's *Oil in the Economic Development of Venezuela* treats the subject from the standpoint of economic rather than political history. George W. Schuyler's *Hunger in a Land of Plenty* examines the tragic irony of poverty amidst Venezuela's vast oil wealth.

Robert L. Gilmore's *Caudillism and Militarism in Venezuela, 1810–1910* remains a valuable source of information on nineteenth-century caudillismo. The crucial period of the transition to democracy during the 1940s and 1950s is examined in *The Venezuelan Democratic Revolution* by Robert J. Alexander and in *Conflict and Political Change in Venezuela* by Daniel H. Levine. Stephen G. Rabe, in *The Road to OPEC: United States Relations with Venezuela, 1919–1976,* provides the most comprehensive look at Venezuela's important relationship with the United States. (For further information and complete citations, see Bibliography.)

Chapter 2. The Society and Its Environment

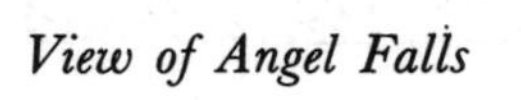

View of Angel Falls

THROUGHOUT MOST OF ITS HISTORY, Venezuela remained a poor country with a rigidly stratified, largely rural population. The political system in the long era of caudillismo (rule by local strongmen, or caudillos) was one in which shifting factions, loosely organized around competing caudillos, vied for dominance over disenfranchised masses. A minuscule upper class of wealthy hacendados, whose income derived from cocoa and coffee plantations, controlled the economy. This group based their superior status on their light skin and on Hispanic cultural and social norms established during the colonial period. Despite its power, prestige, and wealth, however, the upper stratum never formed the sort of cohesive, entrenched oligarchy so common throughout most of the rest of the continent. Venezuela's comparative poverty—its lack of gold or precious stones—limited the attention it received from Spain; fewer Spaniards ventured to Venezuela than to nearby Colombia or more distant Peru. The colonial period, therefore, did not produce an opulent upper class, either Spanish or native born.

Below this small, modestly rich, and fragmented upper class was a somewhat larger, but still limited, middle stratum. This group consisted of soldiers, artisans, craftsmen, bureaucrats, and small traders. Farther down the social ladder was the vast bulk of the population. Persons in this stratum, who were considered and considered themselves lower class, consisted largely of peasants of mixed descent. They had different values, life-styles, family patterns, and religious practices from those of the upper class. These Venezuelans played only a marginal role in the country's affairs. They occupied a subordinate and dependent position in the socioeconomic structure and exercised political influence only by joining the ranks of the local caudillo's personal militia.

Independence effected few changes in the relative position and sizes of these three classes. Indeed, until the discovery and exploitation of large quantities of oil in the first two decades of the twentieth century, Venezuela's economy and society exhibited a traditional agrarian pattern dominated by the production of export crops, such as cocoa and coffee, and some cattle raising. The shift to oil and the subsequent expansion of manufacturing eradicated the old order. In less than a generation, Venezuela became a far more modern, urban-based society. By 1960 some 60 percent of the population lived in cities of over 5,000 inhabitants, and the population of metropolitan Caracas numbered over a million.

Middle-class Venezuelans became a highly mobile people, moving regularly from place to place and job to job. Traditional values changed in ways that made the society more open and class boundaries more flexible. The ongoing process of value modification contributed to changes that accelerated in the 1970s and 1980s, as more women entered the universities and the labor force and more citizens participated in the liberalized political system. In the 1990s, Venezuelan society still exhibited enormous differences between its upper and its lowest strata. But the social system had become more permeable, and the urban middle class had become probably the most effective group involved in the country's vigorous partisan politics. Many Venezuelans therefore felt that the greatest challenge to their sociopolitical system lay not in further involvement of the middle class, but in responding to the concerns of the still large group at the base of the societal pyramid.

Geography

Located at the northernmost end of South America, Venezuela has a total area of 912,050 square kilometers and a land area of 882,050 square kilometers, about twice the size of California. Shaped roughly like an inverted triangle, the country has a 2,800-kilometer coastline and is bounded on the north by the Caribbean Sea and the Atlantic Ocean, on the east by Guyana, on the south by Brazil, and on the west by Colombia (see fig. 2).

Topography

Most observers describe Venezuela in terms of four fairly well-defined regions: the Maracaibo lowlands in the northwest, the northern mountains extending in a broad east-west arc from the Colombian border along the Caribbean Sea, the wide Orinoco plains (llanos—see Glossary) in central Venezuela, and the highly dissected Guiana highlands in the southeast.

The Maracaibo lowlands form a large spoon-shaped oval bounded by mountains on three sides and open to the Caribbean on the north. The area is remarkably flat with only a gentle slope toward the center and away from the mountains that border the region. Lago de Maracaibo occupies much of the lower-lying territory. Areas around the southern part of Lago de Maracaibo are swampy, and, despite the rich agricultural land and significant petroleum deposits, the area was still thinly populated in 1990.

The mountains bordering the Caribbean Sea are actually the northeasternmost extension of the Andes chain. Broken by several gaps, these high mountains have peaks over 4,500 meters; the fertile valleys between the ranges contain most of Venezuela's population,

industry, and agriculture. The discontinuous westernmost range runs along the Colombian border and is the least densely populated part of this region. The ranges southeast of Lago de Maracaibo contain some of the highest peaks in the country (Pico Bolívar reaches 5,007 meters), a few of which are snowcapped year-round.

A broad gap separates this mountainous area from another rugged pair of ranges that parallel the north-central coast. The series of valleys between these two parallel ranges constitute the core area of the country; as the site of burgeoning metropolitan Caracas, this comparatively small area hosts the country's densest population, the most intensive agriculture, and the best transportation network. Another broad gap separates this area from the easternmost group of mountains, a series of dissected hills and uplands that rise steeply from the Caribbean and extend eastward almost to Trinidad.

The great expanse of lowlands known as the Orinoco plains extends westward from the Caribbean coast to the Colombian border between the northern mountains and the Río Orinoco. This region is commonly known as the llanos, although it also contains large stretches of swampland in the Orinoco Delta and near the Colombian border. The area slopes gradually away from the highland areas that surround it; elevations in the llanos never exceed 200 meters. North of the Río Apure, rivers flowing out of the northern mountains cut shallow valleys, leaving eroded ridges that give the land a gently rolling appearance. South of the Apure, the terrain is flatter and elevations lower.

One of the oldest land forms in South America, the Guiana highlands rise almost immediately south and east of the Río Orinoco. Erosion has created unusual formations in this region. Comprising over half of the country, the highlands consist primarily of plateau areas scored by swiftly running tributaries of the Orinoco. The most conspicuous topographical feature of the region is the Gran Sabana, a large, deeply eroded high plateau that rises from surrounding areas in abrupt cliffs up to 800 meters high. Above the rolling surface of the Gran Sabana, massive, flat-topped bluffs emerge; many of these bluffs (referred to as *tepuis* by the Venezuelans) reach considerable altitudes. The most famous *tepui* contains Angel Falls, the world's highest waterfall.

Climate

Although the country lies wholly within the tropics, its climate varies from tropical humid to alpine, depending on the elevation, topography, and the direction and intensity of prevailing winds. Seasonal variations are marked less by temperature than by rainfall. Most of the country has a distinct rainy season; the rainy period

(May through November) is commonly referred to as winter and the remainder of the year as summer.

The country falls into four horizontal temperature zones based primarily on elevation. In the tropical zone—below 800 meters—temperatures are hot, with yearly averages ranging between 26°C and 28°C. The temperate zone ranges between 800 and 2,000 meters with averages from 12°C to 25°C; many of Venezuela's cities, including the capital, lie in this region. Colder conditions with temperatures from 9°C to 11°C are found in the cool zone between 2,000 and 3,000 meters. Pastureland and permanent snowfield with yearly averages below 8°C cover land above 3,000 in the high mountain areas known as the *páramos*.

Average yearly rainfall amounts in the lowlands and plains range from a semiarid 430 millimeters in the western part of the Caribbean coastal areas to around 1,000 millimeters in the Orinoco Delta. Rainfall in mountainous areas varies considerably; sheltered valleys receive little rain, but slopes exposed to the northeast trade winds experience heavy rainfall. Caracas averages 750 millimeters of precipitation annually, more than half of it falling from June through August.

Hydrography

The Orinoco is by far the most important of the more than 1,000 rivers in the country. Flowing more than 2,500 kilometers to the Atlantic from its source in the Guiana highlands at the Brazilian border, the Orinoco is the world's eighth largest river and the largest in South America after the Amazon. Its flow varies substantially by season, with the high-water level in August exceeding by as much as thirteen meters the low levels of March and April. During low-water periods, the river experiences high and low tides for more than 100 kilometers upstream from Ciudad Guayana.

For most of the Orinoco's course, the gradient is slight. Downstream from its headwaters, the Orinoco splits into two; one-third of its flow passes through the Brazo Casiquiare (Casiquiare Channel) into a tributary of the Amazon, and the remainder passes into the main Orinoco channel. This passageway allows vessels with shallow drafts to navigate from the lower Orinoco to the Amazon River system after unloading and reloading on either side of two falls on the Orinoco along the Colombian border.

Most of the rivers rising in the northern mountains flow southeastward to the Río Apure, a tributary of the Orinoco. From its headwater, the Apure crosses the llanos in a generally eastward direction. Few rivers flow into it from the poorly drained region

Angel Falls, the world's highest waterfall, in southeastern Venezuela
Courtesy Martie B. Lisowski Collection, Library of Congress

south of the river, and much of this area near the Colombian border is swampland.

The other major Venezuelan river is the fast-flowing Caroní, which originates in the Guiana highlands and flows northward into the Orinoco upstream from Ciudad Guyana. The Caroní is capable of producing as much hydroelectric power as any river in Latin America and has contributed significantly to the nation's electric power production (see Electricity, ch. 3). Electricity generated by the Caroní was one of the factors encouraging industrialization of the northern part of the Guiana highlands and the lower Orinoco valley.

The Lago de Maracaibo, the largest lake in Latin America, occupies the central 13,500 square kilometers of the Maracaibo lowlands. The low swampy shores of the lake and areas beneath the lake itself hold most of Venezuela's rich petroleum deposits. The lake is shallow, with an average depth of ten meters, and separated from the Caribbean by a series of islands and sandbars. In 1955 a 7.5-meter channel was cut through the sandbars to facilitate shipping between the lake and the Caribbean. The channel also allows salt water to mix with the yellowish fresh water of the lake, making the northern parts brackish and unsuited for drinking or irrigation.

Population Dynamics

Three races contributed significantly to the composition of the Venezuelan population: Indians, whites, and Africans. The Indians of the region belonged to a number of distinct tribes. Those who devoted themselves to agriculture and fishing belonged mainly to the Arawak, Ajaguan, Cumanagoto, Ayaman, and other Carib tribes. The Guajiro lived, as they still do today, in the area that became the state of Zulia (see fig. 1). The Timoto-Cuica lived in the states of Táchira, Mérida, Trujillo, and Lara. The Caquetío, who prevailed in the area of present-day Falcón state, developed probably the highest cultural state of civilization of all the indigenous groups. A number of tribes also lived, as the Guajiro still do, in the Amazon jungle. Compared with other Latin American countries, however, Venezuela never had a large Indian population. After discovery by Spain, this population diminished still further, mainly because the natives lacked immunity to the many diseases brought to the New World from Europe (see Discovery and Conquest, ch. 1). In addition, Indians and Spanish intermarried; the product of this union, the mestizo, often opted for or was forced into assuming Spanish customs and religion. Fewer than 150,000 Indians were counted in the 1981 census, and, of these, over a third were made up of the Guajiro, who, though distinctive, were mostly Roman Catholic, wore their own version of Western-style clothing, and traded openly with other Venezuelans and Colombians.

During the colonial period, white settlers immigrated mostly from Spain. Blacks were brought from Africa as slaves to replace the large numbers of Indians who died from diseases and other consequences of the conquest. The African slaves labored in the hot, equatorial coastal plantations. Although miscegenation was widespread, it did not diminish the importance of color and social origin. In colonial society, *peninsulares* (those born in Spain) enjoyed the greatest prestige and power. Criollos (those born in America of Spanish parentage) occupied a subordinate position. Mestizos, blacks, and Indians made up the large lower end of the social hierarchy. Even at these lower levels, those who could somehow demonstrate a measure of white ancestry enhanced their chances of avoiding a life of penury.

Although the criollos resented the *peninsulares,* they did not identify or empathize with the lower strata. Instead, they remained deeply aware of the potential for trouble from the large mass below them and employed a variety of means to keep the nonwhite peoples at a safe distance. Despite their sometimes disreputable personal backgrounds, *peninsulares* boasted that they had pure white pedigrees. Circumstances rendered the ancestry of some criollos more questionable, and even the wealthiest were conscious of race mixture and anxious to dispel any doubts as to their parentage by remaining as separate from the nonwhite population as possible. Perceptions of race, however, evolved somewhat over time in response to changing social, political, and even cultural interests.

Reforms in the eighteenth century affected race relations by enhancing the social mobility of the crown's nonwhite subjects. During this period, persons of mixed racial origin, or *pardos* (see Glossary), were allowed, for a price, to join the militia, to obtain an education, to hold public office, and to enter the priesthood. They could even purchase legal certification of their "whiteness." These changes eliminated most of the few distinctions that had set the criollos apart from the darker-skinned masses (*pardos* at that time represented more than 60 percent of the population). Feeling their already tenuous position in society threatened, most Venezuelan criollos rejected the social policy of the Bourbons and established themselves in the forefront of the revolutionary movement for independence.

Not all criollos, however, sought to preserve the system in which *pardos* served as virtual vassals of the upper class. Twentieth-century Venezuelan history books proudly recount the late eighteenth-century radical conspiracy of the retired army officer Manuel Gual and the hacienda owner José María España, who advocated a republic that would incorporate all races and peoples equally. Inspired by the rhetoric of the French Revolution, the small group led by Gual and España recruited *pardos,* poor whites, laborers, and small shopkeepers, calling for equality and liberty and for harmony among all classes. They also promised to abolish Indian tribute and black slavery and to institute free trade. Although Gual and España also invoked the example of the newly established United States, they received no encouragement from the young country. When the conspiracy surfaced in La Guaira in 1797, the Spanish authorities terminated the movement in its early stages. Not surprisingly, criollo property owners collaborated with the authorities to suppress the radical movement.

During the wars of independence, both criollo revolutionaries and Spanish loyalists sought to engage blacks and *pardos* in their cause. This competition opened up new paths for advancement, mainly by way of the battlefield. Many of the revolutionary armies depended heavily upon the *pardos* to fill their ranks; many *pardos* also served as officers. Of greater significance for nineteenth-century Venezuelan society, the wars of independence brought to the fore a new class of leaders of mixed social and racial origins, perhaps best exemplified by José Antonio Páez, a fiery *llanero* (plainsman). Páez and leaders like him represented in almost every respect the antithesis to the cerebral, worldly wise, white, and refined Simón Bolívar Palacios and others of his class.

Páez governed Venezuela either directly as president or indirectly through his friends in the presidential office from 1830 to 1848 (see A Century of Caudillismo, ch. 1). It was a period of slow but undeniable transformation of Venezuelan society. Although traditional exports such as cotton, cocoa, tobacco, and beef expanded, coffee soon came to dominate agricultural production. The transition to coffee brought changes to Venezuelan society. Coffee growing was less labor intensive than most agricultural pursuits; even in colonial times, it operated mostly under systems of sharecropping and seasonal labor, rather than slavery. During the nineteenth century, small farmers increased their share of national coffee production and, consequently, they moved upward on the social ladder.

Toward the end of the century, after the years of the Federal War (1858–63), fissures once again appeared in Venezuelan society as new social elements arose, often defying traditional class, racial, and geographic status categories. As in so much of the country's history, a personality, another caudillo, best exemplified the new social order. In this case, the caudillo was Juan Vicente Gómez, a semiliterate Andean who dominated the national political scene from 1908 to 1935. Although often pictured as a traditional caudillo, Gómez did more than merely advance his own interests and those of his clique; he presided over the transformation of Venezuela from a rural to an urban society, from an agrarian to an industrial economy.

The illegitimate son of an Indian mother and a Spanish immigrant, Gómez rose to prominence first as a local and later a national caudillo. Once in control of the national government, he brought prosperity to Venezuela through a regime of repression, austerity, and reform. Perhaps most important, Gómez opened the Venezuelan oil fields for exploration beginning in the second decade of the twentieth century; by 1928 Venezuela had become the world's leading exporter of petroleum, second only to the United States in total petroleum production.

The impact of oil on Venezuelan society was enormous. Gómez used oil revenues to bolster his authoritarian regime. The highway system he built helped to centralize his control over the country. Agriculture rapidly lost its preeminence as petroleum became the country's leading export. Oil profits funded public works programs, industrialization, port expansions, urban modernization, and payment of the public debt. The new revenue also made Gómez and his cronies immensely rich. At the same time, Venezuela entered a new stage in its economic and social development. Traditionally self-sufficient in food, the country began to import even basic foodstuffs. The petroleum workers, never more than 3 percent of the labor force, formed an elite union that served as the nucleus of a new labor movement. The promise of jobs, prosperity, and social advancement drew Venezuelans from every corner of the country to the cities of Caracas and Maracaibo. In just a few short decades, rural agricultural Venezuelan society became urban and industrial; the middle class expanded; ethnic groups mixed more readily; and a once largely isolated society found itself involved with the rest of the world.

Population Profile

Sixth in size among the Latin American countries, Venezuela was one of the Western Hemisphere's least densely populated countries. But despite a low overall population density (21.4 persons per square kilometer in 1987), distribution was extremely uneven (see table 2; table 3, Appendix). Most of its nearly 20 million inhabitants (19,698,104, according to a mid-1990 estimate) were concentrated in the northwest and the mountains along the coast. Although nearly half of the land area lies south and east of the Río

Orinoco, that area contained only about 4 percent of the population in the late 1980s. About 75 percent of the total population lived in only 20 percent of the national territory, mainly in the northern mountains (Caracas and surrounding areas) and the Maracaibo lowlands. In the 1990s, the north, the site of most of the country's first colonial cities, agricultural estates, and urban settlements, remained the administrative, economic, and social heartland of the country. Most of the population was concentrated along the coast and in the valleys of the coastal mountain ranges, and about one of every five Venezuelans lived in Caracas. Only three major inland urban centers existed in the early 1990s: Barquisimeto, Ciudad Guayana, and Valencia. This concentration of population persisted in spite of a number of government programs that provided incentives to relocate industry and tried to expand educational opportunities throughout the rest of the country.

Venezuela's population growth rate (2.5 percent in 1990) remained among the highest in the world, fed by both a high birth rate (28 births per 1,000 population in 1990) and a comparatively low death rate (4 deaths per 1,000 population in 1990)—mainly a result of improved health and sanitary conditions after World War II. The average annual population increase for the period 1950–86 was 3.4 percent. Only in the 1970s and 1980s did it begin to level off somewhat, dropping to 2.7 percent by 1986 and to 2.5 percent by 1990. This still-high growth rate was all the more surprising in light of the widespread availability of contraceptives and Venezuelans' comparatively high education level and standard of living, social indicators that normally correlate with much lower rates of natural increase.

On average, postwar Venezuela roughly doubled its population every twenty years. The prevailing demographic patterns indicated that the population would more than double during the period 1990–2010. The number of births per woman, however, had begun to decline by 1990 (to 3.4), and this decline eventually should be reflected in lower growth figures. But any substantial reduction in the overall growth rate was not expected until sometime in the twenty-first century.

Although population figures based on census data were quite accurate for the decades after World War II, the same could not be said for the figures on mortality, particularly the figures generated at the state level. Deaths were undercounted, particularly those of infants and young children. Thus, one could not reliably compare mortality rates among individual states because a higher mortality rate in one state might not, in fact, reflect greater mortality, but simply better record keeping. Nationally, the infant mortality rate in 1990 was 27 deaths per 1,000 live births, and life expectancy was seventy-one years for males and seventy-seven years for females. Both of these figures ranked among the best in Latin America (see Health and Social Security, this ch.).

In the mid-1980s, about 40 percent of the population was under fifteen years of age; about 70 percent was under thirty (see fig. 3). The last major influx of European immigrants took place in the early 1950s, when large numbers of Spanish, Italian, and Portuguese immigrants arrived, attracted by massive government construction projects. The 1981 census showed that 94 percent of the people were native born. Of the foreign born, most came from Spain, Italy, Portugal, Africa, and Colombia. As of 1986, about 17,000 United States citizens also were living in Venezuela.

Migration

The most striking phenomenon in the distribution of the Venezuelan population has been the shift from a highly rural to an overwhelmingly urban population in response to the process of economic growth and modernization occasioned by the development of the oil industry. Venezuelan census figures defined urban localities as those having more than 2,500 inhabitants, rural areas as those with under 1,000 inhabitants, and areas with between 1,000 and 2,500 inhabitants as intermediate. Most demographers, however, categorized these intermediate areas as urban. The 1941 census indicated that about two-thirds of the population resided in rural areas. By 1950 a major shift had occurred, as the census showed that more than 53 percent of the population was urban. By 1975 the urban population was estimated at over 82 percent; the figure surpassed 85 percent in the late 1980s.

In the thirty-year period between 1941 and 1971, the absolute number of rural people remained almost constant at 2.3 million, and the number of persons in large cities mushroomed. The rural areas experiencing the most intense out-migration were located in the states of Táchira, Mérida, and Trujillo. In 1941 only two cities, Caracas and Maracaibo, had more than 20,000 inhabitants. By 1971 there were eight cities with over 100,000 persons (see table 4, Appendix). In 1981 there were nine such cities. In 1989 the estimated population of the four largest cities was: Caracas, 3,500,000; Maracaibo, 1,350,000; Valencia, 1,250,000; and Barquisimeto, nearly 1,000,000.

In addition to its high natural growth rate, Venezuela also received a considerable number of foreign immigrants during the twentieth century. Influenced by provisions encouraging the immigration of skilled workers under the 1936 Law on Immigration

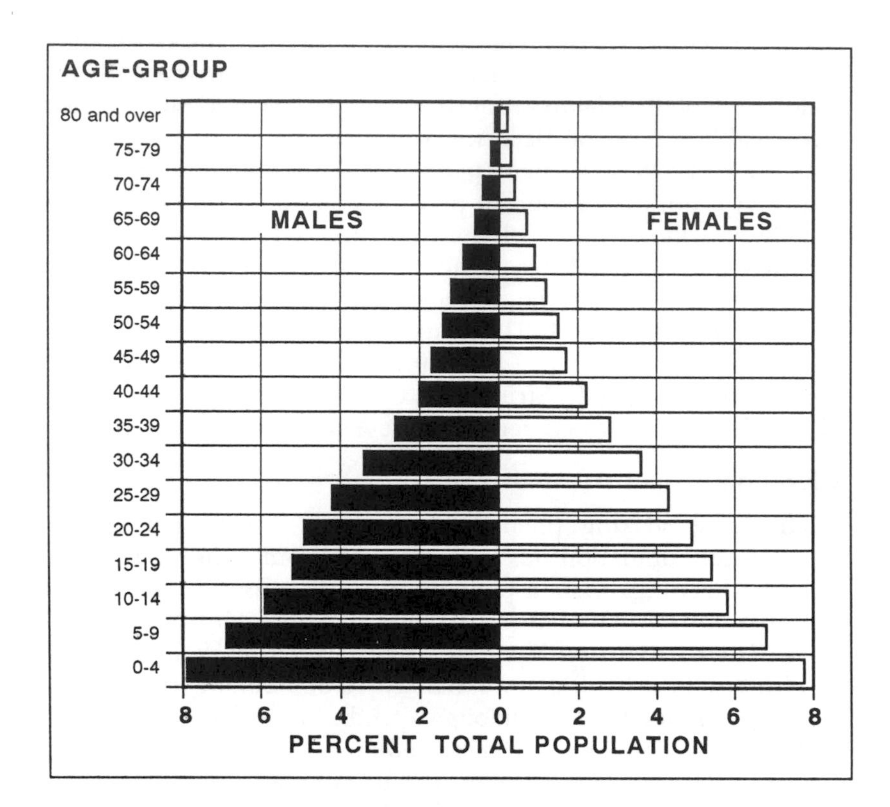

Source: Based on information from Federal Republic of Germany, Statistisches Bundesamt, *Länderbericht Venezuela, 1987,* Wiesbaden, 1987, 18.

Figure 3. Estimated Population by Age and Sex, mid-1985

and Settlement, a wave of immigrants arrived during the first years after World War II. The period of the Marcos Pérez Jiménez dictatorship (1948–58) saw over a million people enter the country. Many of them came to help build major government public works projects; these workers effectively undermined the role of domestic labor and weakened the position of the then-underground labor unions. Many saw the government's 1959 suspension of Pérez's immigration policy as a reflection of the bitterness felt by some groups toward these immigrant workers.

Immigrants to Venezuela tended to come from a fairly small number of countries. About 30 percent of the foreign-born were Colombians. Spaniards accounted for about 25 percent of the total, Italians and Portuguese about 15 percent each. The balance of immigrants came from Africa, the Middle East, Chile, Uruguay, Argentina, or Cuba. Many of these were political or economic refugees who found both economic opportunity and a democratic haven in Venezuela.

In addition to the officially recognized immigrants entering the country, many Colombians (and a far smaller number of Brazilians) have entered illegally. Although the actual number was unknown, it probably ranged between 500,000 and 1,000,000 *indocumentados* (undocumented or illegal aliens). These *indocumentados* suffered exploitation and discrimination; many Venezuelans considered them criminal elements. In reality, most crossed the border simply in search of better economic conditions. Most of them, farm or urban laborers, came in response to the lure of salaries several times as high as those prevailing in Colombia. Others were seasonal workers; about 15,000 reportedly entered each year to work as field hands during the harvest season. Still others entered to take jobs on farms or in factories for a longer time, but with the intention of eventually returning home. Most did stay, however, particularly in the northwestern states of Táchira and Zulia, where most of the border crossings took place. Some eventually migrated farther into the country, to Maracaibo or Caracas. Maracaibo hosted the largest urban concentration of Colombian *indocumentados,* who found work in the construction, petroleum, and other industries.

The illegal migration reportedly slowed down somewhat in the 1980s as a result of Venezuela's extended period of economic depression. Jobs became scarcer, and more Venezuelans found themselves seeking employment in occupations they had previously considered beneath their dignity. At the same time, complaints of mistreatment from Colombians in Venezuela increased, and a growing number of Colombian migrants apparently opted to travel to the United States.

Settlement Patterns

Venezuelans referred to their few major cities as "poles of attraction." These poles indeed functioned as magnets, drawing the population from the interior of the country to the urban centers. The 1971 census evidenced the mobility of the population when it indicated that a larger percentage of urban dwellers had come from some other place in the country than from the city where they lived. For example, less than 30 percent of the population of Caracas had been born there.

By the 1970s, the population of Caracas was spilling over into smaller towns and cities in adjacent administrative units. As a result, the Metropolitan Urban Commission was established in 1973 to be responsible for city planning for the entire metropolitan area.

By the late 1980s, a rapid-rail transportation system connected the capital with some outlying towns. Another means of relieving congestion was the Caracas Metro (Compañía Anónima Metro de Caracas—Cametro), a modern subway system that served a limited area of the capital.

The government sought to encourage reverse migration, the return of urban settlers to rural areas, but the results proved disappointing. The National Agrarian Institute (Instituto Nacional Agrario—INA) conducted a program providing incentives for rural colonization and resettlement, but, ironically, the more economically successful settlements produced such high population growth that they became, in effect, new urban centers. The government also attempted to create other poles of attraction through publicly funded industrialization projects. The best example of this policy was Ciudad Guayana, which at its founding in 1961 was planned to accommodate no more than 300,000 persons. By 1990 the government projected that the city, with its industrial complex and concentration of government services, would boast a population of one million before the end of the twentieth century. During the 1960s, the government also initiated a project to open up the sparsely populated public lands of the Orinoco Delta. Through swamp reclamation, the government expected to make some 1.6 million hectares available for year-round agricultural use. Other programs included the planned settlement of families along the country's frontiers, especially in the state of Bolívar near the Brazilian border.

In spite of these various attempts to manage migration patterns, Caracas continued to overshadow all other cities. In fact, some years the capital grew at the incredible rate of 7 percent annually. Such growth caused tremendous economic and social problems and triggered crises in the delivery of public services, especially as oil revenues dwindled.

Different sections of the country reflected quite different life-styles. Caracas was a modern, sophisticated, cosmopolitan city. Its citizens contrasted sharply with the *llaneros,* persons of the interior plains and cattle-ranching areas, who continued to lead a rugged existence. By the same token, the more conservative Andean peasants also shared few values or perspectives with their fellow citizens from the capital.

The effects of rapid urbanization are strikingly apparent in the poor barrios of Caracas, with their ramshackle *ranchos* (see Glossary). Most of the inhabitants of these barrios came from fairly good-sized towns or were actually born in Caracas, rather than gravitating directly from the hinterland to the capital city. Studies have shown that residents of the barrios were, on average, even younger than

Urban squatter settlements, commonly known as ranchos, *in Caracas*
Courtesy Inter-American Development Bank
View of Caracas
Courtesy Karen Sturges-Vera

Venezuelan society as a whole. In addition, the average family of four children was overwhelmingly the product of informal unions, and many of the children were not recognized by their fathers. In fact, in cases where the father left to form another family or disappeared altogether, prevailing social attitudes held that the mother should support the child herself, perhaps with some assistance from her own family.

The Venezuelan Children's Council (Consejo Venezolano para los Niños—CVN) was the government agency in charge of protecting the welfare of minors, but it seldom instituted judicial proceedings to compel fathers to support their children. In accord with the Hispanic tradition of maternal responsibility for rearing children, mothers were reluctant to complain to the CVN, and the council itself had few means, and perhaps even less will, to seek out those fathers who had left the household and who no longer demonstrated a sense of obligation to their children. The sprawling capital, with its labyrinth of nearly one thousand separate barrios, served as an effective haven for such individuals.

Social Structure

Before the oil era began in the mid-1920s, about 70 percent of the Venezuelan population was rural, illiterate, and poor. Over the next fifty years, the ratios were reversed so that over 80 percent of the population was urban and literate. No group has escaped the impact of this modernization process. Even the most isolated peasants and tribal Indians felt some effects of this economic growth, which opened up access to elite status; expanded opportunities for large numbers of immigrants; increased the size, power, and cohesiveness of the middle class; and created a sector of organized workers within the lower class.

The Elite

Although the traditional gap between rich and poor persisted in democratic Venezuela, the modern upper class was by no means homogeneous. Traditional society—rural, rigid, deeply stratified—changed rapidly during the course of the twentieth century. Perhaps ironically, the man most responsible for giving impetus to this change was the semiliterate dictator Juan Vicente Gómez. The primary catalyst of the social change that began under his dictatorship was economic, and it stemmed not from the established source of land controlled by powerful hacendados, but from the subsoil in the form of petroleum extracted and marketed through the efforts of technicians and technocrats. Gómez, by permitting and encouraging oil exploration, laid the basis for the emergence of an urbanized, prosperous, and comparatively powerful Venezuela from the chrysalis of a traditionally rural, agricultural, and isolated society.

The trends away from traditional society accelerated after 1945, particularly during the decade of dictatorship from 1948 to 1958 and under the post-1958 democratic regime, which is often described as the reign of the middle class. Despite the vast social and economic changes that took place, however, the economic elite remained a small group separated both economically and socially from the rest of society by an enormous income gap and by a whiter and more Hispanicized ethnic makeup.

In general, those who considered themselves the Venezuelan elite, and were thus considered by their fellow citizens, thought of themselves as the upholders of superior values. Most claimed at least one postsecondary degree, possibly with a further specialization abroad. Concentrated in business and the professions, the Venezuelan upper class tended to disdain manual work and to patronize (in both senses of the word) members of the lower classes. In this particular respect, Venezuela was one of the very few countries in Latin America where a number of elite-supported scholarly and community welfare foundations provided support for an imaginative variety of programs and scholarships. These foundations often carried the names of elite families who prided themselves on their sense of civic duty.

The members of the elite also tended to emphasize publicly their devotion to the Roman Catholic Church and faith and to display a more stable family life than did the rest of the society. That is, although divorce did occur in this class, children were usually born within a legally constituted family union. Many of the younger women managed to combine profession and family, often with the help of servants and members of the extended family.

Perhaps surprisingly to those who visit or observe Venezuelan society for the first time, the elite is not a closed and static group. Prominent politicians, even those from humble backgrounds, could easily marry into the elite. Successful professionals could also move up and find acceptance among the upper class. This relative openness of the elite may serve to mitigate to some extent the extremes that persist, particularly in economic terms, between the Venezuelan rich and those considered "marginal."

The Middle Class

Most accounts describe the Venezuelan middle class as the country's most dynamic and heterogeneous class in terms of social and racial origins, and as the greatest comparative beneficiary of the process of economic development. Consisting of small businessmen, industrialists, teachers, government workers, professionals, and managerial and technical personnel, this class was almost entirely urban. Some professions, such as teaching and government service, were traditionally associated with middle-class status, whereas newer technical professions have expanded the options and enhanced mobility within this class. Improved educational and job opportunities since the establishment of democratic government in 1958 have enabled more women to enter the labor force, thus either helping themselves and/or their families to attain middle-class status. Not surprisingly, those who passed from the lower to the middle class in Venezuela often attributed their changed status to their education, and, accordingly, many struggled to send their children to private schools so that they could move still farther up the social ladder.

A few members of the middle class moved into the elite ranks through successful business deals or by marriage. It should be noted, however, that class antagonism in Venezuela has been tempered somewhat as a result of the special efforts made by political parties to appeal to and to co-opt middle-class voters. As a result, the Venezuelan middle class had reason to feel much more politically empowered and significant than did similar groups elsewhere in Latin America. Besides the political parties, active participation in a variety of social groups and organizations further strengthened the commitment of this particular middle class to the overall sociopolitical system.

Constitutional provisions have helped both the middle and the poorer classes fulfill their aspirations in terms of greater personal freedom, expanded economic opportunities, and greater individual involvement in government. At the core of the 1961 constitution is a commitment to social justice; this commitment, in turn, has led to the creation and funding of government agencies designed to provide to the middle class and to the poor many services that had traditionally been reserved to the wealthy prior to the 1958 coup. The implementation of many social justice goals is all the more remarkable because it occurred not only during Democratic Action (Acción Democrática—AD) governments, which, by definition, were center-left, but also under Social Christian Party (Comité de Organización Política Electoral Independiente—COPEI) administrations, which were more center-right in the Venezuelan spectrum.

A short list of government agencies devoted to the implementation of social justice goals sketched in the 1961 constitution would include the Ministry of Health and Social Welfare, which provided free medical care, retirement benefits, and pensions to the disabled;

and the Ministry of Education, which supervised a vast array of goals and programs intended to bring literacy, technical, and professional training to all Venezuelans (see Social Welfare, this ch.). The Venezuelan presidency itself offered a striking illustration of the impact of these social justice goals. Since 1958 all presidents have come from the middle class, and in some cases they could claim, with reason, that they had surmounted rather lowly beginnings.

The Peasants

In the early 1990s, the majority of peasants were wage laborers, sharecroppers, or squatters on private or state-owned lands, and their meager income placed them at the outer margins of Venezuela's general prosperity. Rural life has changed little since colonial times, in spite of concerted efforts by governments committed to agrarian reform. The best land still belonged to a relatively few owners, many of them absentees, while the dwindling rural population eked out a miserable subsistence on inadequate tracts of less-than-prime farmland. Even the agrarian reform, which had distributed millions of hectares of land since 1960, had not as of 1990 gone on to the essential next step of providing the peasants legal title to their parcels (see Land Policies, ch. 3).

Regional variations in settlement patterns reflected geographic conditions, land-use practices, and historical traditions. In the northern mountain region, the heart of Spanish colonial influence, most peasants lived in small, dense settlements. In areas where wage laborers or sharecroppers still worked on large plantations, workers lived in small, centrally located clusters of houses. In the forests of the Orinoco plains, the pattern was usually one of isolated farms and cattle ranches.

Although most peasants were poor, there were gradations determined by such variables as land ownership or job security on a plantation or a ranch. The poorest peasants migrated from farm to farm or from crop to crop. In strict economic terms, the small number of tribal Indians represented the poorest group in Venezuelan society; this characterization, however, was misleading because Indian communities have never been fully integrated into the nation's economy, and therefore the concepts of individual earnings or the use of currency were foreign to their way of life.

For centuries, Venezuelan peasants supported rebel leaders in return for promises of reform. At the time of independence, they were much closer to their own José Antonio Páez than to the aristocratic Bolívar. Since 1958 many have joined the peasant leagues affiliated with the AD and have become much more influential in political terms. Nevertheless, peasants continued to migrate in massive numbers to the cities to escape their poor rural conditions.

The Workers and the Urban Lower Class

Massive rural-to-urban migration has resulted in the emergence of a burgeoning urban lower class, the most successful members of which have become urban workers. In the Venezuelan social view, the lower class consisted of those in low-status occupations (usually manual), the illiterate, and recent immigrants from the countryside. For many, the transition was traumatic and stressful, as epitomized by the presence of innumerable abandoned children in the streets of the capital city. Nonetheless, several studies indicated that most migrants felt that they had made the right move in spite of the hardships and disappointments. Most were confident that the urban environment would help ensure greater prosperity and opportunity for their children.

The urban lower class has not been ignored politically. Political parties made concerted efforts to enlist urban workers into their affiliated unions, and the government has also attempted to ''normalize'' squatter settlements by providing legal title, utilities, and other services. Nevertheless, the 1989 food riots that shook Caracas and left an estimated 300 dead demonstrated that many of the urban poor deeply resented the sociopolitical system in spite of numerous partisan and government efforts on their behalf (see Threats to Internal Security, ch. 5).

The inroads made among the urban poor class by Protestant evangelical and charismatic sects provided another manifestation of this sense of alienation. Perhaps sensing that its traditional hold was being challenged, the Roman Catholic Church renewed efforts during the 1980s to reach out to this group of Venezuelans. Church-sponsored neighborhood organizations, whether Catholic or Protestant, tried to respond to the slum dwellers' immediate needs, such as gaining title to their *ranchos*. The churches also sought to improve the future opportunities for the children of the lower class. For many migrants, the expectation of greater opportunities for children was the major reason for coming to the city in the first place. Slum dwellers also benefited to a limited extent from programs sponsored by political parties. Despite the hardships imposed by poverty and the alienation produced by a consumer culture, Venezuelan slums were surprisingly stable. These communities were socially and politically integrated into the local and national systems, and their inhabitants generally perceived even the mean circumstances of urban slum life as representing improvements over their previous living conditions.

Ethnic Groups

Venezuelan society by the twentieth century was an amalgam of three races; numerically, the country was primarily mestizo (mixed race). Although ethnic background served as an important criterion of status in colonial times, it became less so as genetic mixing involving various combinations of white, black, and Indian made distinguishing among racial types increasingly difficult. Eventually, ethnic categories came to be regarded as points along a continuum rather than as distinct categories, and physical appearance and skin color—instead of ethnic group per se—became major criteria for determining status. No national census has classified Venezuelans according to ethnicity since 1926, so that characterizations of the national composition are only rough estimates. A credible break-down through 1990 would be 68 percent mestizo, which in Venezuela signified a mixture of any of the other categories; 21 percent unmixed Caucasian; 10 percent black; and 1 percent Indian.

Even during the colonial period, native Venezuelan Indians were neither as numerous nor as advanced as their counterparts in Mexico and Peru. Different tribes with varying cultures and languages occupied portions of the territory. The more advanced groups were ruled by a single chief and supported a priesthood to serve the local temples, whereas the more primitive lived as wandering hunters and gatherers or as seminomadic slash-and-burn farmers. The Spanish conquest, either directly or indirectly, resulted in the decimation of many indigenous groups. Many perished from diseases against which they had no immunity; others died of famine or the harsh conditions of enslavement. The nomadic tropical forest Indians were less affected by the Spaniards than were those Indians who occupied a defined territory. Most of the nomadic groups simply moved to less accessible areas. Even they, however, lost many of their number to diseases brought by Europeans, diseases that were airborne or waterborne and therefore did not require direct contact to spread infection. By the end of the first century of Spanish rule, some twenty tribes out of forty or fifty had become extinct.

Also during the colonial period, racial mixture proceeded apace. The earliest conquerors brought no Spanish women with them, and many formed common-law relationships with Indian women. It was not uncommon for the offspring of these unions to be recognized and legitimated by the fathers.

African slavery was instituted in Venezuela to meet the growing labor demands of an emerging agricultural economy. Many of the slaves came to Venezuela not directly from Africa, but from other colonies, especially the Antilles (West Indies). Again, racial mixture was common. The offspring of master and slave often was freed and might even have received some education and been named a beneficiary in the father's will.

As a result of these racial mixtures, Venezuelan society from its very beginnings displayed a more homogeneous ethnic makeup than most other Latin American colonies. The large group of freedmen worked mostly as manual laborers in the emerging cities or lived as peasants on small plots of land. Blacks and mestizos occupied the rungs below Spaniards on the social ladder, but they still enjoyed a number of rights and guarantees provided by Spanish law and customs.

This rather fluid ethnic situation, however, did not equate to a free and open society. Until the latter half of the twentieth century, Venezuelan social structure was quite rigidly organized along class and racial lines. A small number of more or less pure-blooded, unmixed Caucasians occupied the top rung of the social ladder by virtue of their status as landlords and as self-styled inheritors of Hispanic mores and customs. This heritage stressed the importance of the patriarchal extended family, the primacy accorded individual uniqueness and dignity, disdain for manual labor, and a sharp distinction between the roles of men and women. In the traditional society, the lower class was rural, with the majority of its members poor peasants, usually of pure or mixed Indian or black descent. A small middle class, made up of less successful whites and some mestizos, lived mainly in the cities and towns.

By the early eighteenth century, the outlines and bases of the social system had been drawn. Most Indians and a growing number of blacks were losing their ethnic and cultural identities through the processes of racial mixture and societal pressure to conform to Hispanic norms. New generations began to see themselves as Venezuelans, distinct from Colombians, with whom they were associated through colonial administrative structures, or from the dwindling numbers of isolated forest Indians. The criollos, Venezuelan but of direct Spanish descent, formed the leadership cadre of a new national system. The growth of nationalism, however, did not subsume or overcome regional differences. In fact, the devotion to region was often far stronger than devotion to country, a factor that in many ways explains the protracted nature of the war of independence. In addition, both Indians and blacks during this period had reason to feel that they were better protected by the Spanish crown than might be the case under a regime ruled by haughty criollos (see The Epic of Independence, ch. 1).

Venezuelans
Courtesy Inter-American Development Bank

After independence the society changed little; a small, privileged, criollo elite upper class still held sway over a small middle class and a large lower class. The internal wars among competing caudillos during the second half of the nineteenth century served as a leveler to some extent. By the turn of the century, even though Venezuela was still a very traditional society, the upper levels had been breached to the point where a semiliterate peasant caudillo such as Gómez could rise to the very top of the political ladder and rule for nearly three decades (see A Century of Caudillismo, ch. 1).

Given the relative fluidity of Venezuelan society in ethnic terms, few groups have stayed isolated and "pure." Among these were a few settlements of coastal blacks that retained more of their African and West Indian identity than did the vast majority of dark mestizos in many other areas of Venezuelan society, particularly in such cosmopolitan cities as Caracas. Other isolated groups included the tribal Indians, particularly in the Amazon area. A more visible but still distinct group was that of the Guajiro Indians, who could be found mainly in part of the area around Maracaibo, on the Península de la Guajira, and on the Colombian border.

The Guajiro, pastoral nomads who range freely across the Venezuelan-Colombian border region, represented probably the best known and largest tribe of Indians remaining in the country. Owing to their pastoral life, most of the Guajiro lived in temporary villages, often in shelters that were little more than lean-tos. Guajiro society is organized into matrilineal clans, headed by chieftains who inherit their office through the maternal line. The social organization is based on a division of society into classes of nobles and commoners.

Although the Guajiro's style of dress and customs separated them sharply from the larger Venezuelan society, they had adopted many criollo traits and adapted fairly well to a money economy. Most professed at least nominal Roman Catholicism and spoke Spanish. Intermarriage with non-Guajiros also was not uncommon. In this respect, the Guajiro reflected the changes in twentieth-century Venezuelan society as a whole as they adapted to a process of modernization driven by the nation's oil wealth.

Modernization, Social Values, and Religion

Venezuelan society of the late twentieth century was clearly in transition. After centuries of isolation as a rural backwater in Latin America, Venezuela has become a respected voice in world councils because of its oil riches. Most of its population has moved to the cities, and well-to-do Venezuelans have traveled around the world in search of recreation and diversion. Economic growth, urbanization, industrialization, improved education, and expanded opportunities for women have changed the nation's character dramatically. Improved transportation, widespread radio and television access, the availability of numerous national newspapers, and the delivery of government services even in remote areas combined to make regionalism largely a thing of the past. Caracas was greatly influenced by developments in Miami and other foreign commercial and cultural centers; the rest of the country, in turn, felt the reverberations of the capital's growth and change.

The rapid pace of change has had a tremendous impact in such areas as the emerging role of women in Venezuela. Women have occupied positions in the cabinet and have held prominent jobs in the political parties and in labor unions. More than a dozen women representatives have served in the Chamber of Deputies. A number of women have also held top positions in private enterprises. Approximately as many women as men attended postsecondary institutions; in some departments, women outnumbered their male counterparts.

For the middle-class woman who wanted to combine job and family, support continued to be provided by the extended family and the availability of maids, who often were recent migrants from the Andean region or from Colombia. As the extended family progressively shrank and the traditional pool of poor and uneducated women grew progressively smaller, however, Venezuelan professional women had begun clamoring for day-care facilities. As of 1990, more progressive and larger firms were beginning to provide such facilities, but the main push was for the provision of these services by the government. Meanwhile, an active feminist movement was particularly strong in the capital and the major cities, and women's studies were beginning to make their appearance among the university offerings.

Some social observers claimed that the rapid change in women's roles was attributable, at least in part, to the traditional weakness of the Venezuelan Roman Catholic Church when compared, for example, with the church in neighboring Colombia. Some 90 percent of Venezuelans were baptized in the Roman Catholic faith, but most had little regular contact with the church. The number of Protestants continued to grow, mainly as a result of the tremendously successful proselytizing efforts among shantytown dwellers by charismatic and evangelical sects, and had reached about 5 percent of the population in the 1990s. A Jewish population of several thousand was concentrated in the major cities, especially in Caracas and Maracaibo. A minuscule number of Indians, particularly in the Amazon area, continued to practice their traditional religions, but many had adopted Roman Catholicism. This was particularly true among the Guajiro near Maracaibo and on the Colombian border. A few other religions were represented in very small numbers. Religious freedom is guaranteed by the nation's 1961 constitution.

Relations between the Roman Catholic Church and the Venezuelan state have been harmonious throughout most of the twentieth century. They continued to be peaceful even after the 1958 coup d'état against Pérez Jiménez, in spite of the fact that the church had supported the dictator in his early years as president. Relations between the church and AD were somewhat strained during the *trienio* (see Glossary), mainly because the church felt threatened by some of the AD government's liberal reforms. As the corruption of the Pérez Jiménez regime became increasingly apparent, however, the church began to disassociate itself from his rule and to support a return to democracy (see The Transition to Democratic Rule, ch. 1).

Although there is no official state church, the Roman Catholic Church enjoyed close ties to the government and could be perceived as a national church. COPEI, the second largest political party, was originally organized by Roman Catholic lay leaders, even though it has since broadened its appeal to Venezuelans of all religious persuasions.

The Venezuelan church was not well endowed economically. It owned little property and received only limited private contributions. The government contributed a large part of the church's operating expenses through a special division of the Ministry of Justice. Government funds generally covered the salaries of the hierarchy, certain lesser functionaries attached to the more important episcopates, a limited number of priests, and the missionaries to the Indians. In addition, government contributions sometimes paid for religious materials, for construction and repair of religious buildings, and for other projects submitted by bishops and archbishops and approved by the ministry.

Attitudes toward the church varied with education and social class, but it was generally viewed as a traditional institution involved more in ritual than in day-to-day contact with its members. Venezuelans generally practiced a form of Roman Catholicism that adhered loosely to church doctrine but was often deeply emotional in its manifestations. Religious laxity was widespread, as was a low level of general knowledge of the basic tenets of the faith. During the latter half of the twentieth century, Venezuela has become a much more secular and materialistic society, less committed to the traditional social primacy of the church.

In all social classes, religion was regarded as the proper sphere of women. Generally more conscientious in religious practice, women were expected to assume the duty of providing the religious and moral education of children. For girls, early religious and moral training was followed by close supervision in accordance with the socially protected status of women. Boys, however, were not encouraged to pursue the priesthood, and Venezuela historically has had a very low percentage of religious vocations. As a result, most of its clergy were foreign born.

Adherence to traditional Roman Catholic beliefs was stronger in the rural areas, especially in the Andean states, than in the urban centers. Many of the original leaders of COPEI came from the Andean states. Massive internal migration to the cities, however, had lessened considerably the influence of these old strongholds of Roman Catholicism at the national level.

Traditionally, one of the most significant and important areas of church involvement in society was education. Roman Catholic schools historically have educated the children of the middle and upper classes. Because many schools were supported only by tuition fees, their costs were prohibitive for lower-class groups. Spurred by the social encyclicals issued from Rome in the 1960s and challenged by the proselytizing of Protestant groups, the church's hierarchy has sought to establish greater control over the schools, to admit greater numbers of scholarship students, and to increase the number of schools charging little or no tuition. As a result, by the middle of the 1970s an estimated two-thirds or more of Roman Catholic schools and colleges were free or partly free.

The church has always felt a special obligation to help educate and Christianize the Indians. In the 1920s and 1930s, the government entered into a series of agreements with the church that assigned the regions of the upper Orinoco, the western Zulia, the Caroní, and the Tucupita rivers to the Capuchin, Dominican, and Salesian religious orders. Educational work has been carried out in conjunction with the plans of the Indian Commission of the Ministry of Justice.

Although Venezuelan culture was a mixture of Hispanic, Indian, and African elements, comparatively rapid integration of large segments of the population prevented the syncretic blending of animistic and Roman Catholic beliefs so common in other Latin American countries. The culturally embracing nature of Venezuelan Catholicism was symbolized in the national patroness, the mestiza María Lionza, a popular figure among Venezuelans of all social classes. The cult of María Lionza presented a striking synthesis of African, Indian, and Christian beliefs and practices. She was worshipped as a goddess of nature and protectress of the virgin forests, wild animals, and the mineral wealth in the mountains, and certain traits of her character also paralleled those of the Virgin Mary in Roman Catholic tradition.

The worship of María Lionza was particularly widespread among urban dwellers in the shantytowns, many of whom had recently migrated to the big cities and felt the need for a blending of Christian and traditional indigenous beliefs. At the same time, beliefs and practices related to magic and spiritual healing that combined Roman Catholic, African, and Indian elements could be found in remote rural areas, especially in the Andean states. In keeping with the ethnic and cultural background of many coastal communities, African elements predominated in their rituals. Traditional Indian healers still practiced their craft among the remaining tribes.

Social Welfare

Education

In the early colonial era, education by the Roman Catholic Church served a minority of wealthy landowners who, though illiterate or barely literate, sought schooling for their sons in the manner of Spanish aristocrats. The notion of education for a privileged few reflected a rigid, hierarchical social system that distinguished between the man of letters and the man who worked with his hands. The distinction between manual labor and more "artistic" or creative pursuits became deeply ingrained in the value system and affected the educational system as well. The high prestige attached to traditional and philosophical studies channeled resources and talent away from technical and scientific fields at university levels and produced curricula at the primary and intermediate levels that ignored the vocational needs of most of the population. In an abstract sense, the highest ambition was to be a *pensador* (thinker), a man of ideas, an intellectual, rather than an inventor or a *técnico* (technician).

Those who helped shape the struggle for independence and the new constitutions of the early nineteenth century were inspired by the liberalism of the French and American revolutions. Simón Bolívar, who studied in Europe, was greatly influenced by the writings of Jean-Jacques Rousseau and by the French educational system. Such features of Venezuelan education as the degree of centralization, the rigid structure of schools and curricula, and the gaining of knowledge through logic are directly traceable to French practices.

The issue of free, public, and compulsory education at the primary level first arose during the independence struggle. After the initial declaration of independence in 1811, Bolívar issued a series of decrees concerning free education. But by the time of his death in 1830, most of the programs he had proposed had not been implemented. However, the ideal of free, universal education had become inextricably joined to the name of the national hero, and this ideal has since permeated Venezuelan educational policies.

The real beginning of free public education, however, did not come until 1870. Antonio Guzmán Blanco issued a decree in which he recognized compulsory elementary mass education as the responsibility of the national, state, and local governments. The Guzmán regime went on to organize the administration and financing of the school system, establishing the Ministry of Public Education and the first normal schools for training primary school teachers. In 1891 the National University of Zulia in Maracaibo was created, followed in the next year by the National University of Carabobo in Valencia. But these ambitious beginnings came to an abrupt halt. The National University of Carabobo was closed shortly after opening and did not reopen its doors until 1958. The National University of Zulia, closed in 1904, did not function again until 1946.

The long dictatorship of Juan Vicente Gómez, although generally indifferent to education and repressive of student demands, did bring about the reestablishment of cordial relations between the state and the Roman Catholic Church and encouraged church-supported education. Gómez served as a patron to a number of intellectuals who were sympathetic to his regime and increased the support for the national university in Caracas.

During the decade after the death of Gómez in 1935, concern for teacher training prompted the establishment of a new institute for the preparation of intermediate teachers, the National Pedagogic Institute in Caracas. The period also witnessed an expansion of public schools to rural areas. During the *trienio,* a number of teachers' unions grew up. The Pérez Jiménez dictatorship (1948–58), however, represented a low point for education. The regime constantly interfered with and intermittently closed universities in response to perceived opposition among students and faculty. The budget for education was cut, and the number of students entering and graduating from the universities declined.

The return of democratic government in 1958 brought leaders committed to improving both the quantity and the quality of educational opportunities. A number of new universities opened throughout the country, agricultural extension services reached out to Venezuelan farmers, and imaginative education programs broadcast on radio and television further expanded opportunities for learning. In fact, it is generally acknowledged that it was only after

1958 that the ideals and goals of Guzmán began to be systematically pursued. At least six years of primary school were compulsory until 1980, when the Organic Law of Education was passed. This law provided for compulsory preschool education and nine years of basic education, but the implementation of preschool education reform has taken longer than originally intended.

For the upper class, the growing middle class, and those members of the lower class with upward aspirations, an academic education has been indispensable. For this reason, the secondary schools, which prepared students for the universities and subsequently for white-collar jobs or academic careers, were more popular than other intermediate-level schools, such as technical schools or training institutes. Despite government efforts to promote vocational education, university students continued to display a preference for the professions that have always been prestigious and popular rather than for the newer technical fields where the need was greatest. This preference presented a problem in a country that was more industrialized than most in Latin America. In an effort to alleviate the problem and to enhance the prestige of a technical education, since 1969 the government has facilitated the entry into the university system of students with varied backgrounds, including students with a technical education degree. From 1969 on, the changes injected a high degree of flexibility into the education system.

At the same time, the social distinction that has always existed between private and public schools, particularly at the secondary level, has intensified as a result of the expansion of public education. Although the public or official schools often enjoyed better financial support and, as a result, newer equipment and more highly paid teachers, a private-school education still carried far more prestige in the minds of many Venezuelans. In light of the cachet bestowed by affiliation with a private school, some teachers split their time between the two systems.

Since the mid-twentieth century, the natural sciences have been emphasized in education as international organizations, and private foundations have cooperated with the national government in promoting research. The social sciences have been greatly influenced by work done in the United States, especially in the area of economic development.

Overall, Venezuela was among the most literate of the Latin American countries. The literacy rate among Venezuelans fifteen years of age and older was 88.4 percent in 1985. The government distributed training materials such as books and tapes throughout

Fifth-grade classroom, eastern Venezuela
Courtesy Inter-American Development Bank
Science Center at the University of the Andes, Mérida
Courtesy Inter-American Development Bank

the country in an effort to encourage those who could read and write to assist illiterates in acquiring these skills.

Basic education consisted of nine years of compulsory schooling for children six to fourteen years of age. For those continuing their education, the system offered two years of diversified academic, technical, and vocational study at a senior high school, which could be followed by various types of higher education—junior college, university, or technical institute. In addition, adults were encouraged to participate in special night classes conducted at all education levels.

Venezuela's education system, as measured by the number of schools, teachers, and size of the enrollment, expanded rapidly in the 1970s and 1980s (see table 5, Appendix). Enrollments at all levels increased substantially, as did the numbers of schools and teachers at each level. Primary enrollments rose by over 30 percent and secondary by over 50 percent, while university-level enrollments nearly doubled, the latter a reflection not only of population growth but also of the opening of new schools and the easing of entrance requirements. The best-known and oldest university was the Central University of Venezuela, in Caracas. Many of the country's political leaders received their education there, and several of the political parties began as student groups on the Central University of Venezuela's campus. To the west, Maracaibo was the site of the private Rafael Urdaneta University and the public Zulia University. The public University of the Andes was located in Mérida. Carabobo University in Valencia, Eastern University (Universidad de Oriente) in Sucre, and Midwestern University (Universidad Centro-Occidental) in Barquisimeto were all public universities.

Shifts in the economy affected Venezuela's technical education needs. Until the economic downturn of the 1980s, the shortage of skilled workers and managers was a main concern of government planners. Skilled personnel were needed to operate what had been a burgeoning and technologically sophisticated economy. To fill the gap, Venezuela recruited many skilled foreign technicians, expanded its technical education facilities, and sent Venezuelans abroad for training, particularly in the United States and Europe. With the economic decline of the 1980s, however, rising unemployment replaced the continuing lack of technically qualified personnel as the primary manpower concern, and the emphasis on technical education was reduced (see Labor, ch. 3).

Health and Social Security

As in education, Venezuela had, by Latin American standards, an enviable record in health and social welfare and one that had shown tremendous progress. In 1940 the overall life expectancy at birth was forty-three years. By 1990 that figure was over seventy years: seventy-one years for males and seventy-seven for females, both among the highest in Latin America. The death rate was only 4 per 1,000 population, and the average caloric intake was 107 percent of the minimum level established by the United Nations (UN) Food and Agriculture Organization. These indices reflected generally improving health conditions, especially since the end of World War II, and the increase in preventive public health measures undertaken by the government. For example, successful inoculation programs had lessened the incidence of a number of contagious diseases. On the other hand, a comparison between the causes of death in 1973 and 1981 shows that Venezuela, a rapidly industrializing country, was also becoming more prone to causes of death—heart disease, accidents, and cancer—often associated with urban and industrialized countries and a faster pace of life (see table 6, Appendix). Acquired immune deficiency syndrome (AIDS) was also a growing problem, particularly for the major cities, such as Caracas and Maracaibo, and for tourist centers, such as La Guaira and its environs. In 1990 information on the actual incidence of AIDS in Venezuela was unreliable.

Infant mortality, pegged at a relatively low 27 deaths per 1,000 live births in 1990, has also been steadily declining, especially in the years following World War II. The major causes of these improvements were better public health measures, prenatal care, and national immunization campaigns. Overall, health care facilities have grown in number and in quality; at the same time, the population has become more urban and better educated. There has also been a marked increase in the number of medical facilities and personnel offering health care (see table 7, Appendix). The rise in the number of nurses reflected government incentives in this field as well as the selection of this vocation by a greater number of professionally inclined Venezuelan women.

Medicine has traditionally been a highly respected profession, and Venezuelan medical schools turned out adequate numbers of well-trained doctors. At the same time, however, relatively few nurses received proper training, so that doctors often lacked the necessary support system. The availability of care in rural areas represented another gap in the health care delivery system. Doctors tended to concentrate in the large cities, especially Caracas, leaving many smaller provincial towns without adequate medical personnel. The government has attempted to meet these shortcomings, with some success, by providing basic medical services through a system of paramedics. On the other hand, shrinking budgets could take a toll on health services. In the summer of 1990, President Carlos Andrés Pérez himself showed deep concern over the fact that, by government estimates, nearly 46 percent of state-supported hospital buildings were in need of repair.

Private medical facilities, operated for profit, enjoyed greater prestige than public institutions. Charitable organizations, especially the Roman Catholic Church, operated some health facilities. The bulk of the population, however, relied on the Venezuelan Social Security Institute (Instituto Venezolano de Seguro Social—IVSS), which operated its own hospitals, covering its costs out of social security funds. At public hospitals, small fees were charged to those patients able to meet them, but indigents were treated without cost. Services were furnished without charge at public outpatient facilities, with a nominal charge for prescription drugs. Overall, the medical assistance received by most Venezuelans far exceeded that available to the great majority of Latin Americans.

The Ministry of Health and Social Welfare operated hospitals and lesser clinical medical facilities nationwide and coordinated the planning of medical services by the states and the Federal District. Although attempts have been made to provide a unified health system, as of 1990 such plans had not been implemented.

Government campaigns for the prevention, elimination, and control of major health hazards have been generally successful. Venezuela has largely rid itself of malaria; yaws and the plague have been brought under control; and Chagas' disease, carried by a beetle that attaches itself to straw thatch roofing, has been nearly eliminated. Immunization campaigns have systematically improved children's health, and regular campaigns to destroy disease-bearing insects and to improve water and sanitary facilities have all boosted Venezuela's health indicators to some of the highest levels in Latin America.

In addition to providing public health care, the IVSS also administered the country's public welfare program. Launched in 1966, the IVSS provided old-age and survivor pensions. In addition, it sponsored maternity care and medical care for illness, accidents, and occupational diseases for workers in both the public and private sectors. Participation in the program was mandatory for all wage earners with the exception of temporary and seasonal or part-time workers, the self-employed, and members of the armed forces (who were covered under a separate system). The availability of benefits has been extended progressively to all regions of the country so that even farm workers and farmers associated with the agrarian reform program were eligible.

Private charitable and social welfare organizations, which were exempt from the income tax, played an important role in supporting and maintaining charity hospitals and organizations, assisting persons of limited income, and funding scholarships. Among the most active of these organizations was the Voluntary Dividend for the Community, founded in 1964 and supported by contributions from the business community. It subsidized welfare programs, private education, and community development projects. In this instance, as in others, Venezuela benefited from the efforts of community-minded leaders of the private sector, who bolstered government programs and provided further assistance for those in greatest need.

Thus, in the 1990s, Venezuela did not lack for public and private leaders who were deeply concerned about the needs of their fellow countrymen. Rather, the looming problem appeared to be one that Venezuela had not known for decades, that of scarcity. Throughout the 1980s, the state had fewer resources with which to respond to the demands of an expanding young population that had become accustomed to relying on the public sector for employment and social services. For a time, the public was willing to blame the new problems of scarcity on the ineptness and, to some extent, the corruption of politicians. By the end of the 1980s, however, most Venezuelans realized that even a well-intentioned, honest, and capable government would have to adjust to the economic reality of reduced export income and a large external debt. The apparent upward trend in oil prices heralded by the Iraqi invasion of Kuwait in August 1990 represented the one bright spot on the economic horizon. Even that, however, was obscured by concerns over the general health of the domestic economy, the availability of refining capacity for Venezuela's heavy crudes, and other considerations.

Despite these economic setbacks, the legitimacy and the viability of the Venezuelan democratic society did not seem threatened. Racial tension did not divide this largely mestizo society as it did some other Latin American societies. Although poor Venezuelans sometimes demonstrated violently, as in the case of the February 1989 riots against economic austerity, there was no sentiment outside of small extremist groups for a return to an authoritarian government of the right or the establishment of a Cuban-style government of the left. The events of the 1980s, however, shocked Venezuelan society; after decades of increasing prosperity and improving health, education, and economic indices, Venezuelans suddenly found themselves vulnerable to the shifting fortunes of a world economy that had always proved beneficent in the past. This "crisis," although more economic than social, should nonetheless provide the sternest test yet of Venezuela's commitment to a free, tolerant, and socially conscious system.

* * *

A major, comprehensive study of Venezuelan society is still to be written. Although the literature in English is not voluminous, good, but narrow, perspectives can be found in Robert F. Arnove's *Student Alienation: A Venezuelan Study,* G.E.R. Burroughs's *Education in Venezuela,* Lisa Redfield Peattie's *The View from the Barrio,* and John Duncan Powell's *Political Mobilization of the Venezuelan Peasant.*

In Spanish, the offerings are much more promising. Among the best are Federico Brito Figueroa's *La estructura económica de Venezuela colonial,* Sergio Aranda's *Las clases sociales y el estado en Venezuela,* Maritza Montero's *Ideología, alienación e identidad nacional,* Rafael Carías's *¿Quiénes somos los venezolanos?,* and excellent chapters in Antonio Frances's *Venezuela posible.* (For further information and complete citations, see Bibliography.)

Chapter 3. The Economy

Street scene with a view of the harbor, Puerto Cabello

AN UPPER-MIDDLE INCOME, oil-producing country, Venezuela enjoyed the highest standard of living in Latin America. The country's gross domestic product (GDP—see Glossary) in 1988 was approximately US$58 billion, or roughly US$3,100 per capita. Although the petroleum industry has dominated the Venezuelan economy since the 1920s, aluminum, steel, and petrochemicals diversified the economy's industrial base during the 1980s. Agricultural activity was relatively minor and shrinking, whereas services were expanding.

Venezuela possessed enormous natural resources. The country was the world's third largest exporter of oil, the ninth largest producer of oil, and accounted for more oil reserves than any other nation in the Western Hemisphere. The national petroleum company, Venezuelan Petroleum Corporation (Petróleos de Venezuela, S.A.—PDVSA), was also the third largest international oil conglomerate. Because of its immense mineral wealth, Venezuela in 1990 was also poised to become an international leader in the export of coal, iron, steel, and aluminum.

Despite bountiful natural resources and significant advances in some economic areas, Venezuela in 1990 continued to suffer from the debilitating effects of political patronage, corruption, and poor economic management. The country's political and economic structures often allowed a small elite to benefit at the expense of the masses. As a result, Venezuela's income distribution was uneven, and its social indicators were lower than the expected level for a country with Venezuela's level of per capita income. Many economic institutions were also weak relative to the country's international stature. The efforts of the administration of Carlos Andrés Pérez (president, 1974–79, 1989–) to reform the economy, especially if coupled with political and institutional reforms, would likely determine whether the country would reach its extraordinary potential.

Growth and Structure of the Economy

Spanish expeditionaries arrived in what is present-day Venezuela in 1498, but generally neglected the area because of its apparent lack of mineral wealth. The Spaniards who remained pursued rumored deposits of precious metals in the wilderness, raised cattle, or worked the pearl beds on the islands off the western end of the Península de Paria. Colonial authorities organized the local Indians into an *encomienda* system (see Glossary) to grow tobacco, cotton, indigo, and cocoa. The Spanish crown officially ended the *encomienda* system in 1687, and enslaved Africans replaced most Indian labor. As a result, Venezuela's colonial economic history, dominated by a plantation culture, often more closely resembled that of a Caribbean island than a South American territory (see Spanish Colonial Life, ch. 1).

Cocoa, coffee, and independence from Spain dominated the Venezuelan economy in the eighteenth and nineteenth centuries. Cocoa eclipsed tobacco as the most important crop in the 1700s; coffee surpassed cocoa in the 1800s. Although the war of independence devastated the economy in the early nineteenth century, a coffee boom in the 1830s made Venezuela the world's third largest exporter of coffee. Fluctuations in the international coffee market, however, created wide swings in the economy throughout the 1800s.

The first commercial drilling of oil in 1917 and the oil boom of the 1920s brought to a close the coffee era and eventually transformed the nation from a relatively poor agrarian society into Latin America's wealthiest state. By 1928 Venezuela was the world's leading exporter of oil and its second in total petroleum production. Venezuela remained the world's leading oil exporter until 1970, the year of its peak oil production. As early as the 1930s, oil represented over 90 percent of total exports, and national debate increasingly centered on better working conditions for oil workers and increased taxation of the scores of multinational oil companies on the shores of Lago de Maracaibo (see fig. 1). In 1936 the government embarked on its now-famous policy of *sembrar el petróleo,* or "sowing the oil." This policy entailed using oil revenues to stimulate agriculture and, later, industry. After years of negotiations, in 1943 the government achieved a landmark 50-percent tax on the oil profits of the foreign oil companies. Although Venezuela reaped greater benefits from its generous oil endowment after 1943, widespread corruption and deceit by foreign companies and indifferent military dictators still flourished to the detriment of economic development. Nevertheless, despite unenlightened policies, economic growth in the 1950s was robust because of unprecedented world economic growth and a firm demand for oil. As a result, physical infrastructure, agriculture, and industry all expanded swiftly.

With the arrival of democracy in 1958, Venezuela's new leaders concentrated on the oil industry as the main source of financing for their reformist economic and social policies (see The Triumph of Democracy, ch. 1). Using oil revenues, the government intervened significantly in the economy. In 1958 the new government founded a new noncabinet ministry, the Central Office of Coordination and Planning (Oficina Central de Coordinación y Planificación—Cordiplan) in the Office of the President. Cordiplan issued multiyear plans with broad economic development objectives. The government in 1960 embarked on a land reform program in response to peasant land seizures. In 1960 policy makers also began to create regional development corporations to encourage more decentralized planning in industry. The first such regional organization was the Venezuelan Corporation of Guayana (Corporación Venezolana de Guayana—CVG), which eventually oversaw nearly all major mining ventures. The year 1960 also marked the country's entrance as a founding member into the Organization of the Petroleum Exporting Countries (OPEC), which set the stage for the economy's rapid expansion in the 1970s. Throughout the 1960s, the government addressed general social reform by spending large sums of money on education, health, electricity, potable water, and other basic projects. Rapid economic growth accompanied these reformist policies, and from 1960 to 1973 the country's real per capita output increased by 25 percent.

The quadrupling of crude oil prices in 1973 spawned an oil euphoria and a spree of public and private consumption unprecedented in Venezuelan history. The government spent more money (in absolute terms) from 1974 to 1979 than in its entire independent history dating back to 1830. Increased public outlays manifested themselves most prominently in the expansion of the bureaucracy. During the 1970s, the government established hundreds of new state-owned enterprises and decentralized agencies as the public sector assumed the role of primary engine of economic growth. The Venezuelan Investment Fund (Fondo de Inversiones de Venezuela—FIV), responsible for allocating huge oil revenues to other government entities, served as the hub of these institutions. In addition to establishing new enterprises in such areas as mining, petrochemicals, and hydroelectricity, the government purchased previously private ones. In 1975 the government nationalized the steel industry; nationalization of the oil industry followed in 1976. Many private citizens also reaped great wealth from the oil bonanza, and weekend shopping trips to Miami typified upper-middle-class life in this period.

A growing acknowledgment of the unsustainable pace of public and private expansion became the focus of the 1978–79 electoral campaign. Because of renewed surges in the price of oil from 1978 to 1982, however, the government of Luis Herrera Campíns (president, 1979–84) scrapped plans to downgrade government activities, and the spiral of government spending resumed. In 1983, however, the price of oil fell, and soaring interest rates caused the national debt to multiply. Oil revenues could no longer support the array of government subsidies, price controls, exchange-rate losses, and the operations of more than 400 public institutions. Widespread corruption and political patronage only exacerbated the situation.

The government of Jaime Lusinchi (president, 1984–89) attempted to reverse the 1983 economic crisis through devaluations of the currency, a multi-tier exchange-rate system, greater import protection, increased attention to agriculture and food self-sufficiency, and generous use of producer and consumer subsidies. These 1983 reforms stimulated a recovery from the negative growth rates of 1980–81 and the stagnation of 1982 with sustained modest growth from 1985 to 1988. By 1989, however, the economy could no longer support the high rates of subsidies and the increasing foreign debt burden, particularly in light of the nearly 50-percent reduction of the price of oil during 1986.

In 1989 the second Pérez administration launched profound policy reforms with the support of structural adjustment loans from the International Monetary Fund (IMF—see Glossary) and the World Bank (see Glossary). In February 1989, price increases directly related to these reforms sparked several days of rioting and looting that left hundreds dead in the country's worst violence since its return to democracy in 1958 (see Threats to Internal Security, ch. 5). Ironically, Pérez, who oversaw much of the government's expansion beginning in the 1970s, spearheaded the structural reforms of 1989 with the goal of reducing the role of government in the economy, orienting economic activities toward the free market, and stimulating foreign investment. The most fundamental of the 1989 adjustments, however, was the massive devaluation of the bolívar (B; for value of the bolívar—see Glossary) from its highly overvalued rate to a market rate. Other related policies sought to eliminate budget deficits by 1991 through the sale of scores of state-owned enterprises, to restructure the financial sector and restore positive real interest rates, to liberalize trade through tariff reduction and exchange-rate adjustment, and to abolish most subsidies and price controls. The government also aggressively pursued debt reduction schemes with its commercial creditors in an effort to lower its enervating foreign debt repayments.

Economic Policy

Fiscal Policy

The government's fiscal accounts generally showed surpluses until the mid-1980s because of the immense oil income. In 1986, however, the drop in oil prices triggered a fiscal deficit of 4 percent; the deficit exceeded 6 percent in 1988.

The major actors in fiscal policy were Cordiplan, which was responsible for long-term economic planning, and the Budget Office of the Ministry of Finance, which oversaw expenditures and revenues for each fiscal year (FY—see Glossary). Cordiplan also oversaw the fiscal status of the FIV, PDVSA, the social security system, regional and municipal governments, the foreign exchange authority, state-owned enterprises, and other autonomous agencies. But economic planning and budgeting suffered from a serious lack of interagency cooperation, and five-year plans and annual public-sector investments often lacked cohesiveness.

Total government spending reached about 23 percent of GDP in 1988. Current expenditures accounted for 70 percent of overall outlays, compared with 30 percent for capital expenditures. Capital investments, after a decline in the mid-1980s, expanded slowly during the late 1980s. Interest payments, two-thirds of which serviced foreign debt, represented 11 percent of total expenditures in 1988, a typical figure for most of the decade.

The revenue structure in the late 1980s remained excessively dependent on oil income. In 1988 petroleum revenues, both income taxes and royalties, provided 55 percent of total revenue. Although oil's contribution to total revenue had declined in the 1980s, most economists felt that it had not declined sufficiently. Overall, taxes contributed 80 percent of total revenue in 1988, with the remaining 20 percent derived from such nontax sources as royalties and administrative fees. Tax exemptions, deductions, allowances, and outright evasion greatly reduced the effectiveness of fiscal policy. Officials planned to inaugurate a value-added tax in 1990 as another means to widen the revenue base.

Monetary and Exchange-Rate Policies

The Central Bank of Venezuela (Banco Central de Venezuela—BCV) performed all typical central bank functions, such as managing the money supply, issuing bank notes, and allocating credit. As part of the country's overall financial sector reform, the BCV embarked in 1989 on numerous revisions of monetary policy aimed at improving the bank's control over the money supply. The most important policy change was the government's decision to allow the interest rate to fluctuate with market rates. Despite its initial inflationary effect, the policy created incentives for savings and investment, thereby attracting and retaining capital. Deposits swelled noticeably during 1989. In 1990, however, the Venezuelan Supreme

Court declared that the BCV was legally responsible for setting interest rates. The BCV hoped to rescind the law in the early 1990s.

Venezuela traditionally enjoyed general price stability; inflation averaged a mere 3 percent from 1930 to 1970. Annual price increases did not exceed 25 percent until the mid-1980s. During the 1970s, many economists credited the FIV with successfully managing and investing overseas the country's oil windfalls in a way that prevented inordinate price instability. By the 1980s, however, financial deterioration, weakening BCV authority, numerous devaluations, and fiscal deficits had combined to push consumer prices and inflation up dramatically in the late 1980s. The average consumer price index rose by an unprecedented 85 percent in 1989 (see table 8, Appendix). Some price increases were associated with the 1989 structural adjustment program, and thus represented what some economists refer to as "correctionary inflation," the trade-off for eliminating previous distortions in prices. By 1990 only a handful of price controls remained in effect.

The bolívar was traditionally a very stable currency, pegged to the United States dollar at a value of B4.29 = US$1 from 1976 to 1983. The bolívar experienced several devaluations from 1983 to 1988, when monetary authorities implemented a complicated four-tier exchange-rate system that provided special subsidized rates for certain priority activities. The multiple exchange-rate system, however, proved to be only a stopgap measure, eventually giving way to a 150-percent devaluation at the market rate in 1989. The 1989 devaluation unified all rates from the official B14 = US$1 rate to the new B36 = US$1 rate, which was a floating rate subject to the supply and demand of the market. By late 1990, the value of the bolívar had crept down to B43 = US$1.

In a related matter, the Currency Exchange Office (Régimen de Cambio de Dinero—Recadi), the organization that oversaw the various exchange rates, became the focus of one of the largest scandals in the decade. Between 1983 and 1988, businessmen bribed Recadi officials in return for access to half-priced United States dollars to funnel an alleged US$8 billion overseas. When the scandal broke in 1989, law enforcement agents investigated as many as 2,800 businesses, and more than 100 executives from leading multinational enterprises fled the country in fear of prosecution.

Labor

Formal Sector

Venezuela's official labor force in 1989 stood at 6.7 million. The labor force constituted 57 percent of the economically active population (those over age fifteen) and 35 percent of the entire 19.7 million population. Many workers, particularly youth, women, and the elderly, were not recorded in official labor data, however (see Informal Sector, this ch.). Some 6.12 million workers of the total labor force had jobs in 1989, resulting in an unemployment rate of 8.7 percent. Unemployment fluctuated based largely on the health of the oil industry. In 1978 only 4.3 percent of the official labor force was unemployed, compared with the peak level of 14.5 percent in 1984.

Services accounted for the greatest portion of the labor force in 1989 (26 percent), followed by commerce (20 percent), government (20 percent), manufacturing (17 percent), and agriculture (13 percent). Mining and petroleum, the source of most government revenue and nearly all exports, employed less than 1 percent of the labor force (see fig. 4).

Female participation in the labor force was increasing, but represented only 31 percent of the official work force in 1987. A growing cadre of female technicians and laborers worked in heavy industries, but women still generally received lower salaries than men.

The typical rural employee earned 25 percent less than his or her urban counterpart, and white-collar workers averaged more than double the earnings of blue-collar workers. Income distribution was highly skewed, in that the wealthiest 20 percent of the population owned 45 percent of the country's wealth, whereas the poorest 20 percent held only 6 percent of the wealth.

The Venezuelan government passed a rather comprehensive labor law as early as 1936 in response to protracted disputes between workers and foreign oil companies. A new labor law in 1974 further expanded workers' rights, and the country debated a revised labor law in 1990. The nation's 1990 labor law incorporated provisions for organized labor, collective bargaining, generous fringe benefits, and retirement and disability pensions. Venezuela passed a national minimum wage in 1974. As throughout Latin America, however, the Ministry of Labor in Venezuela was generally incapable of adequately enforcing the country's labor code. Conversely, many employers complained of the difficulty of firing a worker after the first three months on the job.

Over one-quarter of all workers were organized, and labor unions played a visible role in society (see Interest Groups and Major Political Actors, ch. 4). The Confederation of Venezuelan Workers (Confederación de Trabajadores de Venezuela—CTV), affiliated with the Democratic Action (Acción Democrática—AD) party, represented the majority of organized labor. There were also

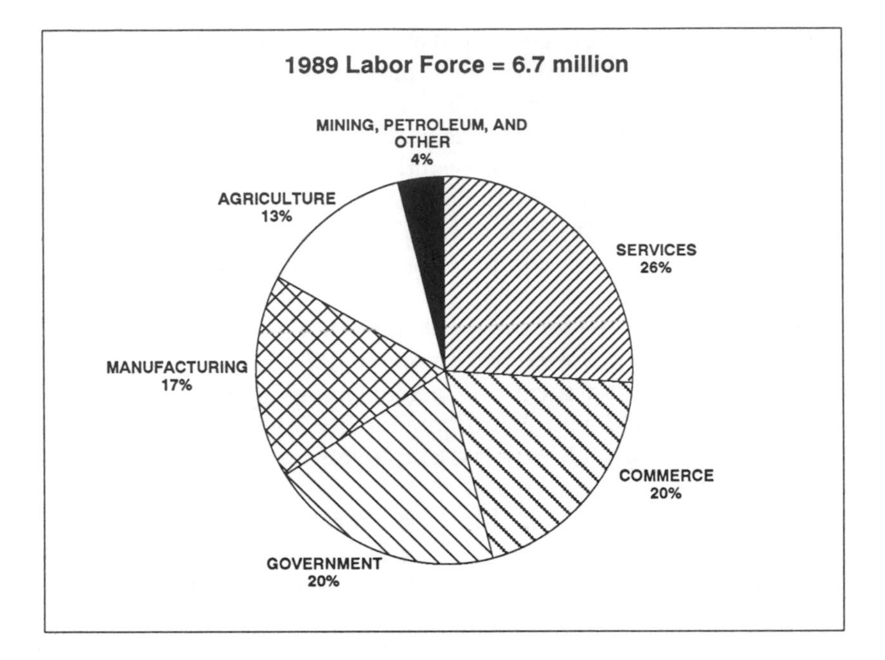

Figure 4. Employment by Sector, 1989

three smaller labor federations and a handful of independent unions. The public sector and heavy industry employed the highest percentages of organized workers.

Unlike what was the case in many Latin American countries, labor relations in Venezuela were consultative rather than confrontational, and the CTV had good working relations with the major business group, the Federation of Chambers and Associations of Commerce and Production (Federación de Cámaras y Asociaciones de Comercio y Producción—Fedecámaras). Strikes were rare, and the government typically did not intervene to resolve labor contract negotiations. Labor's relations with both management and the government soured somewhat after the 1986 fall in oil prices, however. Unprecedented inflation from 1986 to 1990 quickly eroded unionized salaries, further straining these alliances as the country sought to find new mechanisms to compensate for the effects of inflation. In May 1989, the CTV led a general strike to protest the February 1989 adjustment in the value of the bolívar and austerity policies, indicating a growing division between the CTV and its political affiliate, the AD.

Informal Sector

An estimated 2.3 million persons, or 38 percent of all workers, operated outside the formal economy in 1988. Although estimates varied, the informal sector accounted for between 32 and 40 percent of the labor force throughout the 1980s. This sector included nonprofessional self-employed workers, businesses employing five or fewer persons, and domestic workers. So-called *informales* drove taxis, offered door-to-door mechanical services, cleaned homes, sold clothing on downtown streets, and worked as day laborers. Youth, women, and Colombian *indocumentados* (undocumented or illegal aliens) apparently constituted a disproportionate share of the informal sector. According to some analysts, the country's large underground economy stemmed from the government's excessive regulation of the formal economy and the private sector's inability to provide sufficient jobs for the country's burgeoning urban populace.

Agriculture

Agriculture played a smaller role in the Venezuelan economy than in virtually any other Latin American country in the 1980s. In 1988 the sector contributed only 5.9 percent of GDP, employed 13 percent of the labor force, and furnished barely 1 percent of total exports (see fig. 5). Agricultural output was focused almost entirely on the domestic market.

The backbone of the national economy for centuries, agriculture entered a period of steady decline in the early twentieth century as the oil industry eclipsed all other sectors of the economy. As late as the 1930s, agriculture still provided 22 percent of GDP and occupied 60 percent of the labor force. The industrial development of the nation by the 1940s, however, seemed to have relegated agriculture to permanent secondary status.

Agriculture recorded its worst growth in years in the early 1980s, and the decade saw successive programs designed to revive agriculture in the face of a weakened economy. Government policies toward the sector often alternated between deregulation and extensive government intervention, with the latter being the more typical response. In 1984 the Lusinchi administration confronted rural stagnation with a multifaceted program of producer and consumer subsidies, import protection, and exchange-rate preferences. The plan also reduced interest rates on agricultural loans through scores of government development finance institutions serving the sector. Government decrees also required commercial banks to hold at least 22.5 percent of their loan portfolios in agriculture. Farmers

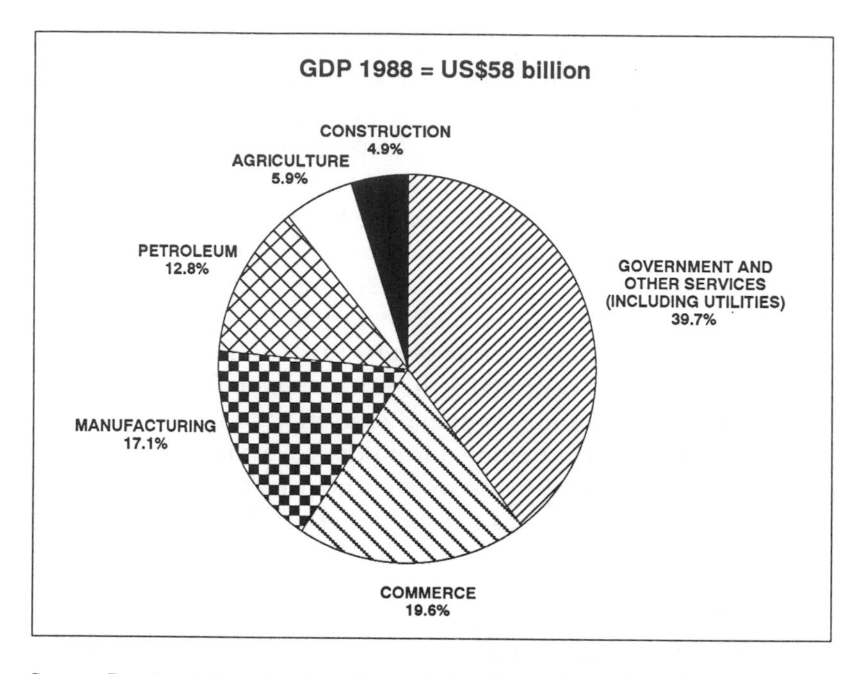

Source: Based on information from Economist Intelligence Unit, *Country Report: Venezuela, Suriname, Netherlands Antilles*, No. 3, London, 1989, 2.

Figure 5. Estimated Gross Domestic Product (GDP) by Sector, 1988

were exempt from income taxes. These measures paid off handsomely in the short run. During one five-year period of expansion, for example, annual growth rates in the agricultural sector reached 8 percent in 1984 and 1985. The government's program to resuscitate the rural economy, however, was extremely costly because it entailed high levels of subsidization.

The Ministry of Agriculture and Livestock (Ministerio de Agricultura y Cría—MAC) designed and implemented the nation's agriculture policy. The most drastic changes in farm policy in 1990 occurred through the devaluation of the bolívar, which automatically eliminated previous preferential rates for certain agricultural inputs. Likewise, the Pérez government's policy of price deregulation affected many basic agricultural commodities, and ensuing price rises were a factor in the February 1989 riots. As a result of government cutbacks in subsidies and price supports, agriculture registered a 5-percent decline in 1989.

Land Policies

Despite agrarian reform efforts beginning in 1960, Venezuela's land tenure patterns in 1990 still portrayed the typical Latin American dichotomy between latifundios and *minifundios* (small holdings). For example, data on land tenancy from agricultural censuses from 1937 through 1971 pointed to a pattern of land concentration. More recent estimates mirrored data from these earlier censuses. One estimate in the late 1980s, for example, held that the smallest 42.9 percent of all farms covered only 1 percent of the arable land, whereas the largest 3 percent accounted for as much as 77 percent of arable land.

The country's major land reform program began with an initial decree in 1958 after the fall of the dictatorship of Marcos Pérez Jiménez. The Agrarian Reform Law of 1960 created the National Agrarian Institute (Instituto Nacional Agrario—INA), which sought to provide land to those who worked it, initially by transferring public lands and later by expropriating private holdings of arable land not under cultivation. Although the government invested substantial resources in an effort to integrate its rural development strategy through the provision of roads, markets, schools, and clinics, new agricultural colonies rarely had the conveniences of earlier farming towns. Accordingly, the land reform experienced a dropout rate as high as one-third. Moreover, few of the peasants who stayed in the settlements actually obtained legal title to their land, which remained in the hands of the state.

Land reform had made only modest adjustments in Venezuelan land tenure through 1990. By the 1980s, over 200,000 families had benefited from the state's distribution of nearly 10 percent of the country's total land area. The average size of the country's 400,000 farming units stood at eighty hectares in 1989, considerably higher than earlier decades. Improved access to land helped expand the country's total land under cultivation and accelerated the country's attainment of self-sufficiency in certain crops and livestock. On the negative side, however, the benefits of land reform were seriously tainted by the program's high failure rate and the fact that as many as 90 percent of participants never gained title to their land. Without land titles, farmers lacked collateral to obtain financing for needed agricultural inputs. These factors, combined with the fact that immense private tracts of land remained intact, demonstrated the relatively minor impact of land reform.

Land Use

Only some 4 percent of Venezuela's total area, or about 3.8 million hectares, was considered readily arable or already under cultivation in the late 1980s. Some estimates claimed that as much as one-third of the country's total land area was suitable for agriculture.

In general, however, Venezuela's vast expanse was better suited to forest or pasture than to crops, and much otherwise arable land had been relatively neglected because of adverse weather conditions or lack of access to markets.

Crops

Food Crops

Despite gains in the production of some grains and cereals, urbanization and changing dietary patterns increased Venezuela's dependence on imports of basic foods during the 1980s. The migration of farmers to urban areas reduced the output of traditional food crops such as cassava, potatoes, and other inexpensive tubers; higher wheat imports compensated for this decline. The growing popularity of wheat products in Venezuela drove imports steadily higher because the country's warm climate was not conducive to the cultivation of wheat.

Corn was the country's major domestic food crop. Most of Venezuela's corn crop came from the central plains, particularly the states of Portuguesa, Barinas, and Guárico. A traditional staple, corn surpassed coffee as the nation's leading crop in the 1960s; by 1988 farmers cultivated corn on some 642,000 hectares. Total production was 1.28 million tons in that year. After declining in the 1970s, corn production flourished in the 1980s, largely because of the agricultural policies of the mid-1980s that provided import protection and stimulated greater food self-sufficiency. Despite the gains of corn producers, however, the costs of corn production remained relatively high, which indicated that domestic production would be vulnerable to the effects of external competition under the market-oriented reforms initiated by the government in the early 1990s.

Sorghum became a major grain in the mid-1970s. A drought-resistant crop, it was introduced to Venezuela because it could tolerate the country's unpredictable precipitation pattern. Sorghum, like corn, was grown nationwide, and sorghum production enjoyed rapid growth during the 1980s. In 1988 sorghum covered some 392,000 hectares, which yielded approximately 820,000 tons of grain. The popularity of sorghum in the 1980s was closely linked with the quick expansion of the national pork and poultry industries, which used sorghum as their major feed grain. Although domestic production increased, however, it could not keep pace with demand. Consequently, imports of sorghum also climbed throughout the decade.

Rice was another major grain. Rice production doubled during the 1970s, mainly because of the increased use of irrigation. In the

Unloading harvested corn
Courtesy Inter-American Development Bank

1980s, however, rice production fell rapidly. Weather variations accounted for some fluctuations in production, but the central cause of the decline was poor technical expertise in both cultivation and irrigation techniques. Rice paddies covered some 116,500 hectares of land and yielded 383 tons of rice in 1988; at its peak in 1981, rice grew on some 243,000 hectares and yielded 681,000 tons. Frustrated by the inadequacy of available technology, many rice farmers had switched to other crops by the late 1980s. Many of these producers had complained about the inadequate levels of credit available from the government, as well as the low prices the government paid for their crops.

Farmers grew rice throughout the country, with the exceptions of the extreme west and south. Farmers who cultivated irrigated rice, especially those in Portuguesa and Guárico, produced as many as 2.5 crops a year, whereas dry rice farmers brought in only one crop, during the May through November rainy season.

Farmers also cultivated a wide variety of tubers, legumes, vegetables, fruits, and spices. Principal tuber crops consisted of cassava, potatoes, sweet potatoes, and taro. In some areas, peasants milled cassava for use as a flour. Legumes included yellow, black, and white beans, as well as a local pulse called *quinchoncho.* Vegetables included tomatoes, lettuce, cabbage, carrots, cauliflower, eggplant, cucumber, beets, and peas. The more moderate regions of Venezuela were also suitable for a wide variety of fruits. Depending on the seasonal crop, the country exported small amounts of tropical fruits.

Cash Crops

Cocoa and coffee provided most of Venezuela's export revenues before they entered a period of prolonged decline in the 1900s. Jesuits introduced coffee in the 1740s, and by the 1800s Venezuela was the world's third largest coffee producer. By the 1980s, however, the coffee industry was in a decline. In 1988 coffee trees occupied 273,200 hectares and produced only 71,000 tons of coffee, one of the lowest yields in the world. The value of coffee exports, mainly to the United States and Europe, was about US$24 million in 1988. Coffee was primarily a peasant crop, grown largely on farms of under twenty hectares in mountainous areas. Low profits prevented most farmers from taking steps, such as the planting of newer coffee bushes, that could improve yields. Worse still, Venezuelan coffee in the 1990s faced the impending introduction of plant diseases from the neighboring coffee crops of Colombia and Brazil.

Cocoa was also characterized by extremely low yields, in part as a result of aged trees and general deterioration in the crop. Once Venezuela's leading cash crop, by 1988 cacao plants covered only about 59,000 hectares and yielded a mere 13,500 tons of cocoa beans. As with coffee, most farmers sold their cocoa through government marketing boards for use domestically and internationally. Exports of cocoa beans and products exceeded US$17 million in 1988, ranking cocoa as the third leading agricultural export (after coffee and tobacco), mainly to Belgium, the United States, and Japan.

Tobacco appeared to be one of the country's few dynamic cash crops in the late 1980s. Although tobacco generally stagnated in the 1970s and early 1980s, output expanded notably in the late 1980s as the industry turned to export markets in the Caribbean. In 1988 farmers in the west-central plains planted about 9,100 hectares of both dark and light tobacco, producing about 15,300 tons of leaf. In 1988 the cigarette industry exported upwards of US$20 million of cigarettes to the Caribbean, ranking tobacco as the second largest export crop.

Other leading cash crops included sugarcane, oilseeds, and cotton. Once a net exporter of sugar, Venezuela by the mid-1970s became a net importer, and in 1988 the country was only 71 percent self-sufficient in sugar. Sugarcane grew on 117,000 hectares in 1988 and produced 8.33 million tons of raw sugar, but annual output fluctuated according to weather conditions, management practices, price changes, and currency devaluations. Many farmers plowed under their cane fields in the 1980s in order to plant more lucrative crops, and the nation's sixteen sugar mills faced ongoing technical obstacles.

Oilseeds, such as sesame, sunflower, coconut, peanut, and cotton, faced a fate similar to other cash crops, and in 1988 the nation was only 21 percent self-sufficient in edible oils. Although Venezuela was once one of the world's leading producers of sesame oil, the industry declined as a result of a deterioration of the genetic content of the country's sesame plants and low market prices. Sesame plants, however, still extended over 148,700 hectares and yielded 68,300 tons in 1988. By the 1980s, Venezuela imported large amounts of soybean oil.

Livestock

The country's livestock industries accounted for nearly a third of all output in the agricultural sector and met the nation's basic meat consumption needs. The pork and poultry industries fared well during the 1980s, but the beef and dairy industries struggled. The cattle industry, a mainstay of Venezuela's central plains for centuries, failed to modernize along with the pork and poultry industries during the 1970s and 1980s. The low prices paid by the government, combined with producer export taxes, hurt cattle ranchers, who did not export for several years during the 1980s. Both cattle ranchers and dairy farmers were unable to maximize production. The government sought to intervene in the case of the dairy industry, providing various levels of subsidies, especially for consumers. These policies proved unsuccessful, however, and did more to promote corruption in milk distribution than efficiency in production. By 1990 the country was only 40 percent self-sufficient in milk. Many of the subsidies were likely targets of market-oriented reforms in the early 1990s.

The poultry and pork industries succeeded in bringing more modern production techniques to Venezuela beginning in the 1970s. Some 2.5 million pigs were slaughtered in 1988, up from 1.7 million in 1980. The poultry industry also increased production, from 156 million broilers in 1980 to 251 million in 1988. The country exported modest amounts of poultry in the mid-1980s. Both the pork and poultry industries, however, faced increased costs after 1989 as a result of the exchange-rate liberalization that raised the cost of imported feeds.

Farming Technology

Venezuelan farmers' use of purchased inputs—such as fertilizers, tractors, and irrigation water—to increase their productivity remained closely tied to government promotional policies. For example, Venezuelan farmers enjoyed generous subsidies for the purchase of domestically produced fertilizers after 1958. As a result, fertilizer use increased greatly. From 1980 to 1986, the application of fertilizers more than doubled, from 64 to 141 kilograms per hectare. In 1989 the Pérez administration reduced fertilizer subsidies from 90 percent to 30 percent. This action had little effect on agricultural production because fertilizer usage already exceeded optimum levels in many areas.

In 1989 MAC administered twenty-four irrigation projects that covered 261,600 hectares. Only 40 percent of this irrigated area, however, actually received water from irrigation projects. Poor management and inadequate maintenance of the irrigation systems prevented the remainder of the land from reaching its full potential. Nonetheless, irrigation projects enabled the country to improve its productivity and self-sufficiency in some crops, most notably rice.

Credit and agricultural extension services were two other tools employed by the government to improve farming practices. Successive governments, beginning in the 1960s, established scores of development finance institutions exclusively for agriculture (see Banking and Financial Services, this ch.). In the 1980s, dozens of such lenders provided finance for agriculture at widely varying rates depending on the loan, the product involved, and the type of institution from which it originated. Commercial banks also held extensive agricultural portfolios as government laws required that 22.5 percent of all credit be allocated to that sector. In addition, bankers and other government finance institutions lent to farmers and ranchers at a rate as low as one-third of the prevailing commercial rate. By contrast, government agricultural extension efforts were less aggressive. The country's extremely low yields in many crops and livestock were attributable, in part, to the inadequacy of extension services. MAC's National Agricultural and Livestock Research Fund (Fondo Nacional de Investigaciones Agropecuarios) performed research and provided some minimal extension services for farmers. Universities and institutes, such as the Simón Bolívar United World Agriculture Institute in Caracas, also contributed to agricultural and environmental research. More typically, farmers obtained technical assistance from producer associations to which they belonged.

Fishing and Forestry

The fishing subsector as a whole provided over one-tenth of the total output of the agricultural sector by the late 1980s. For a country with a 2,800-kilometer coastline, a shallow continental shelf of some

9,000 square kilometers, and a network of more than 1,000 rivers, Venezuela was slow to exploit its coastal and inland waterway resources. It was not until the mid-1980s that a minor fishing boom took place. In 1975 the government established a National Fishing Enterprise to upgrade the traditionally undercapitalized fishing industry. During this period, the growth of domestic shipbuilding and a general industrial expansion benefited fishermen. From 1983 to 1988, the catch of the nation's anglers grew by 54 percent, reaching 354,185 tons. A 300-percent increase in the tuna catch ranked Venezuela as the world's fourth largest producer. Most tuna, however, was sold at sea and did not reach local markets, where meat was still the dietary preference. By contrast, river fishing remained underdeveloped.

Forests covered an estimated 34 percent of Venezuela's land area. During the 1980s, the timber industry modernized and consolidated; from a collection of small saw mills, it developed into several large integrated wood pulp and newsprint plants, especially in the Ciudad Guayana region. Joint ventures with foreign companies sought to harvest several hardwood species for wood products and chemical derivatives. The government's forest protection service wielded little regulatory authority, prompting some concern over the pace of deforestation.

Energy and Industry

Petroleum

Petroleum dominated the economy throughout the twentieth century. In 1989 the petroleum industry provided almost 13 percent of the GDP, 51 percent of government revenues, and 81 percent of exports. Before the sharp drop in international oil prices in the 1980s, these ratios were considerably higher. From 1929 to 1970, the year of the country's peak production, Venezuela was the world's largest exporter of petroleum. In 1990 the country ranked as the third leading oil exporter, after Saudi Arabia and Iran, and contained at least 7 percent of proven world oil reserves.

The country's national petroleum company, the Venezuelan Petroleum Corporation (Petróleos de Venezuela, S.A.—PDVSA), the third largest international oil conglomerate, owned refineries and service stations in North America and Europe. Although Venezuela was only the third largest petroleum producer in the Western Hemisphere, behind the United States and Mexico, its proven reserves, at 58.5 billion barrels in 1989, exceeded those of both countries. Venezuela exported 54 percent of its petroleum to the United States in 1988, representing about 8 percent of American petroleum imports.

The first commercial drilling of petroleum in Venezuela took place in 1917. After World War I, British and American multinational oil companies rushed to Lago de Maracaibo to tap the country's huge petroleum reserves. Oil jumped from 31 percent of exports to 91 percent from 1924 to 1934. The industry proved extremely lucrative to the scores of foreign companies that drilled Venezuelan crude because of the country's low wages and nominal taxes, policies supported by corrupt relations between foreign oil companies and various military dictatorships.

In the forty-year period after the death of Juan Vicente Gómez in 1935, the government and foreign oil companies engaged in a tug-of-war over taxation, regulation, and, ultimately, ownership. Although Venezuela reaped substantially greater benefits from its generous oil endowment after 1943, corruption and deceit on the part of the foreign companies and avaricious caudillos such as Pérez Jiménez still limited the national benefits of the industry. By the early 1970s, the possible nationalization of the oil industry became the focus of debate among labor, businesses, professionals, government, and the public at large. Aware of the conflicts and subsequent difficulties of Mexico's sudden, dramatic nationalization of the entire oil industry in the 1930s, Venezuela pursued its acquisition of the petroleum sector cautiously and deliberately. In December 1974, a national commission created by President Pérez delivered a proposal for nationalization. This proposal formed the core of the 1975 law that nationalized the oil industry. The most controversial element of the new law was Article 5, which gave the government the authority to contract out to multinational firms for various technical services and marketing. Despite the controversy, Article 5 provided technical expertise that proved crucial to the industry's smooth transition to state control beginning on January 1, 1976.

In 1977 the government created a holding company, PDVSA, to serve as the umbrella organization for four major petroleum-producing affiliates. This process consolidated the holdings of fourteen foreign companies and one national company, the Venezuelan Petroleum Corporation (Corporación Venezolana de Petróleos—CVP), into four competing and largely autonomous subsidiaries. Industry analysts have credited the competitive structure of the subsidiaries with increasing overall efficiency to levels well above those of most nationalized companies. The largest subsidiary of PDVSA was Lagoven, which was composed mainly of the facilities previously operated by the United States oil company Exxon. Lagoven

Research and development laboratory, Petróleos de Venezuela, S.A. (PDVSA)
Courtesy Inter-American Development Bank

accounted for 40 percent of national output in 1976. From the holdings of British and Dutch Shell, PDVSA created a subsidiary called Maraven. Four smaller United States companies became Meneven. Finally, PDVSA consolidated six smaller foreign firms and the state oil company into Corpoven.

A slump in world oil prices beginning in 1981 rolled back the substantial revenues acquired, and largely squandered, during the 1970s. The symbolic end of PDVSA's prosperity came in 1982, when the Central Bank of Venezuela seized US$6 billion of the oil company's earnings to help offset the country's growing external debt problems. This action effectively eliminated PDVSA's autonomy. After oil prices dropped nearly 50 percent in 1986, the government accelerated industrial diversification programs in specialized petroleum refining, natural gas, petrochemicals, and mining, and also stepped up oil exploration efforts.

Exploration remained a major focus of PDVSA activities in the 1980s. At the time of nationalization in 1976, exploration efforts had come to a near standstill. Little exploratory activity took place during the 1960s and 1970s because the Venezuelan government did not grant any new oil concessions after 1958 and most foreign oil companies anticipated eventual nationalization. Although financial constraints slowed the pace of exploratory drilling in the 1980s, major new finds of light, medium, and heavy crude by 1986 nearly doubled proven reserves.

The country's 1989 oil reserves were expected to last for at least ninety-three years at prevailing rates of extraction. The Orinoco heavy oil belt accounted for 45 percent of proven reserves in 1989, followed by the Maracaibo region with 32 percent, the eastern Venezuelan basin with 22 percent, and 1 percent in other areas (see fig. 6). Only a small fraction of the Orinoco's total heavy oil deposits, however, were routinely included in estimates of total proven reserves because of the cost and difficulty of extraction. Some estimates of total recoverable heavy crude reserves ran as high as 190 to 200 billion barrels.

PDVSA's early exploration strategy emphasized heavy crude, but by the 1980s the company's efforts shifted toward more valuable light and medium grades. This approach proved successful, as major new discoveries were made in the Lago de Maracaibo area, the Apure-Barinas Basin in southwest Venezuela near the Colombian border, and in the eastern Venezuelan basin in the El Furrial/Musipán area in the state of Monagas. Encouraged by its finds in the mid-1980s, PDVSA launched further drilling operations in the late 1980s, with the goal of adding 14.4 billion barrels of light and medium crude to its proven reserves by 1993. In addition to its land-based drilling, PDVSA established an increasing number of offshore rigs. The Venezuelans also explored off the coast of Aruba and had discussed with the governments of Guyana, Trinidad and Tobago, and Guatemala the prospects of exploratory drilling.

PDVSA not only extracted crude oil, but also refined and distributed a wide variety of petroleum products. In 1988 six active refineries in Venezuela boasted an installed refining capacity of approximately 1.2 million barrels of oil a day. These refineries produced a full range of oil products and specialty fuels, making Venezuela an international leader in petroleum refining (see table 9; table 10, Appendix). PDVSA increased the percentage of locally refined crude from 35 percent to 58 percent between 1979 and 1988. In 1988 the country for the first time exported more refined petroleum than crude. PDVSA diversified its production during the 1980s, increasing the share of petroleum products that fell outside OPEC quotas until the late 1980s, in an effort to enhance price stability and boost profits. Orinoco Asphalt (Bitúmenes del Orinoco), a PDVSA subsidiary, began preliminary shipments in the late 1980s of *orimulsión,* a uniquely Venezuelan synthetic fuel derived from Orinoco heavy crude, water, and chemical additives. PDVSA hoped to export increasing quantities of *orimulsión,* outside OPEC quotas, to Canada and Europe as a substitute for coal or fuel oils used by electric power stations.

From 1983 to 1989, PDVSA acquired overseas refining capacity from at least five multinational oil conglomerates, either through production contracts or outright purchases. For example, in 1983 PDVSA bought a 50 percent share of the West German Veba Oil Company, thereby acquiring 210,000 barrels per day in overseas refining capacity. PDVSA expanded its overseas refining facilities in 1986 with a joint venture with the Swedish lubricant and asphalt producer, Nynas. Beginning in 1986, PDVSA entered the United States oil market by purchasing United States oil firms, refineries, and retail outlets previously held by Citgo, Champlin, and Unocal. PDVSA's overseas refining capacity exceeded 700,000 barrels per day by the close of the decade. By 1990, therefore, PDVSA had the capability to refine nearly all of its crude oil production, either at home or at Venezuelan-owned facilities overseas. Moreover, with PDVSA's purchase of Citgo in 1989, Venezuela became the first OPEC member to wholly own a major United States oil refinery.

The United States has consistently been Venezuela's leading oil export recipient. During the 1980s, however, PDVSA increased its exports to Central America and the Caribbean. In 1980 Venezuela and Mexico embarked on a joint program called the San José Accord, under which the two oil producers exported oil to many countries of the Caribbean Basin (see Glossary) region at concessionary rates. The accord set up a system of compensatory finance and purchases of Venezuelan goods in exchange for crude that amounted to a 20 percent discount on the world market price.

Natural Gas and Petrochemicals

Venezuela also possessed vast reserves of natural gas. Proven gas reserves reached an estimated 3 trillion cubic meters in 1989, the second greatest proven reserves in the Western Hemisphere after the United States. At current rates of extraction, proven gas reserves could meet domestic needs into the twenty-second century. In the late 1980s, the country produced roughly 22 billion cubic meters of gas a year, most of which was used to meet domestic energy needs.

The natural gas industry increased in importance during the 1980s as oil prices declined, as more households received piped gas, as gas-intensive heavy industries came on-stream, and as liberalization of foreign investment rapidly expanded the potential of the petrochemical industry. Natural gas effectively became the property of the state under the Hydrocarbons Reversion Law of 1971, at which time the state-owned CVP oversaw exploration. A major effort to expand consumer sales of gas in the late 1980s involved

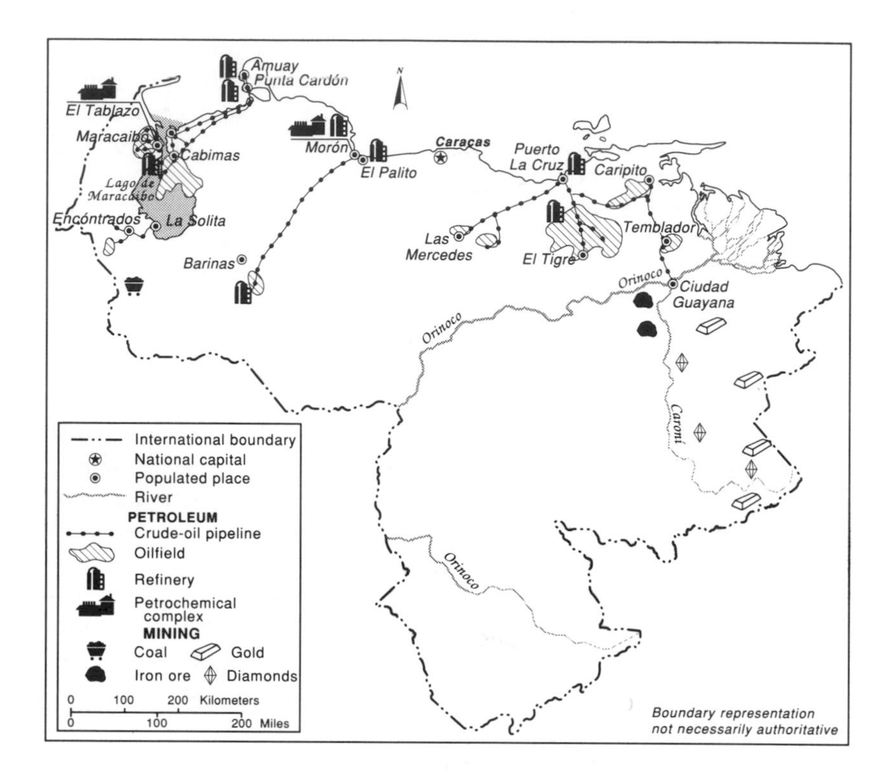

Figure 6. Petroleum and Mining, 1990

gas pipeline construction to provide gas to households. Gas also fueled some of the industries in the mining sector.

Venezuelan Petrochemicals (Petroquímicas de Venezuela—Pequiven), a PDVSA subsidiary established in 1977, oversaw petrochemical development. Pequiven's forerunner institution, the Venezuelan Petrochemical Institute (Instituto Venezolano de Petroquímicas—IVP), was established in 1956. A source of corruption and political patronage, the IVP was reorganized in 1977 in a controversial decision to bring it within PDVSA's nascent structure. The new Pequiven proved successful under PDVSA's guidance, registering its first profit in 1983. Pequiven extended its profits as petrochemical production more than quadrupled from 1979 to 1988, from 540,000 to 2.3 million tons.

In 1990 Pequiven consisted of four major subsidiaries and sixteen associated companies. Numerous joint ventures with multinational firms, however, were slated to begin in the mid-1990s. The three major petrochemical complexes in Venezuela were at El

Tablazo in Zulia, Morón in Carabobo, and José in Anzoátegui. El Tablazo, traditionally the largest complex, produced ammonia, urea, polystyrene, ethylene, and propylene. The Morón plant, the site of the country's first commercial fertilizer production, also fabricated chlorine, caustic soda, and sulfuric acid, all used in heavy industry. The complex in Anzoátegui was scheduled to manufacture liquefied natural gas, methanol, and methyl tertiary-butyl ether (MTBE), primarily for export. Among the three complexes, the country also produced pesticides, insecticides, resins, explosives, aromatics, and dichloroethane and other chemicals. As of 1990, a fourth petrochemical complex in Paraguana in the state of Falcón was also anticipated.

Electricity

In 1990 Venezuela boasted significant electricity production and even greater potential. Besides its plentiful reserves of coal, oil, and gas, Venezuela's cascading rivers provided a hydroelectric potential in excess of 60,000 megawatts (MW), only a small fraction of which had been tapped. The country's total installed capacity in electricity multiplied more than ten times in the thirty-year period from 1960 to 1990, jumping from 1,350 MW to over 18,000 MW. Actual electricity generation paralleled that trend over the same time period, spiraling to more than 52 million MW-hours. During the same time period, the percentage of electric power attributed to hydroelectricity rose to about 50 percent by 1990. Thermal-based electricity declined accordingly.

The national power network encompassed both public and private utilities under the regulation of the Ministry of Energy and Mines. Four major public-sector utilities supplied over two-thirds of the country's electric power, and seven private firms provided the remainder. Until the 1986 opening of the massive Guri hydroelectricity facility, the National Electricity Company (Compañía Anónima de Administración y Fomento Eléctrico—CADAFE) accounted for over 90 percent of the electric power generated by the public sector. CADAFE increased public access to electricity from roughly 30 percent in 1960 to an estimated 92 percent by 1990. The Guri hydroelectric plant, with over 10,000 MW of installed capacity (the world's fourth largest capacity), became the nation's largest single source of electricity upon its completion in 1986. The Guri Dam, located on the Río Caroní, saved the country the equivalent of 300,000 barrels of oil a year.

Venezuela consumed more electricity than any other country in Spanish-speaking South America. Industry consumed 53 percent of all electricity in 1988, followed by private residences (22 percent), commercial entities (13 percent), and federal and local governments (12 percent). Electric rates were highly subsidized until 1989 when the government's structural adjustment policies triggered rate increases of 30 to 65 percent, depending on usage.

The government's plans for the 1990s focused on expanding hydroelectricity output near Ciudad Guayana and reorganizing utilities along more efficient and decentralized lines. The Venezuelan Corporation of Guayana (Corporación Venezolana de Guayana—CVG) oversaw the 360-MW Macagua I plant on the Río Caroní and planned to operate Macagua II, also on the Río Caroní, which was slated to provide an additional 2,500 MW by the early to mid-1990s. In addition, preliminary engineering work on complexes at Caruachi and Tocoma began in 1989; the CVG hoped to further harness the power of the Río Caroní to produce 2,500 MW from each of these facilities. The abundant and cheap supplies of hydroelectricity near Ciudad Guayana represented a significant advantage for Venezuelan heavy industries relative to other South American nations.

Despite these advantages, ambitious long-range expansion plans were hampered by the rigid bureaucracy and centralization of CADAFE. By some estimates, the company wasted nearly 40 percent of its generated power through deficient maintenance, frequent power failures, and theft.

Mining

Venezuela entered the 1990s poised to become a leading international producer of coal, iron, steel, aluminum, gold, and other minerals. In the late 1980s, the industry employed less than 1 percent of the labor force, accounted for less than 1 percent of GDP, and contributed 13 percent of exports. These figures were likely to increase, however, as expanded capacity became operational in the 1990s.

The state historically had played a prominent role in mineral policy and production. Beginning in the 1970s, the government obtained or established scores of mining enterprises in its pursuit of heavy industrial development. By the 1980s, however, the huge debts incurred by these ventures contributed to the government's decisions to reconsider restrictive foreign investment policies and to liberalize mining laws in an effort to expand private-sector participation in mining. The CVG, the country's most prominent regional development corporation and the major player in mining, increasingly entered into joint ventures with foreign companies by the 1990s, when for the first time the CVG agreed to accept a minority share in some ventures. In addition to its role as planner

A petrochemical complex run by the Instituto Venezolano de Petroquímicas in Morón
Courtesy Inter-American Development Bank

and coordinator of most of the country's mining, the CVG was one of Latin America's largest industrial groups, with 30 subsidiaries and 41,000 workers in 1989. According to government sources, the CVG and its affiliates accrued US$1.3 billion in profits from 1985 to 1989 and generated US$3.3 billion in foreign exchange.

The bauxite and aluminum industry, traditionally smaller in size than iron and steel, installed significant new capacity in both mining and processing during the 1980s. As a result, aluminum became the country's second leading foreign exchange earner. By 1990 Venezuela boasted the largest installed capacity in aluminum in all of Latin America. Moreover, the country was believed to be the world's most economical producer of aluminum because of its vast high-quality bauxite reserves, its abundant and cheap energy, and its well-developed infrastructure. Proven bauxite reserves stood at 500 million tons in 1990, with probable reserves as high as 5 billion tons. Overall, the country's smelters, including as many as 1,500 small foundries, produced approximately 443,000 tons of primary aluminum in 1988. About 60 percent of production, or nearly US$1 billion by value, was exported.

Commercial bauxite production, begun in 1987, reached 1 million tons in 1988 and was expected to reach 4.5 million tons in 1991. Much of the bauxite of Bauxita de Venezuela (Bauxiven; wholly owned by CVG) was processed at the Interamericana de Alúmina (Interalumina) plant in Puerto Ordaz. Opened in 1983,

Interalumina produced 1.3 million tons of aluminum in 1988 from its plant's annual capacity of 2 million tons. Jointly owned by the CVG and a Swiss company, Alusuisse, Interalumina also controlled 50 percent of the Belgian Aleurope Aluminum Company, 40 percent of the Costa Rican firm Alunasa, and 20 percent of the United States company Wells Aluminum, thus providing it with worldwide marketing outlets.

Alcasa, the country's first aluminum processing plant, contained plants in Ciudad Guayana and Guacara in Carabobo by the 1980s. Alcasa's installed capacity, on the rise throughout the 1980s, was intended primarily for specialized overseas aluminum markets. In 1990 Alcasa had a 120,000-ton annual capacity for manufacturing primary aluminum. Alcasa's expansion plans for the 1990s foresaw a more than doubling of that capacity to as much as 300,000 tons per annum.

The country's other major smelter, the Industria Venezolana de Aluminio C.A. (Venalum), was also undergoing rapid growth in capacity. Although the CVG enjoyed majority ownership of Venalum, a consortium of Japanese industrial interests held a considerable minority stake.

The iron and steel industries represented the core of the mining sector before aluminum's rapid growth in the 1980s. Large-scale commercial mining of iron ore in Venezuela began in the early 1950s, when the Pérez Jiménez regime granted iron ore concessions to two United States steel companies, Bethlehem Steel and the United States Steel Corporation. Huge iron reserves, located near exploitable hydroelectric resources, combined with a growing national demand for steel to set the stage for the creation of a steel mill in 1955 near the confluence of the Orinoco and Caroní rivers. With the creation of the CVG in 1960, the state gained a greater role in the country's only major steel plant, which at that time produced mainly seamless pipes for the oil industry. One of the landmarks of the government's expanding role in the economy during the 1970s was the nationalization of the Orinoco Steelworks (Siderúrgica del Orinoco—Sidor) steel mill on January 1, 1975. Funding from the Venezuelan Investment Fund (Fondo de Inversiones de Venezuela—FIV) made possible a smooth settlement with the American steel companies.

The nationalized steel industry set ambitious goals for itself, goals it ultimately failed to meet. Slower internal growth dampened local demand, and the proliferation of new steel mills in other developing nations by the late 1970s reduced international demand. As a result, plans to build two new steel complexes were postponed indefinitely by the late 1980s.

The Guri hydroelectric project
Courtesy Inter-American Development Bank

After years of delays, technical bottlenecks, and government mismanagement, Sidor's expansion made the country self-sufficient in steel by 1982. By 1985 steel exports exceeded steel imports fivefold. High initial capital investment, however, made the Venezuelan industry unprofitable, and Sidor accrued a huge debt estimated at US$5 billion to US$10 billion, a substantial portion of Venezuela's debt burden in the early 1980s. Not until 1986 did Sidor show its first profit, US$70 million, but this fell to US$26 million in 1987. In 1990 the government reportedly was considering privatizing Sidor.

Foreign competition for exports remained the major challenge to Venezuela's steel industry in the early 1990s, as steel production continued to increase, rising from 2.7 million tons in 1985 to 3.6 million tons in 1988, and internal demand remained static. Complaints about the dumping of subsidized Venezuelan steel at below-average prices impaired greater market penetration in the 1980s. The government provided subsidies to the Sidor plant, mainly through special foreign exchange rates that allowed the company to purchase imported inputs at a low rate and to pay off its debts at a high rate. In 1982 the United States Department of Commerce accused Sidor of selling its steel in the United States at a 40-percent discount. This complaint led to a 1985 Voluntary Restraint Agreement (VRA) with the United States, which set a maximum export limit of 183,000 tons of steel a year. The two governments reestablished the VRA in 1989 at 280,000 tons a year, two-thirds of which were finished steel products. Venezuela also signed a VRA with the European Economic Community in 1987 after similar dumping allegations were made.

Although the state dominated the industry, some private steel milling went on in 1990. Sivensa, the country's only private steel mill, was generally profitable. In addition, the CVG operated as a minority shareholder in a steel plant called Metalmeg, which manufactured carbon steel products for the petroleum industry. In the late 1980s, the Kobe Steel Company of Japan also converted its Minorca iron briquette plant into a direct reduction steel mill, further expanding steel production capacity.

The basis of the country's controversial steel industry was its enormous iron ore reserves. As of 1990, the government estimates of iron reserves for the state of Guayana were 2.8 billion tons of high-grade ore (80 percent iron). The CVG iron subsidiary, Ferrominera, controlled iron ore mining at numerous mines, most notably El Cerro Bolívar (southwest of Ciudad Guayana), El Pao (south of Ciudad Guayana), and San Isidro. Ferrominera's total installed annual capacity was 20 million tons in 1990. Iron production

Siderúrgica del Orinoco (Sidor) steel mill
Courtesy Inter-American Development Bank
Loading bauxite ore, Los Pijiguaos Mine, Bolívar State
Courtesy Inter-American Development Bank

fell sharply after its peak year of 1974, but was on the rise again by the late 1980s. Iron ore production was 18.9 million tons in 1988. Ferrominera's completion of a floating transportation complex on the Orinoco in the late 1980s facilitated the industry's use of large shipping vessels, thus increasing exports and lowering costs. Exports of iron ore reached 11.7 million tons in 1987, with the United States, Europe, and Japan the leading purchasers.

Coal production also expanded rapidly during the 1980s. As with iron and bauxite, the country enjoyed large reserves of highly pure coal. The state of Zulia alone, for example, contained 900 million tons of proven coal deposits, with probable reserves as high as 2 billion tons. This made Zulia the largest underdeveloped coal field in the Americas. Besides Zulia's coal deposits, the country also possessed significant coking coal to fuel the newer steel mills, coal for thermal electricity generation, and various deposits of clean-burning "hard coal." Most coal deposits were found in the west near the border with Colombia or in the Orinoco Basin.

Three major coal mines accounted for most coal output in the late 1980s. Although not yet fully operational in 1990, the Carbones de Zulia (Carbozulia) mine was already the nation's largest. PDVSA owned roughly half of Carbozulia; a consortium of United States, Italian, and private Venezuelan companies accounted for the balance. The mine produced 822,000 tons of coal in 1988, and plans called for 6.5 million tons-per-year capacity by the mid-1990s. By contrast, the entire country produced only 62,000 tons in 1987. The United States, Italy, and Spain represented the major markets for Carbozulia's coal. The second major mine was the Minas Carbón at Lobatera in Táchira near the Colombian border, with reserves estimated at as much as 60 million tons. The third-leading producer, in Naricual in Anzoátegui, boasted reserves of approximately 50 million tons. In addition to these operational mines, Venezuela had several other key coal zones that remained untapped in the 1980s.

Gold, known to exist since colonial times, did not become a major commercial endeavor until the 1980s. Miners long ignored the country's gold wealth because of its oil. Furthermore, the gold deposits were found mainly in the remote regions bordering Brazil and Guyana. The government, however, increasingly prized its gold reserves, which stood at 11.5 million troy ounces in 1990, or roughly 12 percent of world reserves. Gold existed in Venezuela as an ore with quartz and in alluvial deposits found naturally with diamonds. The government acquired the El Callao gold mine in the state of Bolívar in 1974 to better regulate gold prospecting and sales. The state succeeded in raising official gold production threefold from

1984 to 1989, pushing exports to over US$300 million a year. This figure made gold the second leading nontraditional export. Unofficial production, however, remained as high as 70 percent of total output.

After a decade of closely controlling private gold interests, the state opened up gold prospecting to foreign interests in the 1980s. In 1986 the CVG, in a joint partnership with a Bermuda-based company, formed Monarch Resources Limited to mine gold in the El Callao region. Private Venezuelan entrepreneurs also exploited the nation's gold reserves.

Venezuela also possessed varying amounts of other metals and minerals. For example, the country was a major producer of industrial diamonds, although diamond output fell steadily throughout the 1980s. The country also contained deposits of copper, nickel, zinc, lead, uranium, titanium, palladium, silicon, manganese, and chrome. Quarrying for industrial minerals such as feldspar, gypsum, hydrated lime, salt, phosphate rocks, gravel, barite, pyrophyllite, asbestos, bentonite, and magnesite was also common.

Manufacturing

Government-implemented industrialization policies begun in the late 1950s boosted the manufacturing sector. From the early 1970s to late 1980s, the state's ownership role in manufacturing increased from 4 percent to 42 percent. In 1988 the sector employed 18 percent of the labor force and accounted for 17.1 percent of GDP. Except for the export of processed petroleum and minerals, virtually all manufacturing was consumed locally. Manufacturing previously had been limited to oil refining, food processing, and small-scale enterprises. Domestic manufacturing blossomed somewhat during World War II as the country substituted local production for imports curtailed by the conflict. The expansion of manufacturing accelerated to its fastest pace in the 1950s as the world economy boomed, and the government embarked on the economic diversification and industrial development policies it referred to as "sowing the oil." By the mid-1970s, the nation's enormous oil wealth allowed the government to provide significant aid to industry, especially in the form of subsidized credit. Public-sector participation in industry expanded considerably with the nationalization of iron and steel in 1975 and petroleum in 1976. But after the country had exhausted its reserves from the two oil booms of the 1970s, it was forced to reexamine its industrial policies. Although Venezuela's level of industrialization was impressive by Latin American standards, industry was generally inefficient and productivity low. In 1990 Venezuelan industry faced the difficult task of moving beyond local markets and trying to compete in the international market.

By the end of the 1980s, the structure of manufacturing continued to be dominated by thousands of small firms in the private sector and a few hundred large, mainly public-sector, enterprises. In 1988 large firms employed 64 percent of the sector's workforce and supplied 78 percent of its output. Most smaller firms were family owned. Unlike many Latin American countries, capacity utilization among large, state firms was generally better than in the private sector. Caracas was the home of just under half of all industry, but it provided only 36 percent of its jobs and 26 percent of the country's manufactured goods. By contrast, the Ciudad Guayana region, with only 3 percent of the country's industrial firms, produced 10 percent of all manufactured goods.

Four broad functional categories made up the manufacturing sector: traditional or basic industries, intermediate, capital goods and metals, and other. Basic industries included most traditional manufacturing, such as food processing, beverages, leather, footwear, and wood products. Traditional manufacturing constituted 54 percent of all firms; about three-quarters of these were considered small businesses. Intermediate products, such as paper, petrochemicals, rubber, plastics, and industrial minerals, represented 18 percent of the sector, but their share was growing. The share of the capital goods and basic metals subsector was 19 percent by 1988. These thriving heavier industries included iron, steel, aluminum, transport equipment, and machinery. Other miscellaneous manufacturing accounted for 9 percent of the sector's output.

The automobile industry was one of Venezuela's largest manufacturing activities outside of petroleum refining and mineral processing. The industry consisted of Venezuelan subsidiaries of various foreign-owned companies. United States automobile companies assembled 85 percent of the country's vehicles, and European and Japanese companies produced 10 percent and 5 percent, respectively. The two largest United States car companies, General Motors and Ford, controlled 70 percent of the Venezuelan automobile market, followed by Fiat, Toyota, and Renault.

At the outset, the Venezuelan automobile industry was almost completely an assembly operation, importing most parts. Eventually, local factories supplied a greater percentage of parts to the assembly line, particularly tires, metal products, and motors. A government decree in 1985 required that all car engines be made in Venezuela by 1990.

Venezuela's automobile industry was first established with three vehicle assembly plants in the 1950s. By 1984 cumulative output had reached 1.7 million vehicles. The industry, protected by import tariffs as high as 300 percent, soon became virtually the only source of the country's transportation fleet. In the late 1980s, fifteen producers manufactured scores of models for domestic consumption, ranking Venezuela with Brazil as the largest per capita producers of cars in Latin America.

Venezuelans rushed to purchase vehicles in the 1970s, when generous government price controls on gasoline made driving economical. Production dropped during the less-affluent 1980s, however. As in the manufacturing sector at large, increased competition in the late 1980s forced many lay-offs at automobile factories.

Venezuelan factories manufactured a wide range of new products during the 1980s: specialized rubber goods, new paper products, ships, and aluminum, among others. A growing trend among producers of both new and traditional manufactured goods was overseas marketing. The country's traditional manufacturers began turning to export markets to enhance efficiency. The popular brewery, Polar, for example, turned to the international market after absorbing 85 percent of Venezuela's beer market. Following the success of other foreign beers in the United States, Polar began to export its brew successfully to North America in the late 1980s. Increased sales helped rank it among the world's fifteen largest breweries. The government-owned cement industry likewise expanded exports in the late 1980s, boosting its overall production in the process. Increased production allowed the industry to operate at more than 90 percent capacity, an unusually high rate of efficiency among Latin American industries. Although some manufacturers were expected to succeed in foreign markets, economists predicted that many others would close their doors during the 1990s as a result of reduced import protection.

Having reached a rather advanced stage of physical and human resource development by 1990, Venezuela hoped to turn toward high-technology areas for future manufacturing expansion. One of the country's largest import items, for example, was computer equipment. The Pérez administration promised to create incentives for investment in newer industries, such as information technology, telecommunications, and electronics. One obstacle to this goal, however, was the limited extent of research and development in the economy, particularly in the private sector. The country's expenditure on research and development in 1985 stood at only 0.41 percent of gross national product (GNP—see Glossary), compared with 2.7 percent in the United States. During the 1990s, the country aspired to reach the level of 1 percent of GNP recommended by the United Nations Educational, Scientific, and Cultural Organization.

Construction

The construction industry followed a pattern similar to that of other Venezuelan industries, flourishing during the 1970s as the result of huge government expenditure on physical infrastructure, but contracting severely during the 1980s as the economy waned. Construction employed about 8 percent of the labor force in 1988 and contributed about 5 percent of GDP. After reaching a low in both output and employment by 1985, the construction industry rebounded somewhat by 1987 as a result of new government investments, increased foreign investment, and liberalization of some rent-control policies. The country produced a wide range of inputs—such as wood, cement, basic metals, and industrial minerals—for construction activity. Venezuelan construction firms displayed high levels of technical capability and erected many of the nation's complex, heavy-industry structures.

Although many private construction firms ranked among the country's largest companies, the government played an increasingly more prominent role in the sector by the 1980s. The public sector accounted for 77 percent of construction in 1988, compared with 32 percent in 1978. State-owned enterprises fulfilled a substantial portion of the government's construction activity. Most public-sector construction responded to the needs of PDVSA, various power companies, and the corporations providing sanitation services.

After a frenzy of building in the 1970s, the country still faced an enormous deficit in urban housing in the 1980s. Accelerated urban migration forced millions of Caracas residents to live in *ranchos* (see Glossary), or squatter settlements, made from scrap materials, largely because of the lack of formal housing. As new home starts fell from 35,000 to 15,000 between 1982 and 1983, the Ministry of Urban Development (Ministerio de Desarrollo Urbano—Mindur) and the National Housing Institute (Instituto Nacional de la Vivienda—Inavi) became increasingly involved in residential construction. In 1985 public-sector housing construction exceeded that of the private sector for the first time; private firms, however, produced five times as many single-family homes. One obstacle to more rapid growth in housing was restrictive interest rate policies, which threatened to dry up future mortgage financing.

A thread factory in Guarenas
Courtesy Inter-American Development Bank

Services

Banking and Financial Services

Venezuela's extensive financial infrastructure, distinguished by the specialized nature of its institutions, displayed rapid growth from the 1950s through the 1980s. In 1989 the financial services sector consisted of forty-one commercial banks, twenty-three government development finance institutions, twenty-nine finance companies, sixteen mortgage banks, twenty savings and loan associations, and scores of other related entities, such as insurance companies, liquid asset funds, pension funds, brokerage houses, foreign exchange traders, and a stock exchange. The huge oil profits of the 1970s prompted the rapid expansion of financial institutions. During the less-prosperous 1980s, however, several institutions went bankrupt. These insolvencies greatly disrupted the financial system and led the government to intervene to resuscitate some companies and to force others to close down. The most celebrated of these interventions was the 1982 takeover of the Workers' Bank, which until that year was the country's fastest-growing financial institution.

The Central Bank of Venezuela (Banco Central de Venezuela—BCV) and the Central Office of Coordination and Planning (Oficina

Central de Coordinación y Planificación—Cordiplan), with assistance from the World Bank, sought to modernize, liberalize, and consolidate the private financial system in the early 1990s. One of the main aims of restructuring was to improve the weak supervisory authority of government regulatory bodies such as the Superintendency of Banks, the Superintendency of Insurance, the Deposit Insurance Corporation, and the National Securities Commission. The same policies sought to redefine and eliminate overlapping responsibilities. Financial authorities also attempted to liberalize the BCV's interest-rate policies and strict credit allocation provisions, which restricted financial markets (see Monetary and Exchange-Rate Policies, this ch.). In addition, policy makers contemplated increased participation from foreign banks, which had been limited to a 20-percent equity share since 1970, in order to make local financial institutions more competitive with international counterparts. Financial restructuring also aspired to create new government mechanisms for dealing with ailing financial institutions.

The country's forty-one commercial banks and their hundreds of branch offices represented the core of the private financial system. Commercial banks held about 70 percent of the total assets of the financial system in 1989. Bank lending policies were generally very conservative, favoring high liquidity ratios and emphasizing personal relationships. Banks financed mostly the short-term credit needs of the economy, reserving long-term financing for government development finance institutions. The banking industry was highly concentrated; six major banks, all affiliates of the six leading financial groups, dominated the industry with ownership of 63 percent of total bank deposits and 57 percent of total financial system assets. Banco Provincial, Banco de Venezuela, Banco Mercantil, and Banco Latino were the largest commercial banks in 1989. Fifteen medium-sized banks controlled 29 percent of bank deposits, whereas twenty small banks held only 8 percent of such deposits. Of the forty-one banks present in 1989, thirty were locally owned, private banks; two were privately owned with some foreign interests; and nine were government-owned banks. Many local banks balked at the prospect of outside competition from larger and better capitalized foreign banks.

The nine public-sector banks that operated as commercial entities were the Industrial Bank of Venezuela (Banco Industrial de Venezuela—BIV), the Agricultural and Livestock Development Bank (Banco de Desarrollo Agropecuario—Bandagro), four regional development banks associated with the BIV, and three subsidiaries of the BCV (Banco República, Banco Italo-Venezolano, and Banco

Occidental de Descuento). The BIV, the oldest state-owned bank, served as the major lender to the public sector and to industry. Like its four affiliated regional development banks, the BIV held a great many nonperforming loans. Without continued capitalization from the central government, these five banks likely faced insolvency. Bandagro, also dependent on renewed government capital, faced large debts in 1990 despite several attempts to restructure the institution during the 1980s. Nevertheless, Bandagro remained a key lender for medium-sized agricultural enterprises. The BCV's three banking subsidiaries, also carrying weak loan portfolios, were slated for privatization in the early 1990s.

In addition to public-sector banks, the state also operated twenty-three development finance institutions. Development finance institutions typically funded large, long-term development projects in both the private and public sectors, generally projects that were unable to secure commercial bank loans. Successive governments also had established specialized institutions to propel the development of agriculture, industry, urban areas, tourism, and exports. The names and functions of these financial institutions, most of which were founded after the 1973 oil boom, often changed as successive administrations pursued different development objectives.

Finance companies, a common institution throughout Latin America, met the society's diverse credit needs, ranging from consumer finance to short- and medium-term loans for local industry and commerce. Some twenty-nine finance companies with almost 100 offices in 1989 held about 20 percent of the national assets, ranking them as the second largest type of financial institution in the private sector. In Venezuela these companies tended to be rather specialized, lending primarily to agriculture, industry, and commercial activities. Given the local banking industry's conservative reputation, finance companies often lent where banks did not. At the same time, many of the country's finance companies belonged to larger financial groups affiliated with commercial banks. In addition to finance companies, the major international credit cards did business in Venezuela, thereby supplying another source of consumer credit.

Sixteen mortgage banks served the country's longer-term credit needs with more than 100 offices nationwide. Mortgage banks, which lent for new construction, home improvements, and residential and commercial real estate, contained about 7 percent of the total financial system's assets. Like the commercial banks, mortgage banks faced a serious imbalance of liabilities over assets by the late 1980s, principally as the result of inconsistent interest rate policies on the part of the BCV. The mortgage bank industry was thrown into further disarray in 1989, when the Venezuelan Congress passed a politically motivated Protection Law for Mortgage Owners. As interest rates were liberalized and rose after early 1989, the Protection Law for Mortgage Owners established ceilings on the proportion of monthly salary that mortgage holders could pay, usually no more than 25 percent. This measure aided home owners in the short run, but threatened to squeeze mortgage bank credit for future housing.

Savings and loan associations held about 5 percent of the country's total financial assets in 1989 and were the key to mobilizing the nation's savings. Twenty savings and loans provided short- and long-term lending through nearly 300 branch offices. The weak portfolios of these institutions in the 1980s required substantial government intervention. The National Savings and Loan Bank (Banco Nacional de Ahorro y Préstamo—Banap) intervened in the savings and loan industry on behalf of the government. Banap became the regulator, provider of capital, and guarantor of the industry. By 1990 some institutions owed as much as 40 percent of their overall liabilities to Banap, which itself faced growing financial constraints.

Capital markets constituted the other major component of the private financial system. Unlike other financial establishments, capital markets were slow to develop and remained quite weak in 1990. Among the explanations for the slow growth in capital markets was the traditional, family nature of businesses in Venezuela and the lopsided distribution of income, which limited the savings or capital accumulation of the lower classes. Furthermore, with subsidized interest rates, firms usually preferred debt financing or family borrowing over the mobilization of capital through the sale of equity shares. Investors were also skeptical of inadequate government regulation of publicly traded stocks and the state's history of intervention in industry.

The Caracas stock exchange, founded in the late 1940s, was the country's major capital market. The exchange operated under the nation's 1973 capital markets law, but regulatory changes expected in 1990 would allow foreigners to purchase shares on the Caracas exchange. In 1987, 110 companies were listed on the exchange.

Transportation

Venezuela possessed a relatively well-integrated transportation network that far exceeded that of most of its South American neighbors. Roads were the primary means of transportation for both passengers and cargo, and the country had the highest percentage of paved highways in Latin America. The nation's extensive road

network covered more than 76,600 kilometers in 1988, 34 percent of which was paved and 32 percent gravel. The remaining 34 percent was dirt roads. The southern part of the country lacked a road network and was generally not accessible by land. Bountiful oil windfalls in the 1970s allowed the country to construct modern multilane highways to serve its growing automobile population, which exceeded 2.3 million officially registered vehicles by 1986. The major international highways included the Colombian-Caribbean Highway on the north coast, which connected with the Pan-American Highway in Colombia via San Cristóbal and provided access to Brazil via Santa Elena. There was, however, no direct highway access to neighboring Guyana (see fig. 7). Approximately 55 percent of the capital's streets were paved, and other large cities displayed similar ratios. In addition to the comparatively high volume of automobile traffic, numerous bus services also transported 11.5 million passengers in 1988.

The country's railroad system was not nearly as extensive as its road network, and many industrialists complained that the rail system was insufficient to support the burgeoning mining industry. In 1990 railroads spanned only 400 kilometers, carrying passengers and freight over two major routes. The main passenger route stretched from Barquisimeto to Puerto Cabello. This route also passed through the petrochemical complex at Morón. In 1988 the nation's trains, excluding the Caracas subway, carried 240,000 passengers. The second major rail line ran through the heavy mining area south of Ciudad Guayana.

Caracas also boasted a modern subway system that first opened in 1982. Installed by a French company and managed under private service contracts, the Caracas Metro (C.A. Metro de Caracas—Cametro) was clean, punctual, safe, and financially sound in the late 1980s. Many analysts pointed to the fact that Cametro's employees were not public servants, and therefore not subject to the political patronage system, as the main reason for its success relative to other Venezuelan public-service companies. Construction of the Cametro system continued through 1990, and new lines were expected to open.

Water transport on lakes, rivers, and seas was fairly well developed. The National Port Institute (Instituto Nacional de Puertos—INP) managed the nation's nine major commercial ports, and various government entities administered scores of other ports. INP's ports, located on the various types of waterways, were traditionally the central shipping facilities. The growth of heavy industry in the 1980s permitted CVG-supervised ports, the largest being Puerto

Ordaz, to challenge INP because of their control of heavy minerals exports. Nevertheless, INP ports still handled 90 percent of general cargo and almost all containerized traffic. The port of La Guaira, located in metropolitan Caracas, was the most important INP port, followed by Puerto Cabello and Maracaibo. Other ports on the Caribbean coast and on Lago de Maracaibo were typically specialized ports that served a particular industry.

Venezuelan ports—and INP ports in particular—suffered from extremely high costs, which were closely tied to the strength of the country's longshoremen's unions. A lack of modernization and expansion after the 1970s also contributed to low efficiency. In 1990 the government contemplated increasing the role of the private sector in port management to expand port development, a measure that was likely to spark conflicts with organized labor. The Venezuelan Shipping Company and dozens of private companies provided merchant marine services, including oil tanker service worldwide.

Air transportation was commonplace in Venezuela, which flew nearly 15.7 million total passengers in 1988. Eleven international airports served the nation, along with 36 domestic airports and an estimated 290 private airstrips. The Maiquetía International Airport, located twenty-one kilometers outside the Federal District of Caracas, was the principal international airport, handling about 40 percent of all passengers, 84 percent of air cargo, and as much as 90 percent of all international flights. The other leading international airports were located in Barcelona and Maracaibo. Venezuela International Airways (Venezolana Internacional de Aviación S.A.—VIASA), the government's international carrier, provided regular flights to the United States, the Caribbean, Europe, and South America. VIASA maintained a relatively good reputation and recorded annual profits through 1990. Two domestic carriers, the state-owned Venezuelan Airmail Line (Línea Aeropostal Venezolana—LAV) and the private Avensa corporation, furnished local air service. Beginning in the late 1980s, Avensa also flew a few international routes as well. Numerous air taxis flew to more remote areas. Twenty-seven international airlines flew regularly to Venezuela.

Telecommunications

The national telephone company (Compañía Nacional de Teléfonos de Venezuela—CANTV) was one of the most notoriously inefficient of government enterprises. According to some estimates, CANTV satisfied only 60 percent of national telephone demand in the late 1980s. An estimated 1.8 million telephone lines served 1.4 million subscribers in 1988, and a backlog of at least 1 million persons awaited a telephone line. As a consequence, several utilities, oil companies, and the military maintained their own private telephone networks. To get telephones installed, wealthier consumers placed ads in papers, bribed telephone crews, or paid exorbitant rates for cellular telephones. CANTV's inefficiency stemmed from poor management, deficient maintenance, low quality of service, and pervasive political patronage. As late as 1988, only 40 percent of Caracas residents enjoyed international direct-dial capabilities. The Ministry of Transport and Communications' plan to alleviate the country's telephone crisis called for a US$1.6 billion expansion program from 1989 to 1992, with the goal of providing 1 million new direct-dial telephones in that period. The expansion program also sought to upgrade the country's dialing exchanges and data transmission facilities, and to foster the use of fiber-optic technology. It also pursued new satellite facilities through a joint venture with COMSAT (Communication Satellite Corporation), an American company, to be managed by the Andean Satellite Corporation (CONDOR) by 1994. Other planned reforms called for CANTV to revise its rate structure and to loosen its monopoly by creating several competing companies. Full and eventual privatization was also a possibility.

A subsidiary of CANTV, the Postal and Telegraph Institute (Instituto Postal Telegráfico—Ipostel), provided mail and telegraph services. Both services were generally very slow and unreliable despite the existence of 800 telegraph stations nationwide. As a result, the use of motorcycle mail carriers was common. CANTV also administered 17,500 telex lines for more than 13,000 subscribers, over half of whom were in the metropolitan Caracas area.

Tourism

Tourism was a rather minor and undeveloped industry in Venezuela. In the 1970s, the government targeted domestic vacationers to some extent, but by the late 1980s promotion of tourism focused on the potential foreign-exchange revenues of international visitors. The Venezuelan Tourism Corporation spurred tourist infrastructural development with concessionary financing and international promotional efforts.

Tourist arrivals fluctuated widely in the 1970s and 1980s, mainly in line with prevailing exchange-rate policies. For example, as the bolívar appreciated vis-à-vis the United States dollar prior to the 1983 devaluations, tourist arrivals declined, but arrivals more than doubled from 1984 to 1986. In 1988 an estimated 336,541 tourists visited Venezuela, generating upwards of US$200 million in revenue. The 1989 riots, however, were expected to hurt arrivals in the short run. Approximately 99 percent of all foreign tourists came from the Western Hemisphere or Europe. United States citizens entered with only a tourist card, obtainable on the flight to Venezuela. Cruise ships also visited several ports. In the late 1980s, nearly 2,000 lodging facilities offered 60,000 guest rooms. The peak tourism months were July, August, December, and January.

Foreign Economic Relations

Foreign Trade

The importance of oil exports made foreign trade essential to the country's prosperity. Venezuela benefited from extraordinarily favorable terms of trade in the 1970s—the quadrupling of oil prices in 1973 alone provided the nation with unprecedented wealth. Despite its benefits, the increase in oil exports also exacerbated the country's overreliance on a single export commodity; oil often exceeded 90 percent of total export value in the early 1980s. The oil boom also affected import patterns. Because of the huge foreign-exchange revenues from oil, the country developed a voracious demand for imported luxury goods that persisted even as oil prices ebbed in the mid- to late 1980s. The 50-percent reduction in world oil prices in 1986 underscored these structural weaknesses in the Venezuelan economy.

In 1988 official imports totaled US$10.9 billion; the country also ran a trade deficit in that year of US$758 million, the first since 1978 (see table 11, Appendix). The country's imports peaked in 1982 at US$11.7 billion, before the 1983 economic crisis and the subsequent imposition of multiple exchange rates, higher tariffs, and greater nontariff barriers, all of which stifled new imports. These protective import measures caused imports to drop by 43 percent from 1983 to 1986, before imports surged again to the 1988 level. In 1988 raw materials represented 44 percent of all imports, followed by machinery (26 percent), transportation goods (16 percent), and consumer goods (15 percent). The United States, traditionally Venezuela's leading source of imports, supplied 44 percent of all foreign goods in 1988. Overall, Venezuela ranked as the sixteenth largest trading partner of the United States and was the largest export market for the state of Florida. In 1988 the Federal Republic of Germany (West Germany) trailed the United States with 8 percent of all imports, followed by Italy with 6 percent, and Japan with 5 percent. Brazil, France, Britain, and Canada were other notable suppliers. Imports from members of the Andean

Common Market (Ancom—see Glossary)—Colombia, Peru, Ecuador, and Bolivia—accounted for only a small fraction of total imports.

Import policy traditionally sought to protect local industry and agriculture from foreign competition and to substitute local production for imports. The government accomplished these goals through exchange-rate manipulation, the imposition of tariffs, and through import licensing restrictions. In 1988 there were forty-one different tariff rates on more than 6,000 goods. Although tariffs sometimes exceeded 100 percent, the average was 37 percent. Fiscal policies, however, reimbursed as much as two-thirds of these tariff payments through a complex system that favored priority development activities. Nevertheless, as part of the 1989 structural adjustment policies, the Pérez administration chose to liberalize the import regime to force local industries and farms to be more competitive with international counterparts, much to the displeasure of most local businessmen. In 1989 the government reduced the maximum tariff to 80 percent to simplify tariffs into a uniform structure, expected to include a maximum of 20 percent and a minimum of 10 percent tariffs by 1993. Import liberalization also addressed nontariff barriers, such as import licensing agreements, which further hampered the free flow of imports and often bred corruption. The government abolished most import licenses in 1989, including those of several state-owned enterprises. Economists expected that liberalization policies would hurt the country's balance of payments in the short run, but make the economy more competitive in the long run. Improved access for imports was also expected to increase trade flows from within the Andean region.

Exports declined in the early 1980s, then rose unevenly in the late 1980s, but still did not come close to the peak level of US$20.1 billion in 1981. Both export and import figures excluded substantial contraband trade along the Colombian border. Declining exports in the 1980s resulted almost entirely from lower oil prices. Traditional exports—oil, iron, coffee, and cocoa—averaged about 95 percent of total exports from 1980 to 1985, but fell as a percentage of total exports after the drop in oil prices in 1986. The role of nontraditional exports jumped from 4 percent of total exports in 1980 to 18 percent by 1988. Increased overseas sales of aluminum, steel, and petrochemicals also diversified the country's export base. The public sector produced nearly all the country's exports. The state also exported as much as two-thirds of all nontraditional goods in 1988, but the increasing role of private investment in basic metals and petrochemicals was expected to lower that percentage during the 1990s.

Venezuela shipped half of its exports to the United States in 1988, with another 6 percent destined for West Germany, 4 percent for Japan, 4 percent for Cuba, and nearly another 4 percent for Canada. Ancom countries received an average of about 2 percent of exports in the 1980s. Venezuela exported oil to a large number of other countries, quantities of which were often controlled under OPEC quotas or other agreements, such as the San José Accord (see Petroleum; Natural Gas and Petrochemicals, this ch.).

Trade policy focused on making national exports more competitive and diversifying away from an overdependence on oil. The most consequential reform toward this goal was the 1989 devaluation of the bolívar to market levels. The devaluation made Venezuelan exports cheaper and imports more expensive, thereby favoring export-oriented production over import-dependent activities. The Foreign Trade Institute, a government body, also sought to expedite exporting procedures to encourage entrepreneurs to seek foreign markets.

Trade policy, however, also concentrated on the goal of Venezuela's accession to the General Agreement on Tariffs and Trade (GATT—see Glossary) during the early 1990s. Venezuelan adherence to the GATT entailed several unpopular policy reforms, some of which would come at the expense of exporters. For example, the government reexamined the various subsidies it afforded to exporters, many of which were in violation of GATT regulations. As a result, the government curtailed the amount of subsidized credit offered to merchants for financing exports, credit that paid for as much as 25 percent of exports in a given year during the 1980s. Likewise, exporters received tax rebates, or *bonos de exportación,* which the GATT also considered an unfair export subsidy. The government planned to phase out these rebates in the early 1990s, a decision opposed by various export associations because of the country's already weak export infrastructure for nontraditional items. Other subsidies found throughout the economy, such as subsidized industrial and agricultural credit, were also potentially affected. The tariff reductions begun in 1989 also worked to fulfill GATT requirements.

Venezuela joined Ancom in 1973 and became a signatory to the Latin American Free Trade Association (LAFTA) in 1982. Caracas was the headquarters of Ancom's Andean Development Corporation and the region's Latin American Economic System (Sistema Económico Latinoamericano—SELA); the latter was dedicated to analyzing economic and social policies throughout the hemisphere. Although thoroughly endorsing the aims of these organizations, Venezuela played only a minimal role in regional economic relations because the composition of its trade provided it with only limited interaction with neighboring economies. Venezuela did, however, accept Ancom's provisions to lower the profile of foreign investment by reducing the level of such investment to 50 or 20 percent depending on the sector. Nevertheless, as Chile, Ecuador, Bolivia, and eventually Venezuela embraced more orthodox economic policies in the late 1970s and 1980s, the integration pact diminished in significance. By 1990 Venezuela anticipated liberalizing its foreign investment code to promote new multinational ventures, thereby breaking with Ancom's stipulations.

Balance of Payments

As did its trade, Venezuela's balance of payments experienced wide swings in the 1980s after enormous success in the 1970s. These fluctuations, largely negative, depended primarily on the prevailing value of exports and the level of the country's foreign debt payments. As oil prices fell and interest rates soared in the early 1980s, international accounts recorded a massive deficit in 1982. Greater import protection in 1983 produced renewed balance-of-payments surpluses from 1983 to 1986. But as oil prices fell in 1986, overall payments turned highly negative, culminating in a US$4.7 billion shortfall in 1988. Besides oil price fluctuations, the balance of payments also suffered from huge capital outflows associated with annual, multibillion-dollar debt repayments and private capital flight precipitated by the deteriorating economy. As commercial banks turned away from issuing new loans to Latin America in the 1980s, the country faced a net outflow of capital, exacerbated by the fact that its high per capita income excluded it from multilateral financing.

The current account of the balance of payments moved into a deficit position as exports fell from 1986 to 1988 because of dwindling oil prices. Slightly higher oil prices in 1989 improved the current account again, but large drawdowns on the country's international reserves provided the economy little flexibility. After accruing a level of international reserves equal to that of the rest of Latin America combined in 1975, by 1990 the country's reserves were depleted to such an extent that they covered only a few months of imports. Aside from the large role of merchandise trade in the current account, net services and transfers represented a major drain in the 1980s. Deficits on the services and transfers portion of the current account were largely the result of steep interest payments on the foreign debt. Venezuelans' penchant for foreign travel and costly international freight and insurance expenses also caused the services and transfers deficit to exceed US$3 billion on average during the 1980s.

The capital account experienced large deficits for the first half of the 1980s, but improved after 1985 as new private investment and short-term financing offset some of the outflows of private capital and principal payments on the country's foreign debt. The reduction of capital-account deficits after 1985 was significant because the country could no longer rely on immense current account surpluses, as it had historically, to balance international payments. Despite this trend, average net capital outflows of roughly US$2 billion were registered from 1983 to 1988 as debt repayment proceeded and few new foreign loans were assumed. In 1986 the Japanese Export-Import Bank provided badly needed new monies for import financing, an infusion that also slowed capital outflows. By 1989 the IMF and World Bank also supplied large financial resources in support of the government's structural reforms and in an effort to improve its worsening international financial position.

As the country moved toward a more flexible position on foreign investment in the late 1980s, new inflows of direct foreign investment appeared after near stagnation in the early 1980s. From 1986 to 1989, foreign investment averaged US$300 million a year, an increase that eased the crunch on capital. In 1988 total foreign investment stood at US$2.2 billion; a little over half of this total was attributed to United States investors, followed by British, Swiss, and German investors. Analysts anticipated even greater private capital inflows associated with continuing debt-for-equity swaps. Nevertheless, in 1990 large sums of private Venezuelan capital remained overseas, insulated from the uncertainties of the local economy. During the 1970s and 1980s, more than US$34 billion in private capital left Venezuela, ranking it as one of the world's severest cases of capital flight.

Foreign Debt

Venezuela's public and private sectors owed as much as US$35 billion in debt in 1989, although data on debt varied considerably because of ongoing debt negotiations and reduction plans (see table 12, Appendix). The country ranked as Latin America's fourth leading debtor behind Brazil, Mexico, and Argentina; it was also one of the world's top twenty "highly indebted nations," as defined by the World Bank. Unlike many developing countries, Venezuela could not ascribe its huge indebtedness to the misfortunes of the oil price hikes of the 1970s. On the contrary, Venezuela benefited handsomely from the oil crises of the 1970s. Like several other oil economies, however, Venezuela squandered much of its newly found revenues through poor economic management, corruption, and over-ambitious development projects. Although oil financed economic improvements, the resulting public-sector indebtedness, which skyrocketed from under US$350 million in 1970 to US$10 billion by 1980 to US$25 billion in 1990, in no way compensated for the return on oil-based investments.

The country was atypical of other major debtor nations in other ways as well. Most notably, Venezuela actually paid both the interest and the principal of its debt during the 1980s, and its payments from 1983 to 1988 alone exceeded US$35 billion. These debt payments were pivotal in creating the large capital outflows that the nation suffered during the decade. Although the government temporarily held back debt payments in 1983 and again in 1988 because of ongoing negotiations, many in the international financial community still viewed Venezuela as a model debtor in many respects.

The structure of the country's debt was also distinct, as it was owed almost entirely to commercial banks rather than to multilateral institutions or bilateral agencies. In fact, Venezuela owed a higher percentage of its debt to commercial banks (at least 85 percent) than did any of the highly indebted countries. Another distinction was the large amount of private foreign debt. This private debt, estimated at US$4.5 billion in 1989, was declining under a set of agreements established in the early and mid-1980s. Finally, unlike most other debtors, Venezuela was also a major creditor to other developing countries (see Foreign Assistance, this ch.).

After securing debt rescheduling agreements in 1983, 1986, and 1987 to ease the terms of its repayments, Venezuela concentrated its debt management efforts in 1989 and 1990 on complex debt reduction plans with its more than 450 creditors. By early 1990, the banks, the government, and the government's Bank Advisory Committee had agreed in principle on a series of measures to reduce the country's debt. Although not all provisions were resolved, the plan offered what was termed a "debt reduction menu." Because of the number of creditors involved, the government provided a wide range of reduction options. Debt reduction, aimed at lowering total debt by one-fourth, offered creditors a range of short- and long-term bonds, some guaranteed by the United States Treasury. The various bonds offered highly favorable short-term relief, or conversions into discounted cash, equity, or other debt conversion mechanisms. The reduction plan fell under the auspices of the "Brady Plan," named after United States treasury secretary Nicolas Brady, who devised a worldwide debt reduction program.

As a consequence of the Brady Plan, United States Treasury officials encouraged United States commercial banks to accept the terms of the plan to mitigate the international debt crisis and to strengthen the United States hand in its resolution. American bankers, however, generally frowned upon the Venezuelan plan because of the country's relative prosperity and its track record of questionable economic management. The February 1989 riots, apparently provoked by economic austerity measures, strengthened the Venezuelan government's hand in pressing for debt negotiations. PDVSA's 1989 purchase of the Citgo oil company in the midst of the country's debt negotiations, however, cast doubts in the minds of many United States financiers about the country's genuine need for debt relief.

As early as 1987, Venezuela had initiated a debt-for-equity program to lower its debt, to privatize inefficient semiautonomous government agencies, and to stimulate foreign investment. The plan proceeded slowly because exchange-rate provisions until 1988 offered currency transactions at overvalued official rates rather than market rates. After only three debt swaps in 1988, the Ministry of Finance instituted debt-for-equity auctions in November 1989, where projects previously approved by the state corporation Superintendency of Foreign Investment (Sistema de Inversiones Extranjeras—SIEX) could trade paper debt for discounted bolívares with a monthly limit of US$80 million. Authorities imposed this US$80 million limit to restrain possible surges in the money supply created by bolívar conversions. Such limits, however, prevented debt-for-equity deals in many larger-scale projects in mining and petrochemicals. Debt swaps in 1989 and 1990 financed new investments in cement, paper, steel, aluminum, and tourism. Scores of additional SIEX-approved projects, valued at over US$2 billion, awaited further bidding in 1990.

Foreign Assistance

As the wealthiest country in Latin America and an OPEC member, Venezuela was more frequently a donor than a recipient of foreign assistance. The United States stopped providing aid to Venezuela in the mid-1960s; nor did any bilateral development agency give Venezuela assistance. Instead, Venezuela's bilateral economic relations were characterized by technical cooperation agreements, student exchanges, or commercial accords similar to those signed by the major industrial nations. Its oil wealth in the 1970s, however, did allow the country to become a major provider of bilateral and multilateral financing. From 1974 to 1981, the nation contributed US$7.3 billion to international development, 64 percent of which went to multilateral sources, such as the United Nations Special Fund, the Andean Reserve Fund, the OPEC Fund, the Coffee Stabilization Fund, the Caribbean Development Bank, and the Central American Bank for Integration, among others. In addition, Caracas was the headquarters of the affiliates or institutes of many regional and international organizations. Total annual contributions in the late 1970s averaged 1.88 percent of GDP, above the 1 percent level suggested by the United Nations for developed countries. Most bilateral assistance, funneled through the FIV, went to Andean nations, Central America, and the Caribbean. Venezuela used this oil wealth to enlarge its profile in regional and international affairs, a prestige it aggressively sought.

As its prosperity eroded in the 1980s, Venezuela saw its role as a donor, particularly as a bilateral one, wane. The country's most prominent economic assistance during the decade was dispensed through the joint San José Accord that it administered along with Mexico in order to provide subsidized oil to the Caribbean Basin region. Throughout the decade, Venezuela remained disposed to intervene in Central America. After supporting the Sandinista National Liberation Front (Frente Sandinista de Liberación Nacional—FSLN) against the Somoza dictatorship in Nicaragua in 1979, the Venezuelan government also provided financial assistance to the Sandinistas' opposition, the National Opposition Union (Unión Nacional Opositora—UNO), in its successful bid for power in 1990. Some minimal bilateral funding through the FIV continued in the early 1990s, mainly to promote the country's commercial interests.

In the 1980s, however, Venezuela sought funds from the major multilaterals, such as the World Bank and the IMF, after more than a decade of detachment. The World Bank was active in Venezuela from 1961 to 1974, disbursing thirteen loans worth US$340 million. Because of its high per capita income, however, Venezuela did not become eligible for World Bank financing until 1986. In 1989 it received over US$700 million in the form of a structural adjustment loan and a trade reform loan. Venezuela also used its large and previously untapped reserves at the IMF in 1989, when the IMF disbursed the first installment of a three-year Extended Fund Facility in the amount of US$4.8 billion. These new funds helped ease the country's painful transition to a more open economy, a transition undertaken largely on the advice of the IMF and the World Bank. Another multilateral agency, the Inter-American Development Bank (IDB), also continued to fund Venezuela's development in highway construction, forestry programs, water and sanitation projects, mining, and other infrastructure projects. In cumulative terms, the IDB provided approximately US$1.3 billion from 1961 to 1990.

The economic reforms begun by the Pérez administration in 1989 tracked with the prevailing liberal orthodoxy of international economics, but flew in the face of traditional Venezuelan state intervention. It remained to be seen whether Pérez would be able to weather the political storm created by his restructuring, and whether his program would show enough tangible benefits to warrant its retention and expansion under his successor.

* * *

As of 1990, there was no economic study available in English that examined in depth Venezuela's transition toward a more private-sector and market-oriented economy. Nonetheless, several valuable studies throughout the 1980s provided insight into the nation's evolving political economy. An excellent collection of essays appears in John D. Martz and David J. Meyers's *Venezuela: The Democratic Experience.* Laura Randall's *The Political Economy of Venezuelan Oil* and David Eugene Blank's *Venezuela: Politics in a Petroleum Republic* provide informative analysis on the country's pivotal oil industry. Some outstanding journal articles include Vladimir Chelminski's "The Venezuelan Experience: How Misguided Policies Paralyzed a Prosperous Economy," Rene Salgado's "Economic Pressure Groups and Policy Making in Venezuela: The Case of FEDECAMARAS Reconsidered," and a series of articles by *South* magazine in August 1989. The best source of economic statistics includes the publication of the Oficina Central de Estadística e Informática, *Anuario Estadístico de Venezuela,* as well as numerous publications from the International Monetary Fund, the World Bank, the Economist Intelligence Unit, the United Nations Economic Commission for Latin America and the Caribbean, the Inter-American Development Bank, and the United States Department of Agriculture. (For further information and complete citations, see Bibliography.)

Chapter 4. Government and Politics

President Carlos Andrés Pérez (1974–79; 1989–)

THE DEVELOPMENT OF a stable, democratic political system in Venezuela after 1958 represents a remarkable accomplishment. Few political scientists and historians in the late 1950s would have predicted that Venezuela would become a democratic model. The nation's turbulent past, which saw numerous regime changes, some of them violent, and its tradition of instability and penchant for repeatedly revamping its constitutions gave few hints of its impending transformation.

At the core of this transformation has been the emergence and the strengthening of a diverse party system that has progressively converged toward the center-left in its ideology and its policy orientation without abandoning pluralism. Elections since 1958 have been vigorously contested on a regular and predictable timetable. Political freedoms have been enjoyed by those in and out of power; presidents have been blessed with the sense that their mandate was legitimate. Perhaps even more extraordinary in the context of Latin American politics, outgoing presidents have peacefully handed over power to incoming presidents from another party of somewhat divergent political orientation.

This transformation from an authoritarian past to a healthy and long-surviving democratic regime cannot be understood in a vacuum, however. The political system evolved from a past fraught with instability and authoritarianism. After the heroic years of independence, Venezuelans suffered under the corruption and brutality of caudillismo (rule by local strongmen, or caudillos), fought a major civil war, and saw the constant redrafting of the constitution and changes in the rules of the political game.

Venezuela's independence began with its liberation by Simón Bolívar Palacios, who freed not only his own homeland but also much of the rest of South America. In 1830, with the collapse of Bolívar's dream of a larger Gran Colombia (see Glossary), Venezuela was ruled by General José Antonio Páez, a patriot caudillo from the llanos (see Glossary), or plains (see A Century of Caudillismo, ch. 1). This first postindependence period lasted until about 1858 and was characterized by economic recovery and political stability as the young nation functioned under the reign of a conservative oligarchy. Páez established the model of strongman rule under which an undisputed caudillo governed for a long period, either on his own or through the selection of handpicked loyal subordinates, thus preserving the appearance of constitutional presidential succession. These traditional caudillos, who preserved constitutional appearances while subverting the constitution's spirit, also elevated the role of Caracas as the political and economic center of the country. Throughout the nineteenth century and to this day, the principal goal of traditional and modern caudillos has been to take hold of and control the capital and, from the center, dominate and overwhelm the periphery.

The discovery and exploration of large oil reserves early in the twentieth century accelerated the demise of old-style caudillo rule. But although change took place, emerging constitutional ideals had to compete with the traditional political realities that persisted. Nevertheless, by the time the long-lived dictator Juan Vicente Gómez died in his sleep in 1935, the seeds of democratic transformation had already been planted. The short-lived student protest of 1928 was the first manifestation of democratic stirrings that were to flourish decades later.

The Generation of 1928 that sprang from that experience included future Venezuelan presidents and eminent political leaders of diverse political views, such as Rómulo Betancourt, Rafael Caldera Rodríguez, Jóvito Villalba, Gustavo Machado, and Raúl Leoni. For a brief three years, between 1945 and 1948, many of these leaders experienced their first taste of democratic rule; but they were then perhaps too young and too impatient, and their democratic experiment was short-lived. Exile gave these leaders broader perspectives and provided essential links to other democratic forces. The last decade of dictatorship ended in 1958; by then the Generation of 1928 was prepared to implement democratic reforms without being overthrown in the process.

Since 1958 democracy has survived, although its record has not been uncheckered. Coup attempts, especially in the early years, were fomented by extremists of both the right and the left, sometimes in the pay of or under the inspiration of extremists from outside the country. But the constitution of 1961 has not been rewritten or abolished, even if the spirit of the charter has not always been observed. Corruption has existed as well. At times the oil bonanza has led to a disregard for fiscal responsibility and has also enhanced the notion that the government can always afford the luxury of one more panacea.

An oil-rich nation, Venezuela by 1990 enjoyed the highest annual per capita income in Latin America and a politically moderate labor movement (see Labor, ch. 3). After more than three decades of democracy and a spirited presidential campaign, however, food riots in Caracas and elsewhere in the spring of 1989 shocked Venezuelans and forced them to contemplate the apparent fragility of their socio-political system. The food riots and looting of 1989, in which hundreds of people died violently, presented a stark reminder that Venezuelan democracy, although enviable by Latin American standards, was not without its flaws and its vulnerabilities.

The Governmental System

The Venezuelan governmental system has been characterized by contradictions in theory and practice. Although its constitutions pledged federalism and a separation of powers, political practice and custom gave an undeniable primacy to the government in Caracas and to the president, in particular. Even under the constitution of 1961, which gives extraordinary guarantees and rights to ordinary Venezuelans, the bureaucratic system has continued to favor those with family and political connections. Although the underlying system predates the democratic transition of 1958, it has broadened and become more pluralistic as more individuals and political brokers achieved influence in the drafting and implementation of policies.

The formal constitutional structure is fairly straightforward in its provisions. The pronouncements on individual and group rights, on the other hand, are imaginative, especially those articles dealing with social and welfare rights. This blend of traditional articles and those that reflect commitments to reform and social justice makes the constitution of 1961 an interesting case study.

Under its twenty-sixth constitution, adopted on January 23, 1961, Venezuela is a federal republic made up of twenty states, two federal territories (Amazonas and Delta Amacuro), and a Federal District (Caracas) (see fig. 1). In addition, there are seventy-two island dependencies in the Caribbean. The power of the government is divided between the national government and the states, districts, and municipalities. Throughout most of its history, however, the national governmental power in Caracas has predominated.

Although the states did have some powers of their own and enjoyed some autonomy, until 1989 they were administered by governors appointed by the president. The first direct popular election of governors took place in July 1989. Even though they gained an independent political base, these governors still depended on the national government for their budgets. In contrast, the states had a much longer history of electing unicameral legislative assemblies. States have also been subdivided historically into county-like districts with popularly elected district councils and municipalities with popularly elected municipal councils. The Federal District and the federal territories similarly had elected councils.

Even though the president has considerable power, the constitution does place specific limitations on who may run for the presidency. Further, a retiring president may not return to the presidency until two terms, or ten years, have elapsed. Carlos Andrés Pérez, reelected in 1989, became the first president since 1958 to occupy the highest office twice. Former presidents automatically become life members of the Senate (upper house of the Congress). Traditionally, they have also been viewed as elder statesmen. This was particularly true in the case of Rómulo Betancourt (president, 1959–64), who, with his great prestige, continued to exert considerable influence years after he had left the presidency.

The constitution provides for the direct election of the president, who is chosen under universal suffrage for a five-year term. The president appoints and presides over the cabinet and determines the number of ministries. The office of vice president, which had been at times provided for in earlier Venezuelan constitutions, is not mentioned in the 1961 document. One anecdote holds that wily Juan Vicente Gómez (president, 1908–35) abolished the office of the vice president in a turn-of-the-century constitution after he, as vice president, had moved to the top office during the absence of president Cipriano Castro. Nearly a century later, the Venezuelan governmental system retained in its constitution traditional ways of protecting the president from the possibly fatal ambitions of a second-in-command.

Unlike the constitution followed in the time of the dictator Gómez, however, the 1961 constitution provides for mandatory voting for all Venezuelan citizens who are at least eighteen years old and who are not convicts or members of the armed forces. Generally, more than 80 percent of those registered voted. Each political party had its own ballot with a distinctive color and symbol, so that even illiterate citizens could recognize their preferred party choice. Elections were supervised by an independent, federally appointed electoral commission. Constitutionally assured elections, universal suffrage, and participation in politics for over three decades have made Venezuela a unique and much admired democratic model in Latin America.

Constitutional Development

Until 1961 Venezuela had the unenviable distinction of having been governed by more constitutions than any other Latin American country. This heritage was partly the result of the trauma of a prolonged war of independence that tested the country's fragile social cohesion. Venezuelans are proud of the fact that Bolívar brought freedom to his homeland as well as to the homelands of thousands of other Latin Americans; this epic crusade, however, carried an enormous financial and human burden. The struggle also often pitted the criollo elite, exemplified by Bolívar, against *pardos* (see Glossary), who rightfully felt that they had improved their lot under Spanish rule. In turn, regional elites, resentful of Caracas's ascendancy, refused to join the crusade and often turned to the Spanish side in an effort to curtail Bolívar's power (see The Epic of Independence, ch. 1).

The prolonged war for independence and the subsequent jockeying for power among caudillos, both regional and national, in part accounted for the changes in constitutions and in constitutional provisions to better suit the temper and the realities of the times. Each caudillo scrapped the previous constitution and wrote a basic law that suited him better. Federalism, for example, an ideal in Venezuela since before 1864, was rudely brushed aside whenever a strongman emerged in Caracas who needed to put down opposition from local or regional chieftains. Federalism has enjoyed a more hospitable environment since the promulgation of the 1961 constitution, but no federalist tradition strong enough to challenge the continuing power of the president has yet arisen. Thus, although the possibility of direct election of state governors existed under various constitutions, the actual practice was not implemented until 1989.

The states are considered autonomous and equal as political entities, but their dependence on Caracas for budget allocations ensures that state powers are indeed limited. On the other hand, they do have some symbolic powers. For example, they can change their names, they can organize local governmental entities, and they can perform a few other functions on their own.

Although the division of powers among the executive, the legislative, and the judicial branches has been traditional in Venezuelan constitutions, the executive has overshadowed the other two branches throughout the country's history. A greater break with the past came in the 1961 constitution in its painstaking elaboration of individual and collective duties and rights. No fewer than seventy-four articles deal with human rights and freedoms. Freedom of speech, press, and religion are guaranteed. The right of habeas corpus is recognized, and prompt trials are ensured (although the cumbersome judicial system effectively thwarted the latter guarantee). There are also constitutional prohibitions against self-incrimination, torture, capital punishment, double jeopardy, and discrimination on the basis of sex, creed, or social condition.

The 1961 constitution also places many social obligations on the state, such as responsibility regarding labor, social welfare, and the national economy. Working hours are specified, minimum wages guaranteed, and there is freedom to strike. Special protection is provided women and minors in the labor force.

The government has many powers and responsibilities in regard to national economic development. Private property and private enterprise are protected so long as they do not conflict with national policies. In turn, the national government is given wide latitude in the areas of industrial development and protection of natural resources, and in provisions for the expropriation of property.

It is fairly easy to amend and even rewrite the constitution. Amendments can be initiated by one-fourth of one of the chambers of Congress or one-fourth of the state legislative assemblies. An amendment requires a simple majority for passage by Congress. If passed by Congress, an amendment still requires certification by two-thirds of the states to become part of the constitution. Provisions for reforming or rewriting the constitution are similar; the process may be put into motion by a one-third vote by the states or a congressional chamber, passage by two-thirds vote in Congress, and approval by a national referendum. Rejected initiatives of amendment or reform may not be reintroduced during the same congressional term. The president may not veto amendments or reforms and is obliged to promulgate them within ten days following their passage.

In practice, the 1961 constitution retained many features of previous constitutions. Federalism, for example, has been the nominal basis of constitutional structuring since 1864. Although the 1961 document calls Venezuela a federal state, it also labels the country as the "Republic of Venezuela," whereas earlier charters used the term "United States of Venezuela."

More important, the constitution has served as the basis for expansive government programs that fulfill the mandate for greater social justice and greater use of the central government in all spheres of public policy. Thus, in effect, the 1961 constitution expanded and redefined the central role to be played by government on behalf of the people of Venezuela; it maintained the tradition of powerful presidents and a strong central state.

The Executive

The 1961 constitution continues the long tradition of a powerful president, who serves as head of state and chief executive. He or she must be a Venezuelan by birth, at least thirty years old, and not a member of the clergy. The president is elected by a plurality vote under direct and universal suffrage, serves for five years, and cannot be reelected until after two intervening terms have passed. President Carlos Andrés Pérez became the first Venezuelan elected to serve two terms of office under this provision of the 1961 constitution; he won the December 1988 election after having served as president from 1974 to 1979.

The president commands the armed forces, calls special sessions of the Congress, and exercises sole control of foreign policy. He can authorize expenditures outside the budget and can negotiate loans. The constitution provides for a weak form of ministerial responsibility. This responsibility is rendered meaningless, however, because although the constitution calls upon the president to consult with his ministers, it allows him to appoint and remove them. In fact, through his ministers, the president can adopt whatever regulations he chooses in order to implement the laws. These regulations are not subject to the approval of Congress, and the courts are not empowered to review them.

The major challenges and limitations to presidential power are found not in constitutional restrictions but in the political system as defined by the major Venezuelan political parties. Limitations placed on presidential initiative by the play of forces within the president's party have restricted presidential actions informally but effectively; in practice, therefore, political checks have functioned more effectively than constitutional ones to prevent presidential abuses of authority.

The constitutional power to declare a state of siege and temporarily restrict or suspend constitutional guarantees represents the ultimate exercise of presidential authority under the 1961 constitution. During Rómulo Betancourt's elected tenure (president, 1959–64), he felt compelled to use these constitutionally sanctioned limitations in order to prevail over forces that threatened the survival of his legitimately elected government. It should be pointed out, however, that certain guarantees cannot be constitutionally abrogated under any circumstances. The guarantee against perpetual imprisonment and the prohibition against the death penalty represent two such provisions.

Cabinet and noncabinet ministers serve as advisers to the president; they are appointed and removed by the president without input from the Congress. Ministers may introduce bills in Congress, and they must submit an annual report and an accounting of funds to Congress at the beginning of each regular session. The ministers of energy and mines, finance, foreign affairs, interior, and national defense and the head of the Central Office of Coordination and Planning (Oficina Central de Coordinación y Planificación—Cordiplan) traditionally have been considered the most powerful and prestigious in the Council of Ministers, or cabinet.

The president determines the size and composition of the cabinet. Both Betancourt and Raúl Leoni (president, 1964–69), who succeeded him as the second chief executive in the democratic period, appointed thirteen cabinet ministers. Since then, the number has grown as high as twenty-five. Some observers have noted a correlation between this increase in the number of ministries and the oil bonanza that began in 1973. As the oil money flowed in, the number of ministries also increased. Subsequently, even though the oil boom ended in the early 1980s, presidents have found it difficult to operate with as few ministries as Betancourt and Leoni did.

The growth of the cabinet was not surprising in light of the ambitious list of the government's goals in the 1970s and 1980s. These included preserving democratic institutions, maintaining public order, modernizing the armed forces, managing the external public debt so as to avoid undesirable effects on living standards, and directing the economy and the development of the country's physical infrastructure. All these broad and wide-ranging goals fell within the president's purview and range of legislative initiatives; therefore, when Venezuelans spoke of "the government," almost invariably they meant "the president," or "the executive."

Driven by this mandate, the centralized bureaucracy, under the control of the president, has become by far the largest employer in the country. Commonly cited figures on the number of public servants were inaccurate because they often excluded those employed by the many state corporations, among them those dealing with the Venezuelan Petroleum Corporation (Petróleos de Venezuela, S.A.—PDVSA), the Foreign Commerce Institute, the Superintendency of Foreign Investment (Sistema de Inversiones Extranjeras—SIEX), and many others.

The tremendous growth of bureaucracy provoked controversy, especially as oil revenues declined during the 1980s. Many Venezuelans felt that the growth of bureaucracy contributed to corruption, fiscal irresponsibility, and a declining level of services. And yet, a significant number of Venezuelans worked for the government either directly or indirectly or had close relatives so employed. The Venezuelan press had been vigorous in its exposés of the most flagrant cases of nepotism, but authorities had seldom taken effective action to curtail this practice. The 1989 switch to the direct election of governors lessened the opportunity for presidents to appoint political cronies to these offices. President Pérez's announced policy of privatization of some parts of the public sector could also have an impact on inefficient personnel practices. Through 1990, however, the overall effect of these changes could not be judged.

An early sign of Pérez's intentions toward fulfilling his pledge of greater privatization came with the announced intention to dissolve the Venezuelan Investment Fund (Fondo de Inversiones de Venezuela—FIV), once the most visible institutional symbol of the liberal application of oil revenues. Perhaps ironically, the FIV had been created by Pérez in 1974 during his earlier presidency as a channel to direct the additional income generated by rocketing oil prices into the expansion of non-oil sectors of the economy. Allocations by the government to the FIV funded large-scale projects intended to boost the production of steel, aluminum, and electricity (see Growth and Structure of the Economy, ch. 3). In addition, possibly in an effort to pave the way for an eventual bid by Pérez to become the secretary general of the United Nations, FIV also channeled Venezuelan financial assistance to poor countries in Central America, the Caribbean, and the Andean region.

Early in 1990, the government reallocated FIV's assets among various ministries. This move, however, did not necessarily represent the demise of this powerful bureaucratic entity. Some sources indicated that FIV's technicians would be charged with administering the privatization program. By late 1990, however, the privatization program had yet to sell a single state asset, and some observers questioned the strength of Pérez's commitment to the process.

The Legislature

The constitution establishes a bicameral Congress, comprising a Senate and a Chamber of Deputies. Senators must be at least thirty years of age and deputies at least twenty-one. Both must be native-born Venezuelans. Each body is elected at the same time, with the same congressional ballot, every five years. A party list system of proportional representation is the method of selection for both chambers; voters, therefore, do not cast ballots for individual candidates. The only deviation in the selection of members lies in the fact that the Senate also includes former presidents of the republic. The traditional provision of alternates (*suplentes*) allows persons so designated to hold the position to which a principal has been elected in the latter's absence.

Many felt that the most important unit within the Congress was the party caucus (*fracción*), made up of members of a party's elected delegation to either chamber. A chairman chosen by its members presided over the caucus. Chairmen were effectively preselected by their party's national central committee; balloting by the congressional delegations merely ratified the choice.

Revenue, budget, and taxation bills must originate in the lower house, which also has the authority to censure ministers. The upper house is responsible for the initiation of bills relating to treaties and international agreements. The Senate also approves certain presidential appointments to diplomatic posts and the promotions of high-ranking military officers (see Uniforms, Ranks, and Insignia, ch. 5).

The Venezuelan constitution provides for parliamentary immunity, but this immunity may be revoked by a member's chamber. In 1963 the Supreme Court upheld the right of the president to ban political parties deemed subversive of democracy. Congress, however, has remained responsible for its own organization and regulation. Each chamber elects its own presiding officer. The president of the Senate serves as the president of Congress; the president of the Chamber of Deputies serves as the vice president of Congress.

The political significance of the Venezuelan Congress has increased throughout the post-1958 democratic era. The staffs of congressional committees handle a heavy legislative workload. Initially, each chamber had the same ten permanent standing committees, but in 1966 the Chamber of Deputies created the Committee on Fiscal Affairs. All other committees have continued as parallel structures in both houses of the Congress. Two committees in each chamber deal with internal affairs and foreign relations, four committees with economic matters, and four others with service issues, such as education, tourism, and defense.

The most important committee, however, is the Delegated Committee. An interim body created by the 1961 constitution, it includes the president and vice president of Congress and twenty-one other members selected on the basis of party representation in Congress. The Delegated Committee serves during those periods when Congress is adjourned; it exercises oversight functions and acts for Congress in its relations with the executive. It may convene Congress in extraordinary session if it deems it necessary.

The legislature considers, debates, approves, rejects, or alters legislation. Congress also has the authority to question ministers and to have them explain adopted policies. It can censure executive personnel, with the exception of the president. Moreover, it can impeach the president by agreement between the Senate and the Supreme Court. This has not happened since the adoption of the 1961 constitution, however.

In practice, the legislature does not share equal status with the executive branch. The executive branch, not Congress, introduces most significant legislation. In addition, in certain instances, bills may emanate from the Supreme Court; the constitution also provides that a bill may be initiated directly by the petition of a minimum of 20,000 voters. The president has the authority to veto legislation, although Congress can override that veto. When a veto is overridden, the president may ask Congress to reconsider those parts of the bill he finds objectionable.

Two senators are elected from each state and two from the federal district. Additional members, around five or so, are selected by a system of proportional representation that ensures minority parties a voice in the legislature. Former presidents may serve as senators for life, if they so desire. They are considered elder statesmen and are often consulted by their colleagues on matters of policy and political strategies. All other legislators are elected by universal suffrage for five-year terms concurrent with that of the president. Unlike the president, legislators may be immediately reelected.

The Judiciary

Venezuela has no dual organization of national and state courts. Since 1945, all courts have been part of the federal system, even though at one point a parallel organization of state courts existed. Regardless of their form of organization, the courts have never exercised as much influence as the executive or even the legislative branch in Venezuela.

As is the case with the legislature, the judicial branch in Venezuela does not share equal status with the executive. Although the law provides for the process of judicial review and for coequal status among the three branches of government, the reality is quite different. The Venezuelan brand of federalism does not provide for state courts. The law is perceived as the same, unitary, throughout the national territory. Thus, all courts and virtually all legal officers, from those who arrest to those who prosecute, are federal (i.e., central government) officials.

Broader implications stem from the fact that the Venezuelan legal system is essentially a code law system, and thus the legal system is relatively rigid and leaves little room for judicial discretion. In a system of code law, the jurist is seen as a confirmer of the written code rather than the finder or maker of the law, as is the case in common law systems.

The highest body in the judicial system is the fifteen-member Supreme Court of Justice, which is divided into three chambers that handle, respectively, politico-administrative, civil, and penal matters (see fig. 8). Its members are elected by joint session of the Congress for nine-year terms. One-third of the membership is renewed every three years. Each justice is restricted to a single term

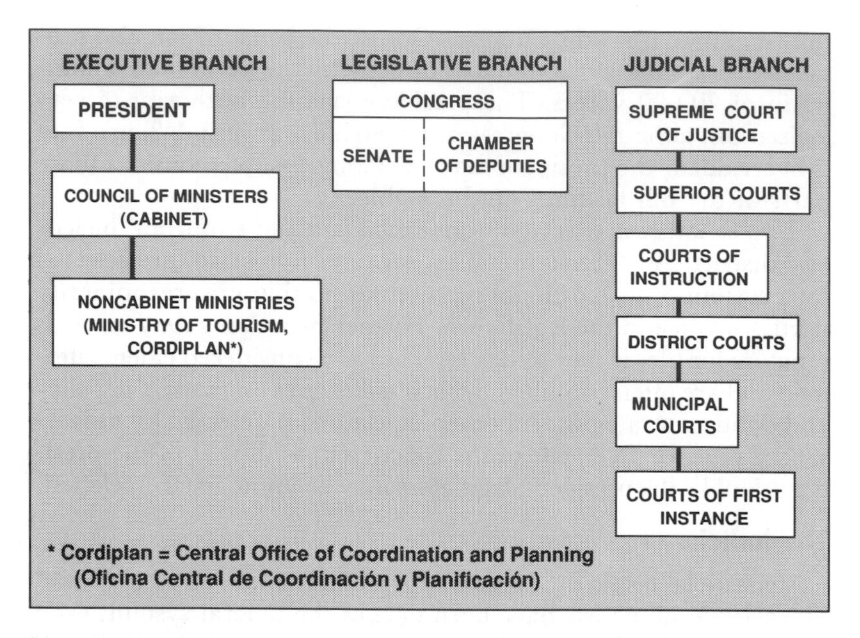

Source: Based on information from Embassy of Venezuela, Washington; and *Encyclopedia of the Third World*, Ed., George Thomas Kurian, New York, 1987, 2098.

Figure 8. Organization of the National Government, 1990

of nine years; this short tenure effectively limits how much a Supreme Court justice can accomplish.

Below the Supreme Court are seventeen judicial districts, each district having its own superior court. Lower courts within a judicial district include courts of instruction, district courts, municipal courts, and courts of first instance. The superior courts are composed of either one or three judges, a bailiff, and a secretary. They serve as appellate courts for matters originating in courts of first instance in the areas of civil and criminal law. Some deal exclusively with civil matters, others with criminal matters, and others with all categories of appeals. The courts of first instance are composed of one judge, a bailiff, and a secretary. They have both appellate and original jurisdiction and are divided into civil, mercantile, penal, finance, transit, labor, and juvenile courts. District courts are composed of one judge, one bailiff, and a secretary; they also operate nationwide. They have original jurisdiction in small bankruptcy and boundary suits, and appellate jurisdiction over all cases from the municipal courts. Municipal courts, consisting of a judge, a bailiff, and a secretary, hear small claims cases and also try those accused of minor crimes and misdemeanors.

They also perform marriages. Although they do not constitute courts as such, instruction judges issue indictments, oversee investigations to determine whether a case merits the attention of the courts and, if so, issue an arrest warrant. Thus, these judges perform a crucial task in the initial stages of all cases that come before the courts.

In addition to the courts of ordinary jurisdiction, several courts of special jurisdiction operate under the Ministry of Justice. Military tribunals, fiscal tribunals, and juvenile courts all fall into this category. Although they operate independently of the ordinary courts, the Supreme Court also acts as the highest court of appeal for the special courts. Juvenile courts throughout the country try those under eighteen years of age.

One of the most interesting aspects of the Venezuelan judicial system is its carryover of medieval Castilian traditions, such as the *fuero militar* (military privilege). Under this centuries-old tradition, members of the military cannot be tried by criminal or civilian courts, although the military has at times intruded into the civilian judicial system. For example, the Armed Forces of Cooperation (Fuerzas Armadas de Cooperación—FAC)—also known as the National Guard—was charged with the function of protecting all national territory and highways. Under this broad mandate, it could and did prosecute contraband cases and in effect became involved in the criminal prosecution of many suspected civilian offenders. This power was likely to increase as drug contraband became a greater problem in Venezuela, especially along its borders with Colombia (see Threats to Internal Security, ch. 5).

Generally speaking, the system for selecting judges tended to limit their independence. The Congress chooses the members of the Supreme Court, and the minister of justice names judges to the lower civilian courts. Neither category of judge enjoys life tenure. Judges' salaries are submitted to Congress as line items in the Ministry of Justice's annual budget and are therefore not guaranteed. Thus, in a number of ways the judiciary was subordinate to and dependent upon the good will of the executive and the legislative branches. Although Venezuelan jurists occupied a highly regarded position in society, they did not hold nearly as much power as their counterparts in those systems where judicial review and common law are the basic determinants of procedures.

Public Administration

The 1961 constitution provides for a career civil service and establishes standards for performance, advancement, suspension, and retirement. The ideals, however, have been largely ignored in practice in favor of a system based on patronage. Scholars of public administration agreed that the bureaucracy was bloated, inefficient, and often susceptible to corruption.

The junta that assumed power after the 1958 overthrow of the dictator Marcos Pérez Jiménez set up a Public Administration Committee that obtained the advice and services of a number of international experts. The committee found the Venezuelan bureaucracy to be unorganized and unprofessional; the experts advised the adoption of a model under which jobs were to be clearly defined, civil service would become divorced from politics, pay scales would be established within accepted guidelines, and the bureaucracy would faithfully follow the directives of government leaders.

Although it became immediately apparent that most, if not all, of the committee's suggestions were unworkable (for example, the notion of a democratic government such as Betancourt's giving life tenure to senior bureaucrats because they had served long years under the Pérez dictatorship), the committee was not totally a failure. As a result of the committee's activities, in 1959 a new Commission on Public Administration undertook the administrative reform of the upper levels of the public service. The commission also established a school in Caracas to train career civil servants, the Graduate Institute of Public Administration (Instituto de Estudios Superiores de Administración—IESA). In spite of IESA's excellent faculty and promising graduates, most of the bureaucracy remained filled with political appointees rather than IESA graduates in the late 1980s.

Cordiplan, in the Office of the President, also was created in 1958. Cordiplan was envisaged as a central agency that would allocate resources within the government and handle budgetary and administrative planning, all on a nationwide basis. Although Cordiplan has been highly regarded and its four- and five-year plans have served as general guides, many of its detailed and imaginative goals for national development have been undercut by a bureaucracy resentful of Cordiplan's clout in budgetary matters.

In 1969 President Caldera charged the Commission on Public Administration with drafting an overall reform plan. The commission submitted a detailed report and plan to the president in 1972, but its sweeping recommendations were never fully implemented. The effort did have some positive results, however. By the end of the 1960s, concepts of regular personnel procedures and civil service tenure had begun to take hold. During the Caldera government, the Central Office of Personnel branched off from the commission and became a force in promoting the professionalization of civil servants.

Carlos Andrés Pérez, during his campaign for the presidency in 1973, promised to further streamline and professionalize the bureaucracy. During the preceding Social Christian Party (Comité de Organización Política Electoral Independiente—COPEI) administration of Rafael Caldera, the bureaucracy had grown and many state enterprises had mushroomed. Pérez reacted by creating a separate reform commission to deal solely with state enterprises; the original reform commission became a subsection of Cordiplan in 1977.

Ministerial and regional reorganization plans also have been enacted into law, but their implementation has been minimal at best. Another strain was added when the oil industry was nationalized in 1976, and a whole new bloc of private workers and managers became government employees. This move initiated a highly political process, as players within the political system sought to exploit the potential of the state-owned oil industry to provide money, patronage, and jobs to the well connected. Whatever the incentives for reform, the incentives for continued corruption almost invariably have proved stronger.

In spite of its many failings, Venezuelans saw the bureaucracy as an integral part of a system in which service and perquisites went hand in hand. Politicians promised services and appointed bureaucrats to provide those services; the appointees themselves, however, more often than not owed their first allegiance to the politicians rather than to the public. Furthermore, the bureaucracy, like everything else, was concentrated in Caracas; therefore it responded more to the needs of the center than to the demands of the periphery.

Local Government

The 1961 constitution provides for a federal republic of twenty states, two federal territories, a federal district, and a federal dependency consisting of seventy-two islands. Each state contains two levels of government, the district and the municipal level. There are 202 districts in the country, between 6 and 16 in each state. Districts are divided into municipalities and are constitutionally independent of the state in economic and administrative matters, subject only to national laws and regulations.

Local government was not strong in Venezuela, and it can be argued that Venezuelans gave greater loyalty to their states than to their local government bodies. The 1961 constitution delegates the establishment of municipalities and other local entities to the states. The municipalities elect their own officials and may collect certain revenues, but they are subject to numerous legal, financial, and political limitations imposed by national officials.

The powers of the states are restricted to those areas not granted to the nation or the municipalities. The states are permitted to merge, cede territory, or change their boundaries with the consent of the Senate. Although it had not done so by the end of 1990, the national Congress may, by a two-thirds vote, expand the powers of the states to include matters previously limited to the consideration of the central government. The states have also remained dependent on the national government for most of their revenue.

In 1990 the direct election of governors was still too recent to indicate to what extent the state executives, now with their own political basis, would be able to exert greater authority than they did as appointed officials. In any case, the governor's powers derive from his or her control of the state's law enforcement machinery, the drafting of the state's budget (which is submitted to the state legislature), and the execution of the directives of the national executive. Unicameral state legislative assemblies are popularly elected and exercise limited powers.

States are divided into districts, the number of districts depending on the size of the state. Districts are governed by popularly elected councils; elections for council members take place at the same time as those for national officials. Like all popularly elected officials, council members serve five-year terms. The number of council members varies, but all councils are presided over by a chairman, who serves in that position for a one-year term. The district councils have limited decision-making powers regarding such matters as the distribution of national funds channeled through the state executives. The councils are charged with providing the local services not provided by the national government.

The districts are divided into municipalities, which are also governed by elected councils. The municipal councils have no decision-making powers and serve as administrative units in charge of garbage collection, sewer construction, and other municipal services. The councils also provide information about local politics to the district council and serve as advocates for local citizens with the national bureaucracy. In Venezuela, however, links between local citizens and the national government have often been more effectively established informally by the political parties rather than by the local bureaucracy.

These links between local citizens and the national government might have to be redefined, however, after the Democratic Action (Acción Democrática—AD) party's major defeat in the December 1989 local elections. These elections were particularly significant because, for the first time, they involved the elections of mayors (a position that previously did not exist) as well as twenty state governors. Another innovation in these elections allowed voters to cast their ballots directly for the municipal councilors of their choice if they preferred this method to the traditional system of voting according to party slates.

President Pérez's AD lost gubernatorial elections in nine key states, including oil-producing Zulia, the industrial state of Carabobo, and the state of Miranda. The opposition made similar inroads at the municipal level, with 95 of the mayoral posts won by COPEI and 24 by other parties, as compared with AD's 150. The immediate result of these electoral setbacks was a renewed and more vocal discussion about the degree to which states should be able to manage their own financial resources.

The Electoral System

The 1947 constitution guaranteed universal suffrage and direct elections by secret ballot, but the Pérez Jiménez dictatorship abrogated these guarantees. Free and fair elections have been held regularly since 1958; voter turnout has been high, especially for national offices.

Voter registration and participation in elections are compulsory for all eligible citizens. Penalties exist for failing to vote, but they were seldom enforced as of 1990. All citizens over eighteen years of age, except members of the armed forces on active duty and persons serving prison sentences, are eligible to vote. There are no literacy, property, or gender requirements for voting.

With the exception of the president, all candidates for national and local offices run on lists as members of a party. Each party issues a party list with its more prominent members at the top. Candidates are elected on a proportional basis according to the number of colored ballots cast for their party and their position on the list.

Elections are supervised and directed by the Supreme Electoral Council (Consejo Supremo Electoral—CSE), which consists of thirteen members chosen every two years by Congress. The CSE heads an electoral system composed of state, district, and municipal electoral boards. The CSE is responsible for registering eligible voters, operating the polling places, counting the votes, ruling on appeals from lower electoral boards, settling controversies between parties, and other electoral matters. No political party may have a majority on the CSE or any of the lower boards.

Presidential, legislative, district, and municipal elections are held once every five years. The president is elected by a simple plurality, and congressional representatives are selected on the basis of a system of proportional representation for the major parties. The minor party representation is determined by dividing the total number of votes cast by the total number of persons directly elected to calculate the number of votes necessary to award a seat to a party. In the 1973 elections, minority parties gained one seat in the Senate for each 98,491 votes they received. In this way, three parties that did not win Senate seats through the direct elections nevertheless gained a total of five seats in the upper house. In addition to the six parties that won seats in the Chamber of Deputies by direct election, six other parties were awarded seats under the quotient system.

Despite efforts, such as the quotient system, that sought to accommodate minority parties, the Venezuelan electorate remained loyal to AD and COPEI, the two major political groups that have dominated the system since 1958. In the congressional elections of December 4, 1988, AD received 43.3 percent of the total, COPEI 31.1 percent. The closest competitor at the polls was the leftist coalition that united the Movement Toward Socialism (Movimiento al Socialismo—MAS) and the Movement of the Revolutionary Left (Movimiento de la Izquierda Revolucionaria—MIR), which obtained 10.2 percent of the total. Small groupings of rightist and personalistic orientations garnered a combined total of only 7.6 percent. The balance went to a variety of very small parties; the Venezuelan Communist Party (Partido Comunista de Venezuela—PCV), attracted only 0.9 percent of the vote.

The elections held since 1958, as a whole, have been noteworthy not only for their high voter turnout, but also for the increasing sense of legitimacy they have conferred upon the winners. Domestic and foreign observers alike have praised Venezuelan elections as fair and highly competitive. Over the years, as AD and COPEI have become the dominant political parties, a return to the traditional fragmentation of the Venezuelan political system has become increasingly unlikely. The fact that on four occasions before the 1990s a president from one party handed over the mantle to the president-elect of another party seemed to augur well for a general acceptance of the democratic system. Increased legitimacy at home has also provided Venezuelan presidents with an international clout they would otherwise lack.

The December 1989 gubernatorial and mayoral elections, however, might presage a certain undermining of this sense of legitimacy. Abstention reached a record level, with estimates suggesting that some 60 percent of the nearly 10 million registered voters did not cast ballots—substantially greater than the 41 percent abstention rate recorded in the previous municipal elections held in 1984. This sense of apathy and alienation may have been heightened by a decline in the quality of life during 1989, by an unprecedented crime wave, and by a deterioration of public services.

Political Dynamics

Political Developments since 1958

Venezuelan political dynamics since 1958 have centered on a strong commitment to the democratic "rules of the game." Although Venezuelans—and foreigners alike—have pointed out that this democratic commitment was not without its blemishes, few Venezuelans still spoke about the days of dictatorship as the golden days of their country. In general, most felt that Venezuela's democracy was strong and robust, but that democracy alone had not brought about social justice or narrowed the gap between the very rich and the very poor. Indeed, the practice of democracy, in and of itself, was perhaps not even capable of achieving such goals.

Both AD and COPEI administrations have committed themselves to developing coherent, overall economic and social development policies. Agencies such as Cordiplan were established to coordinate planning and contributed to rapid social and economic mobilization. Reform rather than revolution has been a goal of both major political parties. By the same token, the policy of *sembrar el petróleo,* "sowing the oil," served as a link uniting different factions within and between the two major parties. Even in the less affluent 1980s, large revenues produced by the petroleum industry continued to contribute to the government's ability to finance and develop ambitious programs in agriculture, education, industrial diversification, and health.

The nationalization of the petroleum industry in 1976, a long-sought goal by both major parties and practically all groups within Venezuela, was accomplished in a measured and tempered manner. Although not all parties to the nationalization accords agreed with every provision, most would admit that nationalization has worked better than many expected. Overall, it has worked well enough to serve as a successful model for other countries with some of the same developmental dilemmas as Venezuela. By ensuring that nationalization did not result in the drying up of foreign investment and, in turn, by ensuring that petroleum revenues served to some extent to underwrite reform programs, Venezuela created a financial cushion that enabled democratic governments to exert primary control over the exploitation of the nation's resources.

AD captured the presidency and both houses of Congress in 1973. Although it lost the presidency in 1978, AD remained the largest political party represented in the Senate and secured the same number of seats as the second largest party (and the winner of the presidency), COPEI, in the Chamber of Deputies. Lesser political parties such as National Opinion (Opinión Nacional—Opina) have won a few seats (usually under ten in the Chamber of Deputies) in various elections since 1958. Since the reestablishment of democracy in 1958, however, the major blocs of senators and deputies have consistently belonged to either AD or COPEI. Possibly because their parties have either held the presidency or have been considered potential winners of the presidency, AD and COPEI legislators have, in general, displayed responsibility in adhering to the political and legislative process and have not gone to extremes to destabilize the executive.

Although Pérez's victory in the December 1988 elections broke the pattern of alternating victories for AD and COPEI, his party lost absolute control of Congress in the legislative vote. AD's share of the legislative vote fell to 43.8 percent, whereas COPEI obtained 31.4 percent, and the leftist MAS doubled its representation. Of a total 253 congressional seats—204 in the Chamber of Deputies and 49 in the Senate—AD won with 121 seats (98 deputies and 23 senators). COPEI won 89 seats (67 deputies and 22 senators) and MAS 22 seats (19 deputies and 3 senators). A center-right group, the New Democratic Generation (Nueva Generación Democrática), won seven seats (six deputies and one senator). Small left-wing parties obtained seven deputies, and small center-right factions also elected seven deputies. Although the loss of absolute control of Congress might restrict some of the president's initiatives, overall it should represent only a minor impediment to the primacy of the executive.

The most outstanding political trend evidenced by six administrations since 1959 has been a commitment to and promotion of representative democracy. To many observers, the elections of 1988 assumed particular significance because they marked thirty years of democracy in Venezuela and indicated that pluralist democracy had a strong chance to survive. The food riots in Caracas in early 1989, which took place in spite of the overwhelming popular vote for the then recently inaugurated president Pérez, revealed a certain popular dissatisfaction. Opinion polls have shown that many Venezuelans felt as though they had little impact on their leaders and the way that policies were drafted and implemented. The alternatives on either the right or left of the political spectrum, however, seemed to hold little appeal, and almost no one desired a return to an authoritarian regime.

AD and COPEI reforms have dramatically benefited large segments of the population. Education and health reforms have opened job opportunities and improved the quality of life. Both literacy and life expectancy figures were among the highest in Latin America. Some other reforms, however well intentioned, have not succeeded. Most Venezuelans admitted that their costly agrarian reform programs had neither provided much land to poor farmers nor managed to feed the nation, which continued to import significant levels of foodstuffs (see Land Policies, ch. 3).

Venezuela's mixed economic picture in many ways served to shape its foreign policy. Venezuela was a founding member of the Organization of the Petroleum Exporting Countries (OPEC). This group brought Venezuela into high-level contact with a number of African countries, such as Nigeria, and with Middle Eastern oil producers. With the downturn of oil prices, Venezuela, like other once revenue-rich countries, had to face a continuing struggle to maintain foreign investment.

Jaime Lusinchi (president, 1984–89) sought to retain Venezuela's creditworthiness by paying the interest on its US$32 billion foreign debt, but was sadly disappointed when his gestures were not tangibly rewarded by foreign bankers. Bankers praised Venezuela's political courage and agreed on the country's long-term prospects, but they declined to approve new loans to Lusinchi's government. The ensuing economic crisis forced the government to devalue the currency; as inflation and unemployment soared, Venezuelans again felt vulnerable at the hands of the "multinationals."

When President Pérez assumed office in 1989, he, too, imposed austerity measures in an attempt to persuade foreign bankers to restructure the old debt and make new loans available to Venezuela. He achieved some initial success; austerity programs, however, have always proven difficult to sustain in the face of political and electoral pressure.

Interest Groups and Major Political Actors

Historically, the decisive arbiters of Venezuelan national politics have been the armed forces. Three governments since the death of Gómez in 1935 have been overthrown by military coups. Minicoups, barracks revolts, and discontent—not always fully reported—have also served as constant reminders to civilian politicians of the fragility of democracy. The armed forces have refrained from partisan political matters, especially since the early 1970s and throughout the 1980s; they have continued, however, their involvement in resolving national crises and in implementing antisubversive campaigns (see Missions, ch. 5).

Although the balance of power among contending factions since 1958 has favored groups committed to upholding the elected government, a few officers from time to time have contended that they are the best guardians of the integrity of the constitution and the nation. These officers, however, have always represented a distinct minority and have posed no real threat to the increasing supremacy of the civilian leadership. In addition, democratically elected presidents have exploited interservice rivalries to survive attempted coups. This strategy proved particularly effective in the years immediately following 1958. Both Betancourt and Leoni survived coup attempts through the loyalty of military factions that failed to rally to the cry of revolt from other factions or branches.

A successful strategy toward the military practiced by both AD and COPEI governments has been that of cooptation. Liberal defense budgets and generous benefits have been the norm. Potential troublemakers were identified and sent to distant outposts or abroad. Generally, the military enjoyed free rein to deal with actual and potential subversives. Presidents have discreetly but deliberately sought the advice of military leaders in drafting and implementing major policies, especially those that affected areas that the military considered as "their" special prerogative, such as control and delineation of borders.

Unlike the military, the Roman Catholic Church has not been a major political force in Venezuelan politics. The church was never as prominent in Venezuela as it was in neighboring Colombia. In addition, the fact that the Spanish clergy, in general, sided with their mother country rather than with the forces of independence did not endear the church to the early Venezuelan patriots.

Until the middle of the nineteenth century, the ranking clergy had close ties with the governing conservative oligarchy, and the church played a dominant role in the educational system. The rise to power of the Liberals in the latter half of the nineteenth century, however, ushered in a period of anticlericalism. It was not until the mid-twentieth century that, under the influence of the Christian social movement that began to criticize the maldistribution of wealth, the church regained some of its former influence.

Roman Catholic laymen played a prominent role in the founding of COPEI in 1946, and the announced disapproval of the church contributed to the fall of the dictator Pérez Jiménez in 1958. In the 1960s, the involvement of the church in education and welfare increased, and, although the church had no formal ties with COPEI,

Military parade on the Paseo los Próceres, Caracas
Courtesy Prints and Photographs Division, Library of Congress

many believed that the support of clergymen and church-affiliated institutions contributed to the electoral successes of COPEI in 1968 and 1978.

The church in Venezuela has been weakened, however, by a traditional lack of vocations. Many priests serving in Venezuela were foreign-born. Charismatic Protestant churches, on the other hand, were beginning to proselyte successfully, especially among the urban poor. The Roman Catholic Church did not have the funds, the personnel, or the enthusiasm to stem effectively this new challenge to its hegemony.

In addition to the military and the church, Venezuela's bureaucracy can be regarded as a major interest group and political power in its own right. The adoption of far-reaching reformist goals since 1958 has generated a proliferation of government agencies and a greatly enlarged bureaucracy. Such entities as Cordiplan, the Venezuelan Development Corporation, PDVSA, the National Agrarian Institute (Instituto Nacional Agrario—INA), and the Office of Integrated Educational Planning acquired institutional objectives that they actively promoted in their dealings with legislators and other policy makers. Overlapping authority among such entities and competing demands on limited resources often led to discord.

According to estimates, the government created an average of about eight new state-owned enterprises each year between 1968 and 1970. That number grew to eleven in 1971, sixteen in 1972, fourteen in 1973, seventeen in 1974, and nearly fifty in 1975. With the explosion of state-financed enterprises came an explosion of bureaucracy and a growing lack of accountability. Scandals were routinely exposed in the freewheeling Venezuelan press. By the end of the 1970s, few doubted that the bloated state sector was a major problem, and all the major presidential candidates in the 1978 campaign promised bureaucratic reform, privatization of inefficient enterprises, and greater efficiency and accountability. Once elected, however, candidates did not pursue their campaign promises with the same vigor with which they were uttered in the heat of the electoral campaign.

The inefficiency and bureaucratization of the economy left it vulnerable in the early 1980s to the downturn in oil prices and the maturation of the significant Venezuelan short-term foreign debt. Fiscal shortfalls threatened the financial viability of many state enterprises; close to 40 percent of the country's foreign debt consisted of short-term obligations incurred by state-owned entities. Again, the government initially temporized and conducted protracted negotiations with international banks and financial institutions rather than actually beginning the painful process of reining in the

The Capitolio, home of the Venezuelan Congress
Courtesy Karen Sturges-Vera

Entrance to the Casa Amarilla, a government building in Caracas
Courtesy Karen Sturges-Vera

bureaucracy. It was not until 1989, perhaps as a result of the shock of the food riots and looting in Caracas that resulted in hundreds killed, that the government of Carlos Andrés Pérez began to make a concerted effort to move toward a leaner and more accountable bureaucracy. The Pérez administration adopted privatization as its new motto; implementation, however, remained a slow, uncertain, and difficult process.

Few disputed that the power of patronage was an important resource for cementing party loyalty and interparty relations. The allocation of available posts for political appointees has been an important factor in forming coalition governments. Furthermore, government employees have played a significant role in electoral campaigns. Although a number of individual ministries set up internal administrative systems, and despite the numerous proposals set forth since 1958 for general standardization of government personnel policies, the bureaucracy still functioned largely on the basis of personal contacts.

Along with the persistence of a powerful and large bureaucracy, commercial and industrial forces have shown a great capacity to adapt to the democratic rules of the game and, at the same time, to use the government system to further their interests. These forces have steadily moved up to replace the traditionally dominant landowning class and have transposed economic power into effective political power. The informal means of exerting pressure through family networks and social clubs have been complemented by linkages forged with the various associational interest groups. Most of the business groups, for example, belonged to the Federation of Chambers and Associations of Commerce and Production (Federación de Cámaras y Asociaciones de Comercio y Producción—Fedecámaras). It represented a great number of interests in the fields of petroleum, agriculture, banking, industry, commerce, and services. Many of its member groups, such as the Bankers' Association, the Ranchers' and Livestock Association, the Chamber of the Petroleum Industry, and the Caracas Chamber of Industry, carried on large-scale lobbying of their own. In 1966, for example, Fedecámaras persuaded President Leoni to allow leaders of the business community to participate in the formulation of economic development policy. It has also been much involved in setting the terms under which Venezuela has entered into various integration and other economic pacts in the region.

In 1962 a group of financiers and industrialists who wanted to participate more directly in electoral politics organized the Independent Venezuelan Association, whose objective was to slow the pace of economic reform. Another group of businessmen joined in a group called Pro-Venezuela, an entity opposed to foreign participation in the exploitation of national resources; it suggested instead the use of foreign experts to train Venezuelans.

Organized labor was the largest and most cohesive of the mass-based political pressure groups that had emerged since the mid-twentieth century. Effectively stifled under military and dictatorial rule, labor did not begin to affect the political balance until the early 1940s. Labor backed the October 1945 coup and benefited much from the short-lived AD government (1945–48). Unionization proceeded apace then, but labor failed to avert the November 1948 coup that brought Pérez Jiménez to power.

Pérez Jiménez further alienated labor by allowing the immigration of thousands of workers from southern Europe. With the return to democracy in 1958, however, organized labor returned to political prominence. All political parties vied to obtain links to labor. By the late 1960s, more than half of the labor force was unionized. The Confederation of Venezuelan Workers (Confederación de Trabajadores de Venezuela—CTV), organized by AD militants, remained the most powerful of the labor confederations. Some of the more militant CTV-affiliated unions who favored severing links to the government split from the CTV to form the United Workers' Confederation of Venezuela. This group never challenged the strength of the CTV. Similarly, the Roman Catholic labor organization, the Committee of Autonomous Unions, remained small and wielded little political clout (see Labor, ch. 3).

Because of the close links between AD and the CTV, the CTV has suffered corresponding splits when AD has been divided. In the 1960s, divisions in AD were reflected in contests for CTV leadership. From time to time, members of COPEI have won certain important leadership posts in the CTV, but AD has remained the major political force.

Students and universities traditionally have been involved in the political process in the twentieth century. Betancourt, Leoni, Villalba, Machado, and other members of the Generation of 1928 were student leaders who dared to openly challenge the dictatorship of Gómez. COPEI itself traced its origins to the National Students Union, created in 1946 to defend the Roman Catholic Church and to oppose the Marxist-oriented Venezuelan Student Federation (Federación Estudiantil de Venezuela—FEV). FEV leaders took part in the protests against Pérez Jiménez and worked closely with the underground Patriotic Junta in the final push against the dictator in January 1958.

When Betancourt assumed the presidency in 1959, student groups participated actively in the establishment of a democratic government. Shortly thereafter, however, many of them became disillusioned with what they perceived as the slow pace of reforms and moved toward the left politically. Some, attracted by the Cuban model, took up arms in abortive attempts to wrest control of the government from Betancourt and the AD reformers.

Of all the national universities, the Central University of Venezuela, in Caracas, has been the major focus of student political activity. Most of the student groups at the university were linked with national political parties, but often the student branches functioned quite independently in their actions and took much more radical stands than did the parties. Students made up a considerable proportion of the membership of MIR, which split off from the AD in 1960, and its militant revolutionary band of irregulars, the Armed Forces of National Liberation (Fuerzas Armadas de Liberación Nacional—FALN) (see The Triumph of Democracy, ch. 1).

The middle class has had a significant impact on government policies in the democratic era. The middle-class origins of most

AD and COPEI leaders helped generate support for their party programs. Many of the new economic elites that have grown up as a result of the benefits produced by the petroleum bonanza had their origins in the middle sectors and generally advocated liberal democracy and public-sector involvement in the economy. With the downturn of oil revenues in the mid-1980s, this mentality began to change somewhat as the government, as well as the middle sectors, considered the potential advantages of privatization.

Political Parties

Contemporary Venezuelan political parties evolved from the student groups formed at the Central University of Venezuela in the capital during the long years of the Juan Vicente Gómez dictatorship. The most prominent of these groups was the FEV. Not surprisingly, the aging dictator swiftly dispatched into exile some of the young leaders of these protests. Abroad, they formed links with activists of similarly democratic inclinations. Other leaders who avoided exile established the bases of clandestine partisan organizations, the most important of which was the Republican National Union (Unión Nacional Republicana—UNR). Shortly after Gómez's death in 1935, these exiled leaders returned, and a spate of new political groups emerged.

Many of the former student leaders helped launch the Venezuelan Organization (Organización Venezolana—Orve); the more radical elements coalesced around the Progressive Republican Party (Partido Republicano Progresista—PRP), a Marxist group. The UNR mostly attracted young businessmen, while the Democratic National Bloc (Bloque Democrático Nacional—BDN) was primarily a regional organization centered in Maracaibo. The Orve, the PRP, and the BDN decided to join forces and, with the remnants of the old FEV, formed the National Democratic Party (Partido Democrático Nacional—PDN). Novelist Rómulo Gallegos ran under the PDN banner in the 1941 presidential election against government candidate Isaías Medina Angarita. Although Medina's victory was a foregone conclusion, as president he did open up the system somewhat, enabling the opposition, under the banner of AD, to make common cause with a reformist faction of the military to launch a crucial experiment in democracy between 1945 and 1948.

The *trienio* (see Glossary) was a time of great political ferment during which two former leaders of the Generation of 1928 came to the fore. Jóvito Villalba called his political group the Democratic Republican Union (Unión Republicana Democrática—URD), and Rafael Caldera founded COPEI. AD also began organizing labor and peasant leagues during this period. Although Betancourt was

Colonial-style church, Caracas
Courtesy Karen Sturges-Vera

the undisputed AD leader, he and others felt compelled to put forward Gallegos as their presidential candidate in the late 1947 elections.

Gallegos won overwhelmingly, but his political inexperience contributed to his overthrow less than a year later. During the reign of Pérez Jiménez (president, 1948–58), political activities were banned, political groups once again had to go underground, and political leaders such as Betancourt once more went into exile. The ten-year hiatus, however, allowed the Generation of 1928 to mature and to deepen its understanding of Venezuelan political and economic problems and realities. After 1958 many of the old organizations revived and reestablished themselves. AD and COPEI went on to hold the presidency a number of times, and Villalba made several runs for the office.

Several other political parties and organizations also were active in 1990. National Opinion, formed in 1958, won three seats in the Chamber of Deputies in 1983 and placed fifth in the presidential elections. New Democratic Generation, a small conservative group formed in 1979, managed to elect one senator and six deputies in 1988. In January 1989, it merged with two smaller groups, Formula One and the Authentic Renovating Organization, under the name of the Venezuelan Emergent Right. The Venezuelan Communist Party (Partido Comunista de Venezuela—PCV), probably the oldest political party in the country, had functioned under the same name since 1931. Accused of involvement in subversive movements that threatened the new democracy, the PCV was banned for several years beginning in 1962. MAS originated as a radical left-wing faction that split off from the PCV in 1971. In the 1970s, MAS became the Venezuelan counterpart of "Eurocommunist" parties. In the 1988 presidential election, the MAS's nominee, Teodoro Petkoff, came in third, after the AD and the COPEI candidates. Still smaller organizations, most of them former factions of the major political parties, included New Alternative, the United Vanguard, the Revolutionary Action Group, the Radical Cause, the People's Electoral Movement (Movimiento Electoral del Pueblo—MEP), the Independent Moral Movement, the People's Advance, the Socialist League, and the Party of the Venezuelan Revolution.

The most noteworthy aspect of Venezuelan party politics, however, was not the proliferation of small parties, but rather the fact that two parties, AD and COPEI, have been the major contenders for power for over three decades. The competition between these two democratic and pragmatically reformist parties gave the Venezuelan political system a great deal of stability; and although the other contenders contributed fresh ideas and at times brilliant leaders, AD and COPEI managed to occupy the broad center, where most Venezuelan voters felt most comfortable.

Formal and Informal Dynamics of Public Policy

Venezuelan public policies reflected the strong contrasts between the goals expounded by practically all major political parties and policy actors and the reality of their implementation. The constitution provides for access of the people to the government, principally via elections; but in its daily operation those with links to powerful groups, such as labor unions and business groups, enjoyed an undeniable advantage in influencing policy formulation. These groups therefore benefited more often and more directly from government policies.

It was not so much that a limited number of families controlled the system. Venezuela long ago ceased to be a rural society in which a few landowners could pick the president and run the country. Rather, through the sophisticated use of the system, certain politicians and political groups achieved a greater say in policy making. Through their various branches, the political parties served as conduits for both policy demands and implementation. Thus, when agrarian reform policies figured prominently in AD's programs, peasant leagues affiliated with the party exercised considerable influence in the formulation and implementation of reforms. These groups also benefited inordinately from these reforms.

This was not to say, however, that certain groups held exclusive access to government and to policy makers. Under the Venezuelan democratic system, various groups participated in the overall process. The system was less than totally open, however, in that certain groups had greater input in the policy-making process, depending on the issues or the status of the group. Thus, even in the modern era of civilian governments, the military would hold veto power in certain policy areas, such as border control or the pursuit of terrorists (see Role of the Military in National Life, ch. 5). In the formulation of economic policy, both the major labor unions and the major business groups affected would be heard at the highest levels of government, where compromises and deals were struck and the political parties and leaders would attempt to preserve their influence among competing constituencies.

The caution and political moderation resulting from the *trienio* and the harsh decade of dictatorship that followed served as a backdrop to the dynamics of policy making in Venezuela. The high hopes and radical reforms of the *trienio* came to naught because too many groups felt threatened; the memory of that period served to deter political actors from pushing too far in one or another public policy area. Both AD and COPEI reinforced this moderating influence by according each other a certain level of participation in policy making and policy implementation.

The Mass Media

The country's first newspaper, the *Gaceta de Caracas,* appeared in 1808, shortly after the arrival of the first printing press and just before the war of independence. The *Gaceta de Caracas,* published by a small group of young intellectuals who advocated a complete break with Spain, presented lively and well-informed discussions of the new political theories emanating from Europe as well as of local news. Around the time of independence and shortly thereafter, a number of newspapers appeared in Caracas, and by 1821 the *Correo Nacional* was being published in Zulia.

These papers emphasized serious political discussions, establishing a tradition that continued during the Conservative-Liberal controversies of the mid-nineteenth century. The literate population of the time, however, was small. With extremely limited readership and often extremely small budgets, many of these newspapers disappeared after a few initial, enthusiastic issues. An exception was *La Religión,* founded in 1890 and still published in 1990.

From early on, Caracas was the undisputed center of influence and the home base of the most significant newspapers. Maracaibo was a strong center for publication of newspapers, but their circulation and impact were still regional in scope. Whether in Caracas, Maracaibo, or outlying areas, newspapers depended heavily on direct and indirect government and/or partisan subsidies. Government advertising, in addition, represented a substantial part of the papers' income.

Only a few families owned and controlled the largest dailies. Family members usually held top administrative positions and often contributed articles. Perhaps the most prominent of these families were the Capriles, who owned a chain of morning and afternoon dailies, in addition to magazines and radio and television interests.

All the major parties maintained official party newspapers, most of them weeklies. Some parties, especially those of the extreme right and extreme left, published newspapers without necessarily identifying their true ownership and control. Organized labor, business, and other major political and economic groups all traditionally produced their own weekly or monthly publications.

Most observers agreed that the Venezuelan media were often sensationalist, and that they exhibited a healthy dose of skepticism toward grandiose government plans. Newspapers and journalists assiduously pursued corruption stories and exposed cases of unbridled nepotism, corruption, and incompetence. Venezuela's press was subject to censorship in times of emergency but was otherwise among the freest in Latin America. About the only consistent taboo was the publication of cartoons or other graphics that denigrated the national hero, Simón Bolívar Palacios.

The major Caracas newspapers in 1990 included *Últimas Noticias,* an independent newspaper with a daily run of 320,000 copies; *Meridiano,* with 300,000 copies; and *El Mundo, El Nacional,* and *Diario 2001,* all independent dailies with a circulation of approximately 150,000. *El Universal,* which used to be among the top Caracas dailies, had fallen to a circulation of 140,000 by 1990. Still influential, though of much smaller circulation, were *Panorama* and *La Crítica* of Maracaibo and *El Diario de Caracas. The Daily Journal,* an English-language newspaper in Caracas, had a print run of about 20,000 copies.

Venezuela had no domestic news agency, but several foreign agencies maintained offices in Caracas, among them the Italian News Agency (ANSA), Associated Press (AP) and United Press International (UPI) from the United States, Reuters from Britain, and TASS from the Soviet Union. The Ministry of Transport and Communications regulated broadcasting; the Venezuelan Chamber of the Broadcasting Industry (Cámara Venezolana de la Industria de Radiodifusión) exercised oversight functions. Most of the country's approximately 180 radio stations were commercial, but the government did operate the Radio Nacional network. The country had 6.7 million radio receivers in 1986 and approximately 2.8 million television sets. Both government and commercial companies operated television stations. The Venezuelan government took advantage of this extensive radio and media network to inform its people, particularly those who lived far away from major urban centers, on educational, agricultural, and civic matters. Stations were concentrated in Caracas, but transmitters were found throughout the country.

Probably even more so than elsewhere in Latin America, television was an established medium. The country had over sixty television stations organized into five networks: two owned by the government, two commercial, and one directed by the Roman Catholic Church. Telecasts began in 1953 on the government-owned Televisora Nacional. The first private commercial station, Venevisión, opened a few months later, followed by another private station, Radio Caracas Television. These two became national networks and were soon joined by the government-owned Venezuelan Television Network and a station directed by the Roman Catholic Church. All had excellent facilities and generally broadcast programs of high quality. Television continued to be extremely popular at all social levels and to represent a status symbol for the rural and urban poor.

Foreign Relations

Former President Luis Herrera Campins effectively described Venezuela's position in the world when he stated that, "Effective action by Venezuela in the area of international affairs must take key facts into account: economics—we are a producer-exporter of oil; politics—we have a stable, consolidated democracy; and geopolitics—we are at one and the same time a Caribbean, Andean, Atlantic, and Amazonian country." After the emergence of a democratic system in 1958, a number of Venezuelan presidents stated the basic principles that guided their foreign policy. These principles included respect for human rights, the right of all peoples to self-determination, nonintervention in the internal affairs of other nations, the peaceful settlement of disputes between nations, the right of all peoples to peace and security, support for the elimination of colonialism, and a call for significantly higher export prices for developing countries' primary products, especially oil. Throughout its history, Venezuela's foreign policy also has been

Figure 9. Boundary Disputes, 1990

infused with Simón Bolívar's ideal of promoting the political and economic integration of Latin America.

In the democratic era, Venezuela has attempted to fulfill these principles through a variety of means. It maintained active membership in the United Nations (UN) and its related agencies, OPEC, the Organization of American States (OAS) and its related entities, the Latin American Integration Association, and a host of other world and hemispheric organizations. In all these forums, Venezuela consistently aligned itself with other democracies. Although Venezuela has been particularly active in the Caribbean area, its foreign policy also has global dimensions.

The first two presidents of the democratic era, Rómulo Betancourt and Raúl Leoni, took courageous stands against tyrannies of the right and the left. Although motivated in part by idealism, these foreign policy positions also responded to the pragmatic need to defend the nascent democracy from foreign intervention. Both presidents saw their country repeatedly subjected to propaganda attacks and actual armed incursions directed or inspired by Cuban leader Fidel Castro Ruz. Although Betancourt and Leoni took a particularly harsh line against Cuba, they expressed equal criticism of the right-wing dictator Rafael Leónidas Trujillo Molina of the Dominican Republic, who nearly succeeded in engineering Betancourt's assassination in June 1960. The Betancourt Doctrine, whereby Venezuela refused to maintain diplomatic relations with governments formed as a result of military coups, was adhered to by both administrations. Although the doctrine was much praised, it gradually isolated Venezuela as most other Latin American nations became dominated by nonelected regimes. Slowly but surely, the doctrine was modified in the late 1960s and early 1970s, allowing for the reestablishment of diplomatic relations with Argentina, Panama, Peru, and most communist countries. In December 1974, President Rafael Caldera announced the normalization of relations with Cuba.

Relations with neighboring Guyana have been strained for decades by Venezuela's claim to all territory west of the Essequibo River, more than half the present size of Guyana (see fig. 9). A 1966 tripartite agreement in Geneva established a Guyana-Venezuela commission to discuss the dispute. In 1970 President Caldera agreed to a twelve-year moratorium on the issue. The dispute was, with the concurrence of both parties, referred to the UN secretary general in March 1983 for a determination of an appropriate means for settlement.

There appeared to be some prospect for improved relations between the two countries during the 1990s. One auspicious indication of this was the talks between the foreign ministers, held both in Venezuela and Guyana, in early 1990. The ministers not only discussed the lingering territorial question, but also committed their governments to greater cooperation in a number of fields, including energy and health. Guyana has expressed interest in importing electricity from Venezuela's mammoth Guri Dam; both countries shared concern over the control of tropical diseases.

Relations with Colombia have also been intermittently tense during the last half of the twentieth century. Caracas and Bogotá have been engaged in a long dispute regarding sovereignty over the Golfo de Venezuela (or the Golfo de Guajira, as the Colombians refer to it). Tensions arising from the dispute contributed to a high-level military alert following the intrusion of a Colombian ship into Venezuelan territorial waters in August 1988. Both countries managed to back away from the brink of open conflict over the incident; in March 1989, the two presidents met at the border to discuss this and other points of contention, most of which arose from the closely linked frontier economies along the vast land border. Venezuelans consistently assumed that most Colombians living in their country were *indocumentados* (undocumented or illegal aliens) and routinely accused them of a variety of crimes, real or imagined.

A constructive outcome of the presidents' meeting at the border in 1989 was the creation of a five-member international conciliation commission, headed by Adolfo Suárez González, the former Spanish prime minister, and including, among others, two former Latin American presidents. Three bilateral commissions were also established to study specific issues. The intensification of drug trafficking added a new urgency to better cooperation between the two countries. Most observers believed that relations improved after 1989 and that intergovernmental cooperation in controlling narcotics trafficking and guerrilla activities along the border expanded. Colombian president César Gaviria used the occasion of his August 1990 inauguration to meet with President Pérez and to reconfirm Colombia's commitment to the agreements signed by the border commissions. For his part, Pérez stressed the need to continue regular meetings between the two heads of state in order to maintain coordinated efforts not only on the resolution of border issues but also in the formulation of regional foreign policy and economic integration efforts.

Under the first Pérez administration (1974-79), Venezuela provided matériel, support, and advice to the Sandinista National Liberation Front (Frente Sandinista de Liberación Nacional—FSLN) during its struggle to oust the dictatorship of Anastasio Somoza Debayle in Nicaragua. President Herrera, who subsequently led the Andean Common Market (Ancom; see Glossary) efforts for a peaceful transition of government in that Central American nation, became increasingly disenchanted with mounting political repression under the Sandinistas. In 1983 Venezuela joined with Colombia, Mexico, and Panama to seek a regional solution to Central America's problems through the Contadora Group (see Glossary) process. In his second administration, Pérez helped to push the Sandinistas into allowing the democratic elections of February 1990, in which opposition candidate Violeta Barrios de Chamorro defeated Daniel Ortega of the FSLN and became Nicaragua's president.

Venezuela bolstered its commitment to Chamorro's government by sending nearly 1,000 soldiers to participate in the UN peacekeeping mission in Nicaragua. This was the first time that Venezuela had sent troops outside the country to demobilize warring factions. In a more traditional vein, Venezuela also cancelled Nicaragua's US$143 million oil debt and resumed oil shipments to the Central

President Carlos Andrés Pérez appears with President George Bush during a visit to Washington.
Courtesy The White House

American country. Venezuela had suspended its oil trade with Nicaragua in 1982 as a result of that nation's default in paying its oil import bill; the cutoff was also intended to signal Venezuela's disappointment with the lack of progress toward democratic government in Nicaragua at the time.

Apart from their differences in relation to Nicaragua and Venezuela's strong support of Argentina during the 1982 Falklands/Malvinas conflict, relations with the United States have been generally close. The minor tensions between the two countries have been exacerbated by trade issues; Venezuela's main objections in this regard concerned United States import policies, which, in the Venezuelans' opinion, raised excessive barriers to Venezuelan products. Also in the economic sphere, the fact that most of Venezuela's foreign debt was owed to United States banks represented a major point of continuing contention between the two countries.

From the United States perspective, Venezuelan efforts at economic reform under President Pérez provided opportunities for an expansion of ties, particularly in the area of foreign investment. To the surprise of many analysts, Pérez, who in his first administration (1974–79) assumed a cool, almost hostile stance toward foreign investment, proved much more favorably disposed to foreign capital in his second term. His administration removed previous limitations on the remittance and reinvestment of profits by foreign companies. The government also approved majority foreign control of companies in several sectors previously closed to foreign investment, such as public services, domestic transportation, and export services. Although the administration hinted at the possibility of foreign participation in oil exploration and refining, it did not immediately enact such measures. After decades of restrictions, however, the new regulations generally opened the local capital market to foreign companies and promised a reduction in the government's discretionary interference in foreign investment decisions.

Because of its long democratic tradition, as well as its support for democratic institutions in other countries, Venezuela was respected and considered a leader among the Latin American nations. It maintained good relations in the Third World, although it had few commercial or other close ties with Third World nations. Venezuela also maintained relations with the Soviet Union and the countries of Eastern Europe and strongly supported the political openings there beginning in the late 1980s. In many ways, Venezuela often felt as close to Western Europe as it did to the United States, but the nature of these relations changed according to who held power in Caracas: AD administrations tended to pursue close ties with the socialist and social-democratic parties and governments in Europe; COPEI governments established close ties with the Christian democratic and more centrist parties and governments of Europe.

Venezuela's domestic breakthrough in 1958 to a functioning democratic system was soon reflected in the conduct of its foreign policy. As that system grew stronger, and as the nation's economic status improved along with rising oil prices in the 1970s, Venezuela's role on the world stage became a more prominent one. Venezuela was a founding member of OPEC and has exercised a responsible role within that organization. Outside of OPEC, Venezuela acted during the 1980s to supply oil to the emerging democracies in the Caribbean in an effort to ease the burden of these often heavily indebted nations. Venezuelan diplomacy also vigorously supported the establishment and strengthening of democracy in the Dominican Republic and in Central America. As a member of the Contadora group of nations dealing with the Central American crisis of the mid-1980s, Venezuela advocated the establishment of democratic systems and procedures in the region as the most beneficial solution both for the countries involved and for Venezuela's own political and economic interests in the region. In the UN, the OAS, and other Third World forums, Venezuela has consistently sought to advance the same basic goals, namely democracy and development.

The future course of Venezuela's foreign policy, regardless of its direction, will undoubtedly depend upon the status of these two factors: the stability of the governmental system and the state of the national economy. The nation's commitment to the overarching principle of representative democracy appeared to be unalterable.

* * *

Venezuela has been the focus of several careful political analyses and studies in English. Among the major titles are John D. Martz and David J. Myers's *Venezuela: The Democratic Experience,* Enrique A. Baloyra and John D. Martz's *Political Attitudes in Venezuela,* and David J. Myers's *Venezuela's Pursuit of Caribbean Basin Interests: Implications for U.S. National Security.* Significant volumes on more specific topics include Robert J. Alexander's *Rómulo Betancourt and the Transformation of Venezuela,* David Eugene Blank's *Venezuela: Politics in a Petroleum Republic, The Nationalization of the Venezuelan Oil Industry* by Gustavo Coronel, *Political Mobilization of the Venezuelan Peasant* by John Duncan Powell, and Luis Vallenilla's *Oil: The Making of a New Economic Order.* (For further information and complete citations, see Bibliography.)

Chapter 5. National Security

Venezuelan weaponry: F–16 fighter, Constitution-class attack craft, and AMX–13 light tank

BY 1990 VENEZUELA REPRESENTED one of the few Latin American countries where a democratic system had produced a military institution that exerted little or no direct influence on the government. When civilian government returned in 1958, the military had been thoroughly discredited in the eyes of the public by the performance of the venal and reactionary regime of Marcos Pérez Jiménez. This rejection of the military strengthened the appeal of civilian politicians, raised the profile of reformist officers within the armed forces, and deterred coup plans by isolated sectors of the officer corps. In short, the return to democracy symbolized a social consensus that supported the concept of civilian control over an apolitical military.

Until Rómulo Betancourt's 1959 inauguration, with the exception of the brief *trienio* (see Glossary) period of 1945–48, Venezuela had been ruled by a succession of military-based caudillos stretching back to "The Liberator" himself, Simón Bolívar Palacios. The nation exhibited all the characteristics of a traditional society—an agricultural economy, a small economic and political elite, and militarism—until the oil industry developed in earnest after World War II. The changes wrought by the influx of oil revenue eventually altered the military institution as much as the society as a whole.

Under a succession of democratically elected presidents, the military improved its capabilities and expertise. It also enhanced its public image. Although defense ministers and other leaders still felt compelled to deny occasional rumors of a coup, such rumors appeared to have no serious basis. And despite popular disillusionment with the economic performance of civilian administrations, there was no indication that Venezuelans would support a return to military rule. Democracy in Venezuela was institutionalized, and no serious threats to its survival, from within or without, were evident.

History of the Armed Forces

During the colonial era, Spain employed only a small army in the area later known as Venezuela. It relied primarily on an elaborate militia system that recruited members of the local population to maintain public order and guard against foreign attack. Militiamen generally were not professional soldiers; they held civilian occupations and met for drill on Sundays, for monthly inspections, and to keep watch on their local communities perhaps one evening a month. The militiamen received a token salary from the crown; service in the militia, however, represented a source of prestige, primarily because of the *fuero militar* (military privilege), which exempted all active militiamen from criminal or civil prosecution and from certain taxes and community work assignments that were obligatory for other citizens.

By 1810 the colony had several thousand active militiamen. These men provided the bulk of the armed force for the independence struggle against Spain that occupied Venezuela for the next twenty years. Many thousands lost their lives as Venezuelans played a dominant role in winning the independence not only of their own future country, but also of Colombia, Ecuador, Peru, and Bolivia. This achievement and the Venezuelan origins of several of the greatest leaders of the revolutionary period—including Francisco de Miranda, Simón Bolívar, and José Antonio Páez—remained sources of national pride for most Venezuelans (see The Epic of Independence, ch. 1).

The militiamen made themselves into a regular army during the independence struggle. After 1830, however, a wave of antimilitary sentiment led to the army's being relegated to a small and comparatively unimportant local security force, a status it retained until the twentieth century. For the bulk of the nineteenth century, successive governments reverted to the old colonial militia system to provide the nation's primary armed force. The nineteenth century was the age of the caudillo in Latin America, and in no other country was caudillismo (rule by local strongmen, or caudillos) more pronounced than in Venezuela (see A Century of Caudillismo, ch. 1). Despite its militaristic trappings, however, caudillismo in Venezuela was more a manifestation of personalistic loyalties than martial aspirations. The employment of personal armies by caudillos rendered the regular standing army superfluous. In 1872 the federal troops were dismissed entirely.

Venezuela did not reestablish a truly professional army until World War II. The transition, however, began under Cipriano Castro (president, 1898–1908). Although otherwise a mediocre and ineffective caudillo, Castro made one important contribution to Venezuelan politics; he established, on a permanent basis, a central authority with sufficient strength to resist all regional challenges to its existence. Whereas earlier caudillos had viewed the development of a strong national army as a threat to their personal control over the country, Castro recognized that a professional armed force could function as an effective guarantor of presidential rule. Among his innovations were the creation of a general staff and a chain of command that extended to the commanders of each state and local contingent. Castro charged these commanders with forcing local caudillos to submit to his authority. The national army granted commissions to most of those who pledged their loyalty and defeated those who resisted. Castro also established the Military Academy in Caracas, at least on paper, in 1903. The academy did not open until 1910, however, two years after Juan Vicente Gómez (1908–35) had seized power from an ailing Castro.

Gómez built on the military policies established by Castro. Although the opening of the academy, the introduction of foreign military training missions, and the procurement of modern armaments brought progress in the development of professional military capabilities, Gómez's most significant achievement was the abolition of the militia system via a 1919 decree. That act signaled the end of the age of caudillismo and the beginning of the age of Venezuelan militarism. Without a militia, soldiers could gain power only from within the ranks of the national army.

Although he improved the capabilities of the army, Gómez never intended to establish a truly professional, apolitical force. Rather, Gómez's army served to enforce the preeminence of the traditional elite by preserving order, quelling opposition, and breaking strikes. After the oil industry became established, Gómez used some of its revenues to purchase modern matériel for the army in order to help preserve a climate of domestic security conducive to continued and expanded foreign investment. The bulk of the increased revenue from oil, however, went not to the army, but to Gómez himself.

After Gómez's death in 1935, Venezuela was ruled first by his minister of war, General Eleazar López Contreras (president, 1936–41), then by López's minister of war, General Isaías Medina Angarita (president, 1941–45). Both of these presidents encouraged the military to move away from direct involvement in politics and toward a more professional role, namely the defense of the country's borders and the maintenance of public order (see The Transition to Democratic Rule, ch. 1). Castro had first brought foreign military missions to Venezuela in the late nineteenth century; succeeding governments maintained this tradition. Venezuelan officers also began to study abroad, in military academies in Peru, France, and the United States. The military also established social welfare measures during this period, as well as a mutual aid fund for officers. Military equipment purchases also modernized the services from a technical aspect. The officer corps, however, continued to be dominated by officers from the Andean state of Táchira, the home state of Castro, Gómez, López, and Medina.

This cliquishness rewarded origins more than professional competence, to the detriment of the corps as a whole.

It was not until near the end of the Medina regime that for the first time a maximum retirement age was set for all military personnel. But the action came too late; such tardy half-measures toward professionalizing the military provoked resentment among junior officers, which eventually split the military. In mid-1945, junior officers founded a secret lodge, the Patriotic Military Union (Unión Patriótica Militar—UPM), which endorsed the establishment of democratic representative government in Venezuela, supported by an apolitical military. One of the principal founders of the UPM was Marcos Pérez Jiménez, then a captain. Other prominent figures were majors Carlos Delgado Chalbaud and Julio Vargas.

The UPM conspired with members of the political party Democratic Action (Acción Democrática—AD) to bring about this new order. Thus, after the successful military rebellion of October 18, 1945, the seven-man ruling junta was made up of four *adecos* (AD members), two military officers, and one independent. Major Delgado was the senior officer on the junta. The leading figure on the junta, however, was AD leader Rómulo Betancourt. Rómulo Gallegos, who was not a junta member, ran for and won the presidency in 1947 on the AD ticket.

During the *trienio* of civilian rule, the military enjoyed relative autonomy in dealing with its own institutional affairs. In turn, officers did not involve themselves in social or economic policy making or in routine political decisions. Nevertheless, the armed forces were among the principal beneficiaries of the 1945 rebellion; from 1945 to 1947, the defense budget tripled, salaries rose dramatically, and matériel procurements increased substantially. Enrollment in the Military Academy more than doubled, and a large United States military mission arrived, making the United States the major foreign influence on the Venezuelan military. The navy was reorganized and the air force was granted autonomy from the army. The young officers now in charge also decided to cashier all officers who had attained ranks above major before the 1945 rebellion, thus leaving room for professionally trained officers to fill the upper ranks.

Despite these concessions and considerations, the AD government proved unable to retain the loyalty of the military. The primary point of conflict between the two camps was the pursuit by AD of what the military leadership considered to be radical social reforms. Many officers also resented AD's active recruiting efforts among the officer corps. When Betancourt floated the idea of establishing a party militia, the military moved directly to preempt this challenge to its authority. The nearly bloodless coup of November 24, 1948, ousted Gallegos and AD from power.

A three-man provisional military junta, headed by Major Carlos Delgado Chalbaud, who had served as defense minister during the *trienio,* assumed power. Allegedly hesitant to repeat the mistakes of 1945 by hastily reestablishing a civilian government, the provisional government gave increasing signals of its intention to establish a permanent military regime. In November 1950, a band of thugs dragged the more moderate Delgado from his home and murdered him. His successor, Caracas lawyer Germán Suárez Flamerich, served as a figurehead for Pérez.

The elections of November 1952 removed any facade of legitimacy from the Pérez regime (see The Triumph of Democracy, ch. 1). After balloting marked by clumsy fraud on the part of the regime, Pérez had himself declared president. No longer directing affairs from behind the scenes, Pérez made no pretense of ruling democratically. Having no political constituency, he ruled in the name of and on behalf of the military. Officers received tremendous salary increases; new and exotic arms were purchased; and the luxurious Officers Club (Círculo de las Fuerzas Armadas) was built in Caracas at a cost equivalent to millions of United States dollars to raise the military's morale.

Pérez ruled in particularly brutal fashion. The regime strictly censored the press and set up an intricate spy network to seek out and punish those suspected of disloyalty. The National Security Police (Seguridad Nacional—SN) became increasingly powerful and threatening to the integrity of the armed forces as they arrested more and more military officers. In a further effort to consolidate his power, Pérez, a native of Táchira, distributed key posts in the government and the military on the basis of personal loyalty rather than professional merit—a throwback to the old days of the *tachirense* (native of the state of Táchira) clique, but even more insidious in its debilitating effect on the military institution. Once again, junior officers grew to resent the incompetence, corruption, and brutality of their superiors. By showing favoritism to the army, Pérez also alienated air force and naval officers. It was these factions within the officer corps that led to military rebellion against Pérez in 1958. Although initially unsuccessful, the rebellion led by the air force triggered widespread popular unrest that brought other elements of the armed forces into the anti-Pérez coalition. The dictator fled the country on January 23, 1958.

The five-man provisional military-civilian junta that emerged under the leadership of Admiral Wolfgang Larrazábal guided the country directly toward what was now clearly the will of the people: a freely elected civilian government. Despite numerous revolts among the armed forces, the junta organized elections that culminated in Rómulo Betancourt's election to the presidency on December 7, 1958. Betancourt's inauguration on February 13, 1959, was a line of demarcation in Venezuelan history between centuries of military dominance and the modern era of civilian democratic rule.

Initially, the Betancourt government faced considerable active opposition from within the armed forces. Right-wing officers, disenchanted with liberal civilian rule, attempted coups on several different occasions, and twice in 1962 officers and enlisted men of the left-wing Infantería de Marina (Marine Infantry) launched unsuccessful rebellions. Such activities eventually subsided, however. The government of Raúl Leoni (president, 1964-69) saw only one small uprising by army officers loyal to Pérez. During periods of political crisis, rumors periodically circulated in Venezuela that the military was preparing to take power. After the 1960s, however, these rumors appear to have been without foundation. By 1990 the democratic order appeared to be well established.

Although the armed forces shunned a direct role in the nation's politics, they continued to act as a powerful pressure group, lobbying in their own corporate self-interest. Their primary concerns included the protection of their share of the national budget, the security of the country's borders, the maintenance of internal order, the operation of the police, and the development of an indigenous military industry. It was in these areas that the civilian government had to consult with and secure the approval of the armed forces leadership before proceeding with any major changes in policy.

Strategic Setting

Like all countries, Venezuela must approach questions of security and defense by considering its geography, its natural resources, its population, and its regional political interests. During the modern era, two such considerations have shaped Venezuelan security policy more than any others. These are the nation's status as a major producer and exporter of petroleum, and its role as a regional power within the Caribbean Basin (see Glossary) area. The country's external defense posture, its internal disposition of forces, and its relations with neighboring states responded in large part to these imperatives.

The development of Venezuela as a major oil producer after World War II transformed the nation both economically and socially. This process of societal transition was reflected in the military

Amphibious vessels
Courtesy Embassy of Venezuela, Washington

institution as well. Long an unprofessional, internal security-oriented force subject to the vagaries of policy as laid down by self-absorbed dictators, the Venezuelan military began a transition under democratic rule.

The growth of the oil industry provided both a legitimate mission for the armed forces in protecting the oil fields and, even more important, the resources with which to accomplish that mission. President Betancourt established the policy of committing significant revenues to the military. Although Betancourt's motivation was largely a political one—keeping the officer corps satisfied so as to forestall future military intervention in affairs of state—his actions yielded a benefit in purely military terms as well. Subsequent administrations have maintained this policy. As a result, the National Armed Forces (Fuerzas Armadas Nacionales—FAN) had become by the 1970s the best equipped military force in Latin America. With this strengthened military posture and the nation's enhanced stature in both regional and international arenas, the concept of Venezuela as an actor with a defined sphere of influence began to take hold in Caracas. At the same time, other South American countries grew to resent, to varying degrees, falling under the shadow of their more resource-rich neighbor.

Venezuela's regional sphere of influence equated roughly with the strategic area that came to be known during the 1980s as the Caribbean Basin. Culturally, the countries of the basin are diverse, ranging from primarily Hispanic Central America to the former British colonies of the Eastern Caribbean to the French and African fusion in Haiti. Despite some variations, all the countries of the basin were economically underdeveloped, and therefore potentially unstable politically. Beginning in the 1960s, the presence of communist Cuba, its major military buildup, and its undisguised intentions to subvert established governments in the area added an urgency to the goal of maintaining Caribbean stability. Cuba's alignment with the Soviet Union also forced strategists in democratic nations such as Venezuela to factor global variables into their security posture.

During the 1980s, Venezuela involved itself actively in the Caribbean Basin. Despite some rhetorical bows to the concept of nonintervention, policy makers generally supported the United States intervention in Grenada in 1983. After the reestablishment of democratic government in that country, Venezuela provided limited economic aid to Grenada, as it had to other island states.

In 1980 Venezuela and Mexico had signed the San José Accord to provide oil at subsidized rates and other economic assistance to designated beneficiary states in the Caribbean Basin (see Foreign Assistance, ch. 3). Their purpose was to cushion the impact of oil price increases on the small oil-importing countries of the basin. Their motivations, however, were as much political and strategic as altruistic. Given the already precarious economic condition of most of these countries, the added burden of oil price increases in 1973 and 1979 had threatened to push many of them from stagnant poverty into widespread social unrest. Although the accord became less economically sustainable for Venezuela and Mexico as oil prices dropped throughout the 1980s, both countries continued to uphold its provisions and expand the number of beneficiaries throughout the decade, mainly because of the perceived political benefits and the potential adverse impact on the importing countries of an oil cutoff.

Although the Venezuelan military was capable of projecting its power to a limited extent within the Caribbean Basin, it has never actively used this power. Instead, Venezuela has applied its efforts to promote regional stability mainly in the diplomatic arena (see Foreign Relations, ch. 4). This approach was epitomized by the Central American crisis of the 1980s. Venezuela was one of the original "core-four" nations—along with Mexico, Colombia, and Panama—that joined together in 1983 as the Contadora Group (see Glossary) in an effort to resolve the tensions in the region through negotiation and avoid armed conflict and possible foreign military intervention.

Venezuela supported the Contadora process as a peaceful path to stability in an area where tensions had escalated following the 1979 seizure of power by the Sandinista National Liberation Front (Frente Sandinista de Liberación Nacional—FSLN) in Nicaragua. The Venezuelan government, led by President Carlos Andrés Pérez, had supported the Sandinistas during the struggle against Nicaraguan dictator Anastasio Somoza Debayle and had cooperated with Cuba, Costa Rica, and other governments to supply arms to the Nicaraguan rebels. The Pérez administration, which had some doubts as to the FSLN's commitment to democratic principles, apparently believed that it could exert sufficient influence over a postrevolutionary Nicaraguan government to ensure some degree of pluralism. As the Sandinistas moved to force moderates out of the government, however, it became clear to Venezuela that the overwhelming foreign influence in Nicaragua was Cuban. Although Pérez had cooperated with Cuban leader Fidel Castro Ruz in arming the Nicaraguans, Venezuela still viewed Cuba as a regional competitor for political influence and as a potential military threat. Therefore, as the FSLN consolidated its rule, set up Cuban-style mechanisms of control, acquired significant amounts of Soviet weaponry to equip a growing military, and increasingly aligned itself with the Soviet Union and its communist allies in political and security matters, Venezuelans looked on with growing alarm.

The Contadora process, however, proved incapable of dealing with the complex Central American situation. Among the core-four nations, Venezuela found itself advocating a much more moderate, security-conscious position than that espoused by the other sponsoring countries. Early on in the process, the government of Colombian president Belisario Betancur Cuartas appeared to take the lead in the negotiating process. But as the talks became protracted, the Mexican government of Miguel de la Madrid Hurtado moved toward the forefront. The Mexicans, however, generally advocated conditions more favorable to the Nicaraguan government than to Costa Rica, Honduras, El Salvador, and Guatemala. From the Venezuelan perspective, the talks became increasingly counterproductive as they dragged on for years without producing an agreement. During the early to mid-1980s, Venezuelans became preoccupied to an increasing extent with their own economic crisis and apparently could not muster sufficient resources or influence to devote to what seemed to many a futile diplomatic exercise. As the United States government refocused its efforts after

1990, working through public and private dilomacy to influence the process toward a resolution that would limit the interventionist nature of the Sandinista regime and promote pluralism in Nicaragua, Caracas came to concur informally with these goals and disengaged itself somewhat from the negotiations.

Venezuela and the United States

The strategic relationship between Venezuela and the United States has changed as rapidly as has Venezuela itself during the latter half of the twentieth century. Before World War II, Venezuela was a relatively traditional Latin American society, ruled by a succession of dictators and dependent on the cycles of an agriculturally based economy. As its growing oil wealth changed and modernized Venezuelan society, however, Venezuela became a more important strategic consideration for the United States. As Venezuela began to develop its own limited sphere of influence, the United States began to consider it as a potential strategic partner in the Caribbean area.

The basic strategic assumptions of the two countries, although not identical, tracked closely enough to make possible a supportive and cooperative relationship during the 1960s. As an emerging democracy, Venezuela opposed authoritarian governments of both the right and the left. In the early 1960s, Venezuela came to share the United States conviction that the Castro regime in Cuba presented the most compelling threat to the stability of Latin America and the Caribbean. Cuban backing of Venezuelan insurgents confirmed this belief. Counterinsurgency training provided by the United States contributed to the successful quelling of the insurgency by the late 1960s.

During the 1970s, Venezuela and the United States followed more divergent paths with regard to security matters. The global strategy of containing communism had drawn the United States into a debacle in Vietnam. As the prestige and perceived influence of the United States waned, lesser powers such as Venezuela moved to pursue policies of independent outreach to the Third World. Although largely political in nature, Venezuela's relations among Third World nations had distinct security connotations as well, seeking as they did to promote development within a democratic framework that would yield a broader market for oil exports.

By the 1980s, Venezuela had articulated such a significant range of differences with the United States regarding security matters—on such issues as intervention in the affairs of other states and the relative influence of external versus internal factors on regional stability—that the kind of close identification of interests that characterized the relationship in the 1960s was no longer workable. Nevertheless, the two countries continued to share certain basic strategic interests that bound them in a shifting and sometimes uneasy partnership. These shared interests included the safety and free passage of shipping through Caribbean sea-lanes, concern for the Caribbean region as a market for exports, a desire to promote political stability by encouraging and supporting democratic governments, and opposing the expansion of Cuban presence and influence.

Some of these shared interests came to the fore in the debate that preceded the United States sale of F-16 jet fighters to the Venezuelan air force in 1983. Despite some concern expressed by such other regional powers as Colombia, the administration of United States president Ronald Reagan pushed for the sale on the grounds that Venezuela needed advanced aircraft to help protect the Caribbean sea-lanes, to secure its oil resources against external attack, and to help secure the approaches to the Panama Canal. The Reagan administration argued that regional allies such as Venezuela should be encouraged to share strategic responsibilities and to complement United States military forces. Military advances in Cuba and Nicaragua, along with the potential at that time for the Soviet Union's military use of an expanded airport base on Grenada, further buttressed these arguments.

Despite such public characterizations of Venezuela as an active contributor to regional defense, both countries accepted the proposition that Venezuela fell under the strategic umbrella of the United States. As crucial as Venezuela's oil resources were to the nation's economic well-being, they were also of significant strategic interest to the United States, the primary consumer. The United States therefore fulfilled the role of unacknowledged guarantor of Venezuelan sovereignty if for no other reason than to maintain access to this important source of petroleum in the Western Hemisphere.

The threat of communist expansion that had undergirded security policy even before the advent of the Castro regime in Cuba appeared to have waned considerably by the 1990s. Nevertheless, it appeared likely that Venezuela and the United States would continue to cooperate in maintaining stability in the Caribbean Basin. Venezuela's economic setbacks, however, seemed to indicate that it would not soon return to the regional prominence it enjoyed in the 1970s.

Venezuela and Colombia

These two neighbors shared many points in common. Both were large South American states with security concerns that encompassed the Caribbean area as well. Both have functioned under representative democratic systems for decades. Associated under the Spanish colonial Viceroyalty of New Granada, both nations could point to Bolívar as their liberator (see Spanish Colonial Life, ch. 1). The disparities between Venezuela and Colombia, however, have contributed to a fluctuating undercurrent of tension over the years.

The most visible irritant in the relationship was the dispute over the boundary demarcation in the Golfo de Venezuela (Golfo de Guajira as the Colombians refer to it—see fig. 9). The roots of the maritime boundary issue stretch back to colonial times. The borders of the nations that emerged from the wars for independence were not clearly defined. As these nations grew, disputes became unavoidable. In 1881 Venezuela and Colombia appealed to King Alfonso XII of Spain to arbitrate their conflicting claims. Venezuela rejected the eventual 1891 arbitration decision because of a disagreement over the location of the source of the Río Oro. Fifty years later, the two nations signed a treaty that defined the border along the Península de la Guajira. This 1941 treaty, however, has been criticized by many Venezuelans for granting too much territory to Colombia. This attitude has hardened the stance of the armed forces with regard to the Golfo de Venezuela; it has also rendered more tentative the attempts of subsequent governments to negotiate the boundary in the gulf. Moreover, the development of oil resources in the area and the expectation of further expansion also raised the stakes involved in a potential resolution.

After an abortive effort in the early 1970s and an adamant refusal by Venezuela to submit the dispute to international arbitration, the two governments announced in 1981 a draft treaty designated the Hypothesis of Caraballeda. When President Luis Herrera Campíns's foreign minister presented the draft to representatives of the officer corps, however, he received an extremely negative reaction. Opposition to the treaty quickly spread, forcing the government to withdraw from further negotiations with the Colombians. There have been no formal talks dedicated to the maritime boundary since that time.

In the mid- to late 1980s, Caracas and Bogotá rose above their diplomatic failure on the boundary issue to effect greater cooperation on security issues. In January 1988, the interior ministers of both countries met in the Venezuelan border town of San Antonio de Táchira. The meeting produced an agreement to increase the military presence on both sides of the border and to expand cooperation in such areas as counternarcotics and counterinsurgency. The movement toward cooperation grew out of a shared realization that Colombia's internal security problems—namely drug trafficking and insurgency—were spilling over the border.

On several occasions in the late 1980s, Colombian guerrillas attacked posts manned by the Venezuelan Armed Forces of Cooperation (Fuerzas Armadas de Cooperación—FAC)—also known as the National Guard. Drug trafficking activity, always attended by increased levels of violence, also picked up.

Venezuelans generally have tended to view Colombia as a violent and unstable country whose problems and people washed over the border into more peaceful and prosperous Venezuela. News of attacks on border posts, kidnappings of wealthy Venezuelan ranchers by Colombian guerrillas, and drug seizures during transshipment have reinforced this conception. Another issue, Colombian *indocumentados* (undocumented or illegal aliens), underscored for Venezuelans the disparities in both internal security and economic development between themselves and their neighbors. Estimates of the number of illegal Colombians in Venezuela varied, but most ran in the hundreds of thousands (see Migration, ch. 2). Although some Venezuelans saw Colombians as a threat to law and order, their major impact was economic. During the boom years of the Venezuelan oil economy, the Colombian immigration issue constituted a minor irritant. As the economy constricted during the 1980s, however, Venezuelans grew more resentful of the Colombian presence. Nevertheless, it was highly unlikely that this problem, even in combination with the Golfo de Venezuela dispute, would provoke active hostilities between the two countries.

Venezuela and Guyana

Over the years, Venezuela's claim to the Essequibo region of Guyana has been a much more bitter issue than the maritime dispute with Colombia. Historical and cultural dissimilarities between Venezuela and Guyana explained this fact to some extent. Formerly British Guiana, Guyana represented for Venezuela the unfair intrusion of an extrahemispheric colonial power into the Caribbean region. Originally settled by the Dutch, the Essequibo region was claimed by the Spanish, seized by the British, and subsequently restored to the Netherlands by France. Britain finally took firm possession in 1803 during the Napoleonic Wars. After achieving independence from Spain, the Republic of Gran Colombia, and later Venezuela, petitioned Britain for a resolution of the border question. The Venezuelans held that the Essequibo River should mark their eastern boundary; the British favored a line from the mouth of the Río Orinoco to Mount Roraima on the Brazilian border as the demarcation line. Negotiations failed to achieve a compromise. A protracted period of proposals, threats, and brief skirmishes yielded in 1897 to international arbitration, a step strongly urged on the British by the United States.

The final decision of the arbitral tribunal awarded Punta Barima and the mouth of the Río Orinoco to Venezuela, but granted the vast majority of the Essequibo territory to Britain. The Venezuelan representatives, claiming that Britain had unduly influenced the decision of the Russian member of the tribunal, protested the outcome. As a poor country with comparatively limited military capabilities, Venezuela could not press its claim against the British empire by force of arms. Periodic protests, therefore, were confined to the domestic political arena and international diplomatic forums.

In 1962 Caracas began to make more forceful efforts to resolve the Essequibo dispute. Britain agreed in November to hold tripartite negotiations, including representatives of British Guiana, which would review the record of the 1899 arbitration. After numerous ministerial conferences, the parties agreed to procedures by which the conflicting claims could be resolved definitively. Subsequent negotiations were complicated by Venezuela's occupation in 1966 of a portion of Ankoko Island in the Cuyuni River that had previously been claimed by Guyana (which became independent that same year). In 1968 Venezuela extended its maritime claim to include a portion of the Atlantic Ocean beyond Guyana's three-nautical-mile claim. The Guyana government also accused Caracas of aiding an insurrection in southern Guyana the following year. This incident prompted reports of a Venezuelan military buildup near the Guyanese border. Against this backdrop of conflict and recriminations, the tripartite commission that had been negotiating the territorial dispute declared itself incapable of producing a settlement. The two governments began bilateral talks in 1970.

In 1970 leaders of both countries signed the Protocol of Port-of-Spain after talks hosted by the government of Trinidad and Tobago. Under the terms of the protocol, Caracas agreed to suspend its territorial claims for twelve years. The two nations established diplomatic relations and continued their talks. In 1981, however, Venezuelan president Herrera reasserted the historical claim to the Essequibo and refused to renew the protocol. Venezuelan political and military leaders began to make bellicose statements with regard to the Essequibo; there was much speculation in the press that Venezuela might take the region by force. This saber rattling aroused the concern of the Brazilians, who also considered Guyana within their sphere of influence. In September 1982, Guyanese president Forbes Burnham visited Brasília and agreed to a project whereby the Brazilian government would build a road northward through the Essequibo region. If the Venezuelans had entertained notions of reclaiming the territory by force, this demonstration of concern by their giant neighbor to the south apparently deterred them from taking action. Accordingly, both governments submitted the dispute to the United Nations secretary general under the terms of the 1966 tripartite agreement signed in Geneva. The issue lay dormant through 1990.

Although the Venezuelan claim to the Essequibo stemmed in large part from nationalistic and anticolonialist sentiments, it also involved the control and exploitation of natural resources. Long unexplored, the Essequibo reportedly contains important mineral and petroleum deposits. Its crude oil reserves, according to some sources, are of a lighter grade than most of those produced in Venezuela. Lighter oils are more easily extracted and refined, and they command a higher price on the world market. It was highly unlikely, however, that Venezuela would annex the Essequibo by force, risking regional conflict and international condemnation, merely to add to its already considerable petroleum and mineral reserves.

Venezuela and Brazil

Historically, the strategic postures of Venezuela and Brazil have proven to be largely exclusive, with few points of intersection or friction. In contrast to Venezuela's inclination toward the Caribbean, Brazil's external focus lay to the east, toward the southern Atlantic Ocean. As Brazil has begun to emphasize the extension, exploitation, and protection of its Amazon resources, however, minor potential conflict areas have emerged.

The Brazilian interest in the Essequibo dispute served as a signal of peripheral friction. Some Venezuelan observers have claimed that Brazil harbored a desire to extend not only its influence but also its territorial access northward to the Caribbean. It is not clear whether governments in Caracas have shared this concern. Brazilian outreach to previously neglected areas such as Guyana and Suriname, however, has highlighted for Venezuelan strategic planners the vulnerability of the southern and eastern frontiers. In this context, the movement to develop and populate areas more remote from the Caribbean heartland, such as Ciudad Guayana, could be viewed not only as a response to economic circumstances, but also as a move to bolster the nation's security posture.

Although neither government has stressed the issue publicly, the question of itinerant Brazilian gold miners plying their trade illegally across the border has been an irritant to Venezuela. Although the strategic effect of this phenomenon was negligible, its implications appeared serious to some Venezuelan policy makers. The situation touched on two nationalistic sore points: Venezuela's inability to police effectively its long southern border and its apparent inability to protect its natural resources. The latter issue was a particularly resonant one in light of Venezuela's dependence on one resource—petroleum—for its economic existence.

Role of the Military in National Life

Missions

Broadly speaking, the FAN by the 1990s had two major missions: external defense and internal security. The counterinsurgency mission of the 1960s and 1970s had ended with the successful resolution of the conflict with leftist guerrillas. After that time, the military's approach to its missions became less focused, and the armed forces became a more technocratic and bureaucratic institution that was more susceptible to the pressures of politics. Although Venezuela's oil resources lent a certain impetus to the external defense mission of the FAN, the absence of a viable external threat dulled the response of policy makers and shifted the motivation of defense planners away from contingency planning and more toward political considerations, such as maintaining military pay and benefits. This phenomenon appeared likely to persist and to intensify as the potential conventional threat from Cuba, which had seemed viable during the early 1980s, continued to wane during the 1990s.

Venezuelan military doctrine, in keeping with the perceived role of the armed forces in a democratic state, theoretically emphasized readiness for external defense. Strategic planners attempted to prepare their forces to engage in a conflict of limited objectives. Tactically, the doctrine called for the employment of combined forces capable of employing significant firepower and shock capability, while also displaying adequate mobility. It stressed an active defense in which regular forces would engage the enemy and reserves would man static defensive positions. The FAN's amphibious and air transport capabilities, though limited, extended its strategic reach somewhat; naval forces also lent a degree of support to a ground effort in the areas of sealift and antisubmarine warfare. Although the FAN's ability to implement its doctrine was hampered by equipment shortages, maintenance problems, and other logistical shortcomings, these problems generally were less severe than those exhibited by most other Latin American military institutions.

Venezuelan marine infantry
Courtesy Embassy of Venezuela, Washington

Although the probability of external conflict was low, the role of the FAN in national life was still significant. Even under the democratic system reestablished in 1958, the FAN (including the National Guard) retained certain traditional responsibilities. Among these were the regulation and control of national highways; the security of basic industries such as petroleum and petrochemicals, energy production, and steel production; the administration of the prison system; the enforcement of federal taxes on alcoholic beverages; and the regulation of customs and immigration. In response to the FAN's traditional concern with the national borders, an active-duty officer usually headed the Directorate of Frontiers of the Ministry of Foreign Affairs. According to law, Venezuelan frontier regions were considered security zones; accordingly, foreigners could not own land in these areas, and no construction or industrial development could take place there without the approval of the government as expressed by the Ministry of National Defense. Other security zones included coastal areas, territory surrounding lakes and rivers, and areas adjacent to military installations and to industrial facilities engaged in basic industrial production. In a more limited sphere, the FAN also conducted small-scale civic-action projects. Most of these projects were confined to the dispensing of medical care—immunization and dental and medical attention—to residents of isolated rural areas. The army has also provided literacy programs for these citizens.

In theory, the internal security mission of the FAN involved the National Guard more than the other branches of service. This fact stemmed from the purely domestic orientation of the National Guard. In practice, however, the delineation of mission blurred somewhat. National Guard posts in frontier regions have responded to cross-border attacks and incursions by Colombian insurgent forces, thereby fulfilling an external defense mission. Some observers also have characterized National Guard efforts against drug trafficking as an external defense effort. By the same token, Venezuelan governments have accepted the fact that regular military forces at times may have to be employed in order to maintain order in major cities. When riots or violent demonstrations have broken out, the public routinely has demanded a response from the minister of national defense in addition to the efforts expended by local police.

Manpower

The FAN consisted of a well-paid professional officer corps, a well-paid nucleus of career noncommissioned officer (NCOs), and two-year conscripts who comprised the bulk of the noncommissioned officers and all of the privates and seamen. The National Guard was an exception to this pattern; it was made up completely of volunteers, many of whom had already completed their conscriptive service in one of the other services.

According to the Laws and Regulations of the FAN, all Venezuelans between the ages of eighteen and fifty shared an equal obligation to military service. All citizens, including women, were required to register for conscription. In practice, however, conscription drew disproportionately from young men in rural areas and from among the poor. This situation was partially a result of the numerous categories of deferments allowed potential draftees. Recruits could be deferred for illness or disability, marriage, a sibling already in service, status as sole support of one's family, pursuit of higher education, and membership in certain religious denominations advocating pacifism. Other explanations for the nonrepresentative nature of draftees included the relatively low manpower needs of the FAN and the comparative benefit of a military salary for youths of the lower class.

The role of women changed slightly in the Venezuelan military after the passage of a revised conscription law in 1978. Although the law required women to register for the draft—an unprecedented development—it stated that military service for women was mandatory only in time of war. As Venezuela has never engaged in a war with any of its neighbors, it appeared unlikely that women would ever be called to service in any significant numbers. As for those women who elected voluntary military service, the minister of national defense determined which units could accept these recruits. The categories of service open to women included support positions, health, civil defense, police, transport, and refugee services.

The pay and perquisites of Venezuelan military personnel were generous by Latin American standards. Traditionally, pay scales have been maintained at a rough parity with those of the United States armed forces. In addition, officers and career noncommissioned officers and their immediate families enjoyed access to a military social security system administered independently by the FAN. The system provided medical care to military personnel at little or no cost. Pension benefits were also generous. The categories of pensioners included those with certified disabilities, those who reached the limit of their time-in-grade without promotion, retirees, and surviving family members of deceased military personnel. Members of the FAN became eligible for retirement after ten years of service. Retirement became mandatory after thirty years, at which point one could retire at full salary. The president had the authority to extend the careers of certain officers beyond the thirty-year limit with the approval of the Superior Board of the FAN. No one, however, was allowed to serve more than thirty-five years in the military.

Defense Spending

Although there is some evidence that military spending tightened in response to the fiscal crisis of the 1980s, the process of drafting and approving the defense budget has remained largely closed to public scrutiny. The FAN submitted its budget requests directly to the president through its own comptroller general. Much of the budget was approved or amended by the executive with only limited consultation with the Congress. The heads of the various branches of service reportedly exercised broad control over their budget requests. They were restricted as to the overall level of those requests, however, by several factors. One was the traditionally high percentage of the military budget devoted to salaries and benefits; in times of fiscal austerity, military equipment and readiness suffered disproportionate cutbacks. Another budgetary limitation was the high cost of the entitlements and other benefits accorded civilians; these outlays and the maintenance of a large government bureaucracy also tended to limit the funding available to the military. As a result, the military portion of the overall government budget rarely exceeded 10 percent.

From 1950 to 1986, Venezuelan military spending as a percentage of gross domestic product (GDP—see Glossary) averaged between 1.5 percent and 2 percent. Increases in this figure in the late 1980s appeared to be attributable to the government's efforts to maintain a stable military budget amid a contracting overall economy. This effort continued a pattern of several decades' standing, whereby during austerity periods the military portion of the budget was cut by a lower percentage than was the remainder of the budget. By the same token, during periods of expanding revenue, military expenditures generally rose by a lower percentage than did other outlays. This pattern indicated a desire on the part of both AD and Social Christian Party (Comité de Organización Política Electoral Independiente—COPEI) administrations to insulate the military, at least to some extent, from budget cuts. The comparative restrictions on military expansion during boom times might also have indicated a preference by the civilian executive for limiting the role of the military in the overall government. Even in an established democracy such as Venezuela's, presidents felt compelled to continue a political balancing act with regard to the military.

Venezuela's lack of a significant domestic arms industry and its consequent importation of almost all of its weaponry represented another constraint on defense spending. The FAN attempted to address this deficiency in 1975 by establishing the Venezuelan Military Industries Company (Compañía Anónima Venezolana de Industrias Militares—CAVIM). Despite initial expectations of channeling government revenues into the development of a significant domestic arms industry, by the 1990s CAVIM had made little progress. Domestic arms production consisted of small arms ammunition, explosives, some spare parts, and coastal patrol craft for the navy. CAVIM's development fell victim to the oil revenue crisis of the 1980s and the purchase of big-ticket advanced weaponry such as the F-16 fighter. Further expansion of the domestic arms industry appeared unlikely during the 1990s.

Armed Forces Organization, Training, and Equipment

According to Article 190 of the constitution of 1961, the president serves as commander in chief of the National Armed Forces (Fuerzas Armadas Nacionales—FAN). The day-to-day administration of the FAN, however, falls to the minister of national defense, traditionally a senior general officer. Other officials with responsibilities for the entire FAN were the FAN's inspector general and comptroller general.

The National Security and Defense Council, established in the 1970s, functioned as a planning and advisory body for the president on military and security matters. Its membership included the minister of national defense, the minister of interior, the minister of foreign affairs, the minister of finance, the inspector general of the FAN, the chief of the joint general staff of the FAN, and other ministers designated by the president. The council recommended policy to the president, prepared measures for its implementation, drafted mobilization and demobilization orders, and coordinated the defense efforts of national, state, and local authorities. The president appointed a permanent secretary of the council, who administered a political committee, an economic committee, a social committee, a military committee, a mobilization committee, and other committees that might be created by the president. The National Intelligence Service was a functional department of the council.

The military chain of command extended downward from the president to the minister of national defense to the commanders of the individual services (see fig. 10). The Superior Board of the FAN was a purely military organization that advised the president, the National Security and Defense Council, and the Ministry of National Defense on security and defense matters. The board consisted of the minister of national defense, the inspector general, the chief of the Joint General Staff, and the service commanders. The chief of the Joint General Staff acted as the secretary of the board. The approval of the board was required for major weapons acquisitions.

The Joint General Staff of the FAN did not exercise operational control over the services. It functioned as an advisory body and as the planning organ of the National Defense Ministry under the direction of the minister of national defense and the Superior Board. The Joint General Staff prepared strategic planning, logistics, intelligence, training, and educational policies and plans for the entire FAN. It did not have budget authority, however; each branch of service handled its own budget planning.

The assets of the FAN were assigned and deployed in five geographically defined military regions, which functioned as unified commands. Most of the forces were deployed in Military Region One, headquartered in Caracas. Military regions two, three, four, and five were headquartered in San Cristóbal, Maracaibo, San Fernando, and Ciudad Bolívar, respectively. All air and naval assets were located in either region one or region two (San Cristóbal).

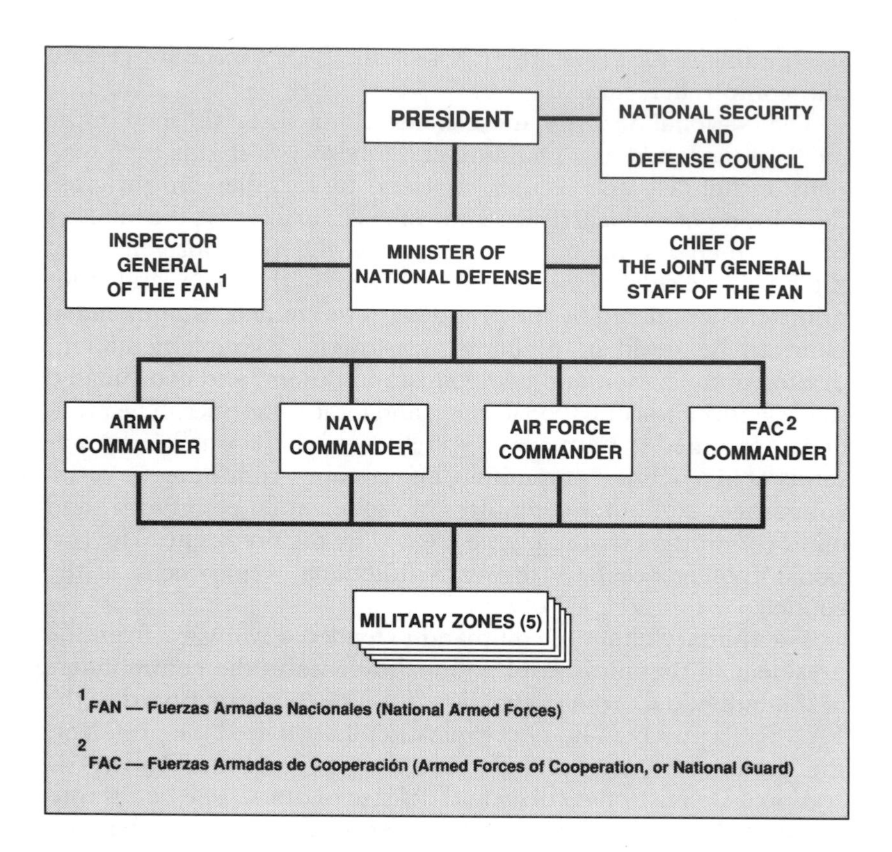

Figure 10. Structure of the Armed Forces, 1990

The Army

Traditionally the predominant branch of service, the army during the 1970s and 1980s lost a certain amount of prestige vis-à-vis the air force and the navy, the two services that benefited most from the purchase of upgraded weaponry during that period in the FAN. Nevertheless, the army remained in 1990 the largest of the services, and its general officers still dominated top leadership posts in the FAN.

In 1990 the army consisted of approximately 34,000 personnel of all ranks under the direction of the commander of the army. The bulk of these troops were organized into five divisions. Four of these were infantry divisions, each of which encompassed four to six battalions. The remaining division—the First Cavalry Division, headquartered at San Juan de los Morros, some fifty kilometers

South of Maracay, or about eighty kilometers south-southwest of Caracas—included most of the army's armored units. An independent airborne regiment and ranger brigade also maintained their headquarters in Military Region One (Caracas). Other deployments in and near the capital included the Fourth Infantry Division, headquartered at Maracay, an armored brigade stationed at Valencia, and an infantry brigade and the First Antiaircraft Artillery Group, both headquartered in Caracas. Additional independent units included the Presidential Guard Regiment, an aviation regiment, an engineer regiment, and a military police regiment. As of the late 1980s, the army's long-range plans called for the establishment of one additional infantry division. The placement of forces reflected the traditional political importance of the capital, as well as Venezuela's strategic orientation toward the coastal area and the Caribbean.

The army's mechanized and artillery assets were somewhat dated in comparison with the newer, higher-technology equipment employed by the air force and the navy (see table 13, Appendix). For example, the only main battle tank in the inventory was the French-made AMX-30, of immediate post-World War II vintage. The standard-issue infantry weapon was the Belgian-made FN FAL 7.62mm assault rifle. Elite and specialized units carried Israeli Uzi, Italian Beretta, German Walther, and American Ingram submachine guns. The army's single antiaircraft artillery group relied on rather ineffective 40mm guns rather than surface-to-air missiles, indicating a heavy reliance on the air-to-air interception capabilities of the air force. This posture responded to the lack of a significant regional air-strike threat aside from that posed by Cuba, which was distant enough to allow for adequate warning and response time.

Army officers received their initial training at the Military Academy at El Valle outside Caracas. Officers could pursue postgraduate training at civilian universities (although only a small percentage did so) or at the Polytechnic University of the Armed Forces. The Staff College prepared officers for advanced command responsibilities. Some officers also studied abroad, particularly at the United States Army's School of the Americas at Fort Benning, Georgia. The army also administered an NCO school and other specialized schools for enlisted personnel at Maracay.

The Navy

In 1990 the navy maintained a force level of approximately 10,000, a figure that included a marine infantry corps of some 5,000 personnel. The branch was headed by the commander of naval operations, who exercised administrative and operational control over a number of subordinate commands, among them the main naval squadron at Puerto Cabello, the marine infantry corps, the naval aviation command at La Carlota Airport near Caracas, a River Forces (Fuerzas Fluviales) Command at Ciudad Bolívar on the Río Orinoco, and the Coast Guard at Puerto Cabello.

After years of subordination to the army, during which it struggled with antiquated equipment, the navy began to benefit from civilian democratic rule in 1960, when it purchased a submarine from the United States Navy. Concerted upgrading of naval matériel did not really begin, however, until 1972, when Venezuela purchased an American "Guppy II"-type submarine; another was purchased in 1973, along with two decommissioned American destroyers. From 1974 to 1975, the navy purchased six "Constitution"-class patrol fast attack craft from Britain. It also acquired two German-built Type 209 submarines from 1976 to 1977. Six Italian "Lupo" missile frigates ordered in 1975 were delivered and in service by the early 1980s (see table 14, Appendix).

Venezuelan naval aviation was not established as a distinct element until the late 1970s. With the exception of helicopters, all of its assets were stationed at La Carlota Airport near Caracas. Marine infantry personnel were deployed in four battalion-sized units, referred to as "tactical combat units," headquartered at Maiquetía, Puerto Cabello, Carúpano in Sucrey, and Punto Fijo. The River Forces Command was also subordinate to the Marine Infantry Command. The Coast Guard, established in 1982, maintained its headquarters at Puerto Cabello.

The Venezuelan Naval Academy (Escuela Naval de Venezuela) at La Guaira offered a five-year course of study culminating in a commission. Other naval schools at La Guaira included the Naval Postgraduate School and the Naval Superior War College. The Naval Training Center for enlisted personnel was located at Puerto Cabello. In addition, there were a Naval Infantry Training Center, a Naval Armament Training Center, and a Naval Police School.

The Air Force

The air force benefited greatly from purchases of upgraded hardware in the 1970s and 1980s. The most highly publicized defense acquisition of the 1980s was the purchase of twenty-four F-16 fighters from the United States. At the time of their delivery in 1984-85, the F-16s represented the most advanced military aircraft in the inventory of any South American air force. In 1990 other comparatively advanced aircraft in service in Venezuela included the French Mirage 50 and older-model Mirage IIIs and Mirage Vs, retrofitted to meet the more advanced performance standards of the Mirage 50s (see table 15, Appendix). In June 1990, the air force also let a contract with Singapore Aerospace Industries to upgrade its older, American-made CF-5A and CF-5B fighter aircraft.

In 1990 the ranks of the air force included some 5,000 personnel, very few of whom were conscripts. The service, headed by the commander of the air force, was organized into three commands: the Air Combat Command, the Air Logistics Command, and the Air Training Command. Combat aircraft were organized into three attack groups: one bomber group and two special operations groups. The bomber group included one squadron equipped with Mirage fighter-bombers and based in Palo Negro; two squadrons, based in Barquisimeto and Barcelona, equipped with CF-5s; and two F-16 squadrons, also based in Palo Negro. Two squadrons of heavier bombers, British-made Canberras, were based in Barquisimeto and Barcelona.

The Air Logistics Command controlled three transport groups, including the Presidential Squadron based in Caracas. The logistics command also owned reconnaissance aircraft and transport helicopters. The primary transport aircraft were the American-made C-130H and C-123.

The Air Training Command included Air Training Group Number 14, which was attached to the Military Aviation School at Maracay. The primary training craft were the T-34, the T-2D, and the EMB-312 Tucano. The six F-16B two-seat trainers were attached to the fighter squadrons. The air force required its officer candidates to complete a four-year course of study at Maracay before receiving their commissions. The air force also had a number of specialist schools as well as its own Command and Staff School for advanced military studies.

The Armed Forces of Cooperation (National Guard)

The Armed Forces of Cooperation (Fuerzas Armadas de Cooperación—FAC)—also known as the National Guard—was a domestic paramilitary force that was incorporated into the FAN in 1954. In 1990 the FAC numbered approximately 20,000. Its operational commands included the Logistics Command, the Air Operations Command, and the Operations Command. The tactical chain of command ran from commander of the FAC downward through three regional commands headquartered at San Antonio de Táchira in the western Andean region, Maracaibo, and

Caracas. Regional commanders, in turn, exercised authority over local battalion-sized detachments. Eight mobile detachments functioned as a reserve force, available for deployment to any area of the country in response to threats to internal security or border security. FAC personnel also provided static defense of certain public buildings, oil installations, and penal institutions. In addition, the FAC patrolled the nation's highway system, functioning as a federal police force.

The FAC was equipped as a light infantry force, with the standard FN FAL assault rifle and mortars up to 81mm. Its armored assets consisted of forty armored personnel carriers (see table 16, Appendix). It also employed seventy-seven small craft for coastal and river patrol duties. Air assets included both fixed-wing craft and helicopters.

FAC recruits, all volunteers, underwent a one-year training course at the Ramo Verde School at Los Teques. Officer candidates were required to study for an additional four years at the Officers Training School in Caracas. Postgraduate studies for officers were available at the Advanced Officers School at Caricuao, near Caracas.

Uniforms, Ranks, and Insignia

Officers of the four services had a series of uniforms, including full dress, dress, parade, garrison, work, and field uniforms (the last four assigned to all ranks). White and beige cotton uniforms were authorized for summer wear. The army winter garrison uniform was dark green, the navy midnight blue, and the air force light blue. Cap covers for all navy uniforms were white. Cadet uniforms were distinctive; their parade uniforms consisted of white trousers and a single-breasted, high-collar shirt, light grey for the Military Academy and dark blue for the others. Cadets at the military, naval, and air force academies wore service caps; cadets at the FAC Officers Training School wore shakos similar to those of the United States Military Academy.

The FAN had nine officer ranks: three general, three field grade, and three company grade. Ranks from second lieutenant through lieutenant colonel were conferred directly by the president. Above that level, promotions required the approval of the Senate. There were seven enlisted ranks and also eight cadet ranks.

Army officer rank insignia were silver for officers up to and including captain, gold for higher ranks. All insignia were worn on gold shoulder boards. Navy officer rank insignia were rendered in gold on black shoulder boards. Air force officer insignia were silver up through captain and gold for higher ranks, worn on a blue shoulder board (see fig. 11). Enlisted rank insignia consisted of chevrons worn on the sleeve: red with black or gold markings for the army; blue with black or gold markings for the air force; and black with blue, red, or gold markings for the navy (see fig. 12).

Internal Security and Public Order

Threats to Internal Security

In the early 1990s, Venezuela demonstrated comparative domestic tranquility by Latin American standards. It did not exhibit the severe disturbances of leftist guerrilla insurgency and widespread drug trafficking so evident in neighboring Colombia. Generally speaking, threats to internal security could be cited as follows: the activities of radical leftist student groups and political parties, the expansion of drug trafficking and domestic drug abuse, and popular discontent resulting from economic restructuring.

Venezuela has had a number of small radical leftist student groups and political parties (see Political Parties, ch. 4). Although the parties achieved little support among the electorate, student groups attracted a more activist membership that sometimes exercised disproportionate influence among the university population. Student demonstrations always had the potential to erupt into violence, whether their inspiration was domestic—student privileges or other parochial concerns—or foreign, as in protests against United States foreign policy. Although university students eventually became the political and technocratic leaders of the country, the general public has shown no inclination since the reestablishment of civilian democratic rule in 1958 to look to student leadership as a political vanguard. In more general terms, the Venezuelan consensus in favor of social programs has long had the effect of diluting the appeal of violent leftist ideology. By the early 1990s, the collapse of socialist regimes in Eastern Europe had also had an effect in this regard.

The expansion of illicit drug production and transportation appeared to have the potential to disrupt Venezuelan internal security significantly in the 1990s. As the decade began, most illegal drug activity in Venezuela resulted from a spillover effect from Colombia, the world's leading distributor of cocaine. Venezuela's long Caribbean coastline and large expanses of sparsely populated territory made it attractive as a transshipment point for cocaine products in transit from Colombia to the United States. The gravity of the security situation along the western border was brought home to the Venezuelan public during the presidential election campaign

VENEZUELAN RANK	SUBTENIENTE	TENIENTE	CAPITÁN	MAYOR	TENIENTE CORONEL	CORONEL	GENERAL DE BRIGADA	GENERAL DE DIVISIÓN		GENERAL EN JEFE
ARMY	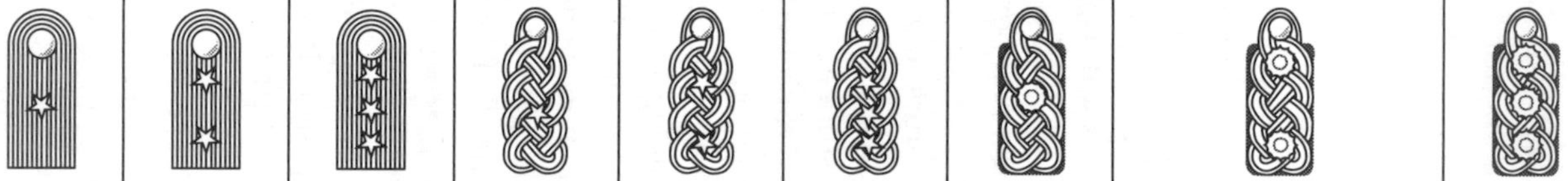									
UNITED STATES RANK TITLES	2D LIEUTENANT	1ST LIEUTENANT	CAPTAIN	MAJOR	LIEUTENANT COLONEL	COLONEL	BRIGADIER GENERAL	MAJOR GENERAL/ LIEUTENANT GENERAL		GENERAL
VENEZUELAN RANK	**SUBTENIENTE**	**TENIENTE**	**CAPITÁN**	**MAYOR**	**TENIENTE CORONEL**	**CORONEL**	**GENERAL DE BRIGADA**	**GENERAL DE DIVISIÓN**		**GENERAL DE FUERZA**
AIR FORCE										
UNITED STATES RANK TITLES	2D LIEUTENANT	1ST LIEUTENANT	CAPTAIN	MAJOR	LIEUTENANT COLONEL	COLONEL	BRIGADIER GENERAL	MAJOR GENERAL/ LIEUTENANT GENERAL		GENERAL
VENEZUELAN RANK	**ALFÉREZ**	**TENIENTE DE FRAGATA**	**TENIENTE DE NAVÍO**	**CAPITÁN DE CORBETA**	**CAPITÁN DE FRAGATA**	**CAPITÁN DE NAVÍO**	**CONTRA-ALMIRANTE**	**VICE-ALMIRANTE**	**ALMIRANTE**	**NO RANK**
NAVY										NO RANK
UNITED STATES RANK TITLES	ENSIGN	LIEUTENANT JUNIOR GRADE	LIEUTENANT	LIEUTENANT COMMANDER	COMMANDER	CAPTAIN	REAR ADMIRAL LOWER HALF	REAR ADMIRAL UPPER HALF	VICE ADMIRAL	ADMIRAL

Figure 11. Officer Ranks and Insignia, 1990

VENEZUELAN RANK	SOLDADO	SOLDADO DISTINGUIDO	CABO SEGUNDO	CABO PRIMERO	SARGENTO SEGUNDO	SARGENTO PRIMERO		SARGENTO AYUDANTE		
ARMY	NO INSIGNIA									
UNITED STATES RANK TITLES	BASIC PRIVATE	PRIVATE	PRIVATE 1ST CLASS	CORPORAL / SPECIALIST	SERGEANT	STAFF SERGEANT	SERGEANT 1ST CLASS	MASTER SERGEANT	SERGEANT MAJOR	COMMAND SERGEANT MAJOR
VENEZUELAN RANK	SOLDADO	SOLDADO DISTINGUIDO	CABO SEGUNDO	CABO PRIMERO	SARGENTO SEGUNDO	SARGENTO PRIMERO		SARGENTO AYUDANTE		
AIR FORCE	NO INSIGNIA									
UNITED STATES RANK TITLES	AIRMAN BASIC	AIRMAN	AIRMAN 1ST CLASS	SENIOR AIRMAN / SERGEANT	STAFF SERGEANT	TECHNICAL SERGEANT	MASTER SERGEANT	SENIOR MASTER SERGEANT	CHIEF MASTER SERGEANT	
VENEZUELAN RANK	MARINERO	MARINERO DISTINGUIDO	CABO SEGUNDO	CABO PRIMERO	SARGENTO SEGUNDO	SARGENTO PRIMERO		SARGENTO MAYOR		
NAVY	NO INSIGNIA									
UNITED STATES RANK TITLES	SEAMAN RECRUIT	SEAMAN APPRENTICE	SEAMAN	PETTY OFFICER 3D CLASS	PETTY OFFICER 2D CLASS	PETTY OFFICER 1ST CLASS	CHIEF PETTY OFFICER	SENIOR CHIEF PETTY OFFICER	MASTER CHIEF PETTY OFFICER	

Figure 12. Enlisted Ranks and Insignia, 1990

of late 1988, when the media publicized an incident that took place on October 29 near the town of El Amparo along a tributary of the Río Arauca. What was originally reported as an ambush of Colombian guerrillas by Venezuelan troops eventually turned out to have been the inadvertent murder of sixteen Venezuelan fishermen. The revelation that security forces had mistakenly fired on peaceful residents, then apparently attempted to cover up their error, caused a political furor. It also highlighted the increasing confusion along the frontier that resulted from the activities of drug traffickers and Colombian guerrillas. The overreaction of the Venezuelan forces also suggested that they were not properly prepared to deal with the situation.

Although Venezuela's role in the international drug trade was limited in 1990 to the transshipment of drugs and precursor chemicals, there were signs that this role was expanding. In November 1989, authorities made the largest cocaine seizure in the country's history, taking 2,220 kilograms in transit through Valencia. It has been estimated that 130 tons of cocaine and *basuco* (semirefined paste) entered the country during 1990. There was no evidence that Venezuela was a major drug-producing country in 1990, but some marijuana was grown along the Sierra de Perijá, in the northwestern part of Venezuela along the border with Colombia. The National Guard has carried out eradication programs in the area, with financial and material assistance from the United States.

The Pérez administration appeared to take seriously the threat of increased drug activity. In July 1990, the president raised the National Drug Commission to the status of a cabinet ministry. In November of the same year, the governments of Venezuela and the United States signed a bilateral agreement to restrict money laundering by Venezuelan banks. Some elements of the FAN assisted law enforcement agencies in counternarcotics efforts; the navy, in particular, stepped up its interdiction activity in conjunction with the coast guard. As in other countries, however, the effort has been hampered by judicial, and possibly political, corruption. In September 1987, a penal judge of the Supreme Court was arrested and dismissed after he ordered the release of seven drug traffickers in return for a bribe of 10 million bolívars (B; for value of the bolívar—see Glossary). At the time, the justice minister publicly claimed knowledge of 400 other similar cases of corruption.

The riots in Venezuelan cities following President Pérez's second inaugural in February 1989 shocked many Venezuelans and made headlines across the world. Many observers described these disturbances as a precursor of further violence in heavily indebted Third World nations. The riots began in response to government

Army troops with riot-control helmets and Uzi submachine guns
Courtesy Embassy of Venezuela, Washington

austerity measures that included a jump of almost 100 percent in domestic gasoline prices and a 30 percent increase in public transportation fares. In less than a week of rioting and looting, some 300 Venezuelans died and some 1,800 were wounded. The army reinforced police forces in the capital and elsewhere in order to restore order. The riots, which were marked by widespread looting, apparently expressed the frustration of the Venezuelan urban poor with their lack of economic progress. The disturbances had been preceded by a week of student demonstrations, some of which had resulted in violence.

Disturbances of a similar character but more limited scope erupted in February and July 1990. The February riots followed student protests in Caracas, scheduled to mark the one-year anniversary of the 1989 riots. Police contained the looting and sporadic violence. President Pérez called in National Guard and air force units to reinforce the police in the eastern port cities of Barcelona and Puerto La Cruz, where rioting was more intense. Scattered violence in July followed another increase in bus fares. The most serious disturbances took place in Maracaibo and Maracay. In both instances, university students were reported to have been the primary instigators of the violence.

As of 1990, Venezuela had only one insurgent/terrorist group, the Red Flag (Bandera Roja—BR), and it was largely inactive. The BR, a splinter group of the Movement of the Revolutionary Left (Movimiento de la Izquierda Revolucionaria—MIR), continued the armed struggle against the democratic system after the MIR put down its arms in 1969. In the early 1980s, the BR staged a number of terrorist actions—kidnappings, bank robberies, and airline hijackings. Counterstrikes by the police and army eventually eliminated BR's urban capabilities and drove the remnants of the group into the Colombian frontier region, where some members reportedly still operated, perhaps in association with Colombian guerrilla groups.

Law Enforcement Agencies

Many different organizations carried out Venezuelan law enforcement in 1990. Including the paramilitary National Guard, there were four national-level police forces (see The Armed Forces of Cooperation [National Guard], this ch.). In addition, over 450 state and municipal police forces functioned throughout the country. Although state and municipal police normally operated independently, they could be mobilized under emergency conditions into a Unified Police Command.

The Directorate of Intelligence and Prevention Services (Dirección de Seguridad e Inteligencia Policíal—Disip) was a nonuniformed force of some 3,000 personnel under the Ministry of Interior. Disip's nationwide jurisdiction included the investigation of crimes involving subversion, narcotics, and arms smuggling. Disip's responsibilities include operations against terrorists and other potentially violent groups, including organized crime. Disip's director was appointed by the minister of interior. The organization maintained its headquarters in Caracas, with field offices in principal cities throughout the country.

The Technical and Judicial Police (Policía Técnica y Judicial—PTJ) was a component of the Ministry of Justice. It fielded over 3,000 plainclothes personnel in 1990. The PTJ handled most of the country's investigative police work; other police agencies passed on all cases requiring investigation to the PTJ. The president, on the advice of the minister of justice, appointed the organization's director, who was required to be a lawyer. Most PTJ personnel were assigned to its headquarters in Caracas. Numerous divisions and subdivisions throughout the country handled field work. New agents were required to have completed at least three years of secondary education and to undergo several months of training at the National Academy in Caracas before assuming their duties.

The Traffic Police was a force of about 2,000 under the Ministry of Transport and Communications. In addition to national traffic control, the Traffic Police were responsible for issuing and regulating drivers' licenses and for determining public transportation routes and services.

Venezuela's state, metropolitan, and municipal police forces totaled some 18,000 personnel. The largest such force was the Metropolitan Police Force of Caracas, with about 9,000 members. All local police forces received their funding through the Ministry of Interior but responded to state governors under normal conditions. The Metropolitan Police Force, which maintained a Police Academy in El Junquito near Caracas, was comparatively well trained. In contrast, other state and municipal forces fielded largely untrained personnel and suffered from deficiencies in communications, transportation, supplies, and facilities.

The Criminal Justice System

Many observers believed that the Venezuelan criminal justice system was inadequate to deal with the rising crime rate of the late 1980s and through 1990. The most glaring deficiency of the system was the high percentage of incarcerated prisoners awaiting trial. As of 1989, only some 25 percent of all prisoners had been tried and convicted.

This situation appeared to be attributable to a shortage of judges, the automatic review of lower-court decisions, and the general inability of the courts to keep pace with an increasingly crowded calendar. The highly bureaucratized court system, which generated thick written records for each case, sometimes delayed trials for years.

The Venezuelan system also suffered from corruption and political influences. Although the judiciary was an independent branch of government, the system of appointing judges traditionally introduced political considerations and personal connections into the process. A five-member Judicial Council attempted to regulate this process by way of its power to nominate, train, and discipline judges. One member of the council was named by the Congress, one by the president, and three by the Supreme Court.

The criminal justice system was based largely on Spanish, Napoleonic, and Italian influences. Under this system, the burden of proving innocence fell upon the accused. Defendants theoretically had access to legal representation through the public defenders program. In the late 1980s, however, there were only 350 attorneys employed under this program. This fact further delayed legal procedures and made for inadequate representation for many prisoners.

Venezuelans could be tried for criminal offenses under two categories: felonies (*delitos*) and misdemeanors (*faltas*). Penalties were divided into the categories of corporal and noncorporal. Corporal punishment included imprisonment, relegation to a penal colony, confinement to a designated place, or expulsion from the country. Noncorporal punishments included fines, supervision by the state, the loss of civil rights, or the loss of the right to practice a specific profession. The death penalty is prohibited under the 1961 constitution. Venezuelan citizens also cannot be extradited; foreigners cannot be extradited for political crimes or for offenses not considered crimes under Venezuelan law.

Military tribunals customarily handled cases involving crimes committed by military personnel on military installations or at sea. Under a law passed during the guerrilla disturbances of the 1960s, however, civilians could be tried under military jurisdiction for crimes of armed subversion. The Martial Court, located in the capital, was a permanent institution that exercised national jurisdiction. Decisions by the Martial Court could be appealed to the Supreme Court. The preponderance of cases brought against security forces personnel for abuses allegedly committed during the riots of February 1989 were remanded to military courts.

The Prison System

The Venezuelan prison system, which consisted of twenty-five institutions, suffered from overcrowding and understaffing as well as from graft and corruption. In the mid-1980s, the annual average prison population was about 15,000, exceeding the intended capacity of the system. As a result, prison conditions generally were inadequate, and prisoners commonly endured hardship and sometimes were subjected to physical abuse. As the national crime rate rose during the 1980s, the problems of the prison system became more acute.

The twenty-five prisons were essentially of three kinds: judicial detainment centers, which numbered seventeen; national jails and penitentiaries, which numbered seven; and the National Institute of Female Orientation located in Los Teques. Ostensibly, the prisons were designed to house those awaiting trial, those convicted, and women, respectively. In fact, however, several of the prisons had separate wings for each kind of inmate, although Los Teques housed the majority of female inmates and contained no males. Minors were interned in separate institutions. Prisons were staffed by civilian employees of the Ministry of Justice, although exterior guard duty was entrusted to National Guard personnel.

Inmates at the San Juan de los Morros Penitentiary gathering corn
Courtesy United Nations (J. Littlewood)

By law the rehabilitation of convicted criminals was based on their having meaningful work, an opportunity to receive at least a minimal education, and adequate medical assistance and living conditions. In fact, however, the overcrowded conditions precluded rehabilitation efforts. The idleness of many inmates, it is theorized, led to corruption, drug abuse, and homosexuality, all of which were growing problems in the prisons. One large Caracas prison had an entire wing that housed homosexuals exclusively.

Conditional liberty was granted to prisoners who had served at least three-fourths of their sentence and had a favorable conduct record. Prisoners who reached seventy years of age and had completed half their sentence were eligible for conditional liberty. Several organizations existed to help prisoners who had been released to find jobs and readjust to society. Nevertheless, the ex-convict encountered a generally hostile society on the outside, and the high rate of criminal repeaters was attributed largely to the stigma attached to the ex-convict.

The criminal justice system represented a glaring example of an area that lagged behind the many other comparative advances in Venezuelan society during the latter half of the twentieth century. Given the government's emphasis on reforming the bureaucratic structure that underlay the nation's economic shortcomings, it did not appear that judicial reform would be accorded a high priority during the 1990s. As with most of Venezuela's problems, however, the resources existed with which to effect reforms. Only the political will and the legislative procedure remained to be hammered out.

* * *

Aside from the section on Venezuela in Adrian English's *Armed Forces of Latin America,* there is no comprehensive source in English on the Venezuelan armed forces. Good historical background can be gleaned from Winfield J. Burggraaff's *The Venezuelan Armed Forces in Politics, 1935-1959.* David J. Myers's *Venezuela's Pursuit of Caribbean Basin Interests* is an excellent overview of the country's strategic situation and thinking. Jacqueline Anne Braveboy-Wagner in *The Venezuela-Guyana Border Dispute: Britain's Colonial Legacy in Latin America* and John D. Martz in his article "National Security and Politics: The Colombian-Venezuelan Border" effectively address Venezuela's border disputes. Robert E. Looney has produced good studies of Venezuelan military expenditures from an economic standpoint. Several periodicals occasionally report on technical and organizational developments within the FAN. These include *Jane's Defence Weekly, Military Technology,* and *Defense and Foreign Affairs.* (For further information and complete citations, see Bibliography.)

Appendix

Table

1 Metric Conversion Coefficients and Factors
2 Population by Administrative Division, 1971, 1981, and 1985
3 Population Density by Administrative Division, 1971 and 1985
4 Population of the Largest Cities, 1971 and 1981
5 Schools, Teachers, and Enrollments by Public and Private Institution, 1974–75 and 1983–84
6 Mortality Rate for the Ten Most Common Causes of Death, 1973 and 1981
7 Medical Facilities and Personnel, Selected Years, 1974–81
8 Consumer Prices, 1986–90
9 Oil Production, 1985–90
10 Petroleum Refining Capacity of the Venezuelan Petroleum Corporation, 1988
11 Trade and Current Account Statistics, 1985–89
12 External Debt, 1985–89
13 Major Army Equipment, 1990
14 Major Navy and Coast Guard Equipment, 1990
15 Major Air Force Equipment, 1990
16 Major Armed Forces of Cooperation Equipment, 1990

Appendix

Table 1. Metric Conversion Coefficients and Factors

When you know	Multiply by	To find
Millimeters	0.04	inches
Centimeters	0.39	inches
Meters	3.3	feet
Kilometers	0.62	miles
Hectares (10,000 m^2)	2.47	acres
Square kilometers	0.39	square miles
Cubic meters	35.3	cubic feet
Liters	0.26	gallons
Kilograms	2.2	pounds
Metric tons	0.98	long tons
	1.1	short tons
	2,204	pounds
Degrees Celsius (Centigrade)	9 divide by 5 and add 32	degrees Fahrenheit

Table 2. Population by Administrative Division, 1971, 1981, and 1985
(in thousands)

State, Territory, or District	1971 [1]	1981 [1]	1985 [2]
Amazonas Territory	22	46	71
Anzoátegui	506	684	783
Apure	165	188	231
Aragua	543	892	1,109
Barinas	231	326	413
Bolívar	392	668	824
Carabobo	659	1,062	1,341
Cojedes	94	134	166
Delta Amacuro Territory	48	57	83
Falcón	408	504	576
Federal District (Caracas)	1,861	2,071	2,451
Guárico	319	393	439
Lara	671	945	1,096
Mérida	347	459	552
Miranda	856	1,421	1,714
Monagas	298	389	452
Nueva Esparta	119	197	236
Portuguesa	297	425	519
Sucre	469	586	676
Táchira	511	660	765
Trujillo	381	434	507
Yaracuy	224	301	340
Zulia	1,299	1,674	1,982
TOTAL	10,720	14,516	17,326

[1] Census figures.
[2] Midyear estimates.

Source: Based on information from Federal Republic of Germany, Statistisches Bundesamt, *Länderbericht Venezuela, 1987,* Wiesbaden, 1987, 19.

Table 3. Population Density by Administrative Division, 1971 and 1985
(inhabitants per square kilometer)

State, Territory, or District	1971 [1]	1985 [2]
Amazonas Territory	0.1	0.4
Anzoátegui	11.7	18.1
Apure	2.2	3.0
Aragua	77.4	158.1
Barinas	6.6	11.7
Bolívar	1.6	3.5
Carabobo	141.7	288.4
Cojedes	6.4	11.2
Delta Amacuro Territory	1.2	2.1
Falcón	16.5	23.2
Federal District (Caracas)	964.2	1,269.9
Guárico	4.9	6.8
Lara	33.9	55.4
Mérida	30.7	48.8
Miranda	107.7	215.6
Monagas	10.3	15.6
Nueva Esparta	103.5	205.2
Portuguesa	19.5	34.1
Sucre	39.7	57.3
Táchira	46.0	68.9
Trujillo	51.5	68.5
Yaracuy	31.5	47.9
Zulia	20.6	31.4

[1] Census figures.
[2] Midyear estimates.

Source: Based on information from Federal Republic of Germany, Statistisches Bundesamt, *Länderbericht Venezuela, 1987,* Wiesbaden, 1987, 19.

Table 4. Population of the Largest Cities, 1971 and 1981
(in thousands)

City	1971 [1]	1981 [1]
Caracas		
City limits	1,035	1,817
Metropolitan area	2,184	2,944 [2]
Total Caracas	3,219	4,761
Maracaibo	652	889
Valencia	367	616
Barquisimeto	331	497
Maracay	255	440
San Cristóbal	152	199
Cumaná	120	192
Ciudad Bolívar	104	182
Maturín	98	155

[1] Census figures.
[2] 1980 figure.

Source: Based on information from Federal Republic of Germany, Statistisches Bundesamt, *Länderbericht Venezuela, 1987,* Wiesbaden, 1987, 19.

Table 5. *Schools, Teachers, and Enrollments by Public and Private Institution, 1974–75 and 1983–84*

	1974–75			1983–84		
	Public	Private	Total	Public	Private	Total
Preschool						
Schools	n.a.	n.a.	n.a.	n.a.	n.a.	n.a.
Teachers	2,986	1,252	4,238	15,440	4,008	19,448
Enrollment [1]	108,500	43,800	152,300	442,700	80,600	523,300
Primary						
Schools [2]	9,982	1,116	11,098	11,397	1,285	12,682
Teachers	54,276	8,922	63,198	71,454	9,176	80,630
Enrollment [1]	1,764,100	226,000	1,990,100	2,338,400	303,000	2,641,400
Secondary [3]						
Schools	735	438	1,173	1,486	710	2,196
Teachers	24,222	9,133	33,355	41,350	13,964	55,314
Enrollment [1]	513,100	118,100	631,200	786,200	177,200	963,400
Higher education [4]						
Schools	26	12	38	53 [5]	27 [5]	80 [5]
Teachers	13,228	1,376	14,604	24,633	4,072	28,705
Enrollment [1]	172,100	21,200	193,300	320,800	63,900	384,700

n.a.—not available.
[1] Rounded off to nearest hundred.
[2] Includes preschools.
[3] Middle schools and high schools.
[4] Universities, teachers' colleges, technical colleges, polytechnical institutes, and other comparable institutions.
[5] 1981–82 figures.

Source: Based on information from Federal Republic of Germany, Statistisches Bundesamt, *Länderbericht Venezuela, 1987,* Wiesbaden, 1987, 25–26.

Table 6. Mortality Rate for the Ten Most Common Causes of Death, 1973 and 1981
(in percentages)

Causes of Death	1973	1981
Heart disease	10.9	14.8
Cancer	7.9	9.4
Accidents	7.8	11.7
Diarrheal diseases	7.5	3.8
Perinatal complications	6.7	7.5
Pneumonia	6.6	4.7
Cerebrovascular diseases	4.5	5.5
Suicides and homicides	2.1	2.7
Congenital anomalies	1.6	1.9
Diabetes	1.4	2.2

Source: Based on information from Hernán Castellano Méndez, *Aproximación a la salud de la Venezuela del siglo XXI,* Caracas, 1985, 77–84; Venezuela, Ministerio de Sanidad y Asistencia Social, *Anuario de epidemiología y estadística del Ministerio de Sanidad y Asistencia Social,* Caracas, 1973; and *Anuario de epidemiología y estadística del Ministerio de Sanidad y Asistencia Social,* Caracas, 1981.

Table 7. Medical Facilities and Personnel, Selected Years, 1974–81

	1974	1976	1978	1979	1981
Hospitals	353	n.a.	444	n.a.	446
Hospital beds	34,263	36,163	41,386	40,575	n.a.
Inhabitants per hospital bed	345	n.a.	n.a.	378	n.a.
Physicians	13,017	n.a.	14,771	15,368	n.a.
Inhabitants per physician	908	n.a.	1,004	999	n.a.
Dentists	3,439	n.a.	4,342	n.a.	n.a.
Inhabitants per dentist	3,435	n.a.	3,417	n.a.	n.a.
Pharmacists	3,175	3,187	3,187	n.a.	n.a.
Registered nurses	8,426	8,833	9,077	n.a.	11,885
Nurses aides	22,993	26,804	29,984	n.a.	n.a.
Midwives	2,503	*	*	n.a.	n.a.

n.a.—not available.
* 1977 figure was 1,200.

Source: Based on information from Federal Republic of Germany, Statistiches Bundesamt, *Länderbericht Venezuela, 1987,* Wiesbaden, 1987, 11, 23

Table 8. Consumer Prices, 1986-90

	1986	1987	1988	1989	1990
Average consumer price index	124.3	159.2	206.1	380.2	534.8
Percent change from previous year	11.6	28.1	29.5	84.5	40.7
Percent change in wholesale prices	20.1	48.1	17.0	106.2	n.a.

n.a.—not available.

Source: Based on information from Economist Intelligence Unit, *Country Profile: Venezuela, Suriname, Netherlands Antilles, 1990-91,* London, 1991, 14; and information provided by United States Embassy, Caracas.

Table 9. Oil Production, 1985-90
(in thousands of barrels per day)

Year	Crude	Condensates	Liquefied Natural Gas	Refined
1985	1,558	119	63	864
1986	1,626	152	102	903
1987	1,556	176	83	797
1988	1,680	188	109	1,095
1989	1,812	112	112	942
1990	2,357	37	114	993

Source: Based on information provided by United States Embassy, Caracas.

Table 10. Petroleum Refining Capacity of the Venezuelan Petroleum Corporation, 1988
(in thousands of barrels per day)

Subsidiary and Location	Capacity	Processing
Lagoven		
Amuay	600	415
Maraven		
Punta Cardón	291	286
Corpoven		
Puerto La Cruz	195	129
El Palito and El Toreño	110	110
San Roque	5	5
TOTAL	1,201	945

Source: Based on information from Economist Intelligence Unit, *Country Profile: Venezuela, Suriname, Netherlands Antilles, 1989-90,* London, 1990, 21.

Table 11. Trade and Current Account Statistics, 1985–89
(in millions of United States dollars)

	1985	1986	1987	1988	1989 [2]
Merchandise imports (f.o.b.) [1]	7,501	7,862	8,832	10,872	7,145
Merchandise exports (f.o.b.) [1]	14,283	9,122	10,567	10,114	12,935
Trade balance	6,782	1,260	1,735	- 758	5,790
Current account balance	3,327	- 1,471	- 1,125	- 4,692	2,295

[1] f.o.b.—free on board.
[2] Preliminary.

Source: Based on information from United States, Department of Commerce, *Foreign Economic Trends and Their Implications for the United States: Venezuela,* Washington, 1989, 2; United States, Department of Commerce, *Foreign Economic Trends and Their Implications for the United States: Venezuela,* Washington, 1990, 1; and Economist Intelligence Unit, *Country Profile: Venezuela, Suriname, Netherlands Antilles, 1990-91,* London, 1991, 36.

Table 12. External Debt, 1985–89
(in millions of United States dollars)

	1985	1986	1987	1988	1989 [1]
Total external debt	35,240	34,550	35,205	34,657	34,108
Public disbursed debt	17,645	25,241	25,088	25,413	26,177
Debt service	4,740	5,088	4,743	5,512	6,497
Debt service ratio [2]	27.0	42.8	37.4	43.0	44.4
Private debt as a percentage of total external debt	24.5	22.4	17.3	14.1	12.6
Short-term debt as a percentage of total external debt	25.4	4.6	11.5	12.6	8.3

[1] Estimated.
[2] In percentages.

Source: Based on information from Economist Intelligence Unit, *Country Profile: Venezuela, Suriname, Netherlands Antilles, 1990–91,* London, 1991, 39.

Table 13. Major Army Equipment, 1990

Type and Description	Country of Origin	In Inventory
Tanks		
AMX-30	France	81
AMX-13 (light)	-do-	36
M-18 (light)	United States	35
Armored personnel carriers		
AMX-VCI	France	25
V-100	United States	70
V-150	-do-	50
M-113	-do-	46
Self-propelled artillery		
M-109 (155mm)	-do-	10
MKF3 (155mm)	France	20
Field artillery		
Model 56	Italy	40
M-101	United States	30
Multiple-rocket launchers		
LARS AMX-13 (160mm)	Israel/France	25
Fixed-wing aircraft		
BN-2	Britain	1
Cessna 172	United States	3
Cessna 182	-do-	3
4206	-do-	6
King Air	-do-	1
Queen Air	-do-	1
Super King Air 200	-do-	1
G-222	Italy	2
Helicopters		
A-109	Italy	6
AS-61R	United States/Italy	4
Bell 205	United States	3
UH-1H	-do-	6
Bell 476	-do-	2
Bell 206	-do-	2

Table 14. Major Navy and Coast Guard Equipment, 1990

Type and Description	Country of Origin	In Inventory
Navy		
Submarines		
209 class (type 1300)	West Germany	2
Guppy II class	United States	1
Frigates		
Lupo class	Italy	5
Amphibious craft		
Capana class	United States	4
Terrebonne Paris class	-do-	
Utility landing craft (LCUs)	-do-	2
Patrol craft		
LCVP landing craft	Venezuela	12
Shipborne aircraft (helicopters)		
Agusta AB12 antisubmarine warfare aircraft	Italy	10
Land-based maritime aircraft		
CASA C-212A/MR	Spain	4
Grumman S-2E Tracker	United States	6
Coast Guard		
Patrol craft		
Almiante Clemente class	Italy	2
Constitution class	Britain	6
Cherokee class	United States	2

Table 15. Major Air Force Equipment, 1990

Type and Description	Country of Origin	In Inventory
Fighters		
F-16A	United States	18
F-16B	-do-	6
CF-5A	-do-	10
CF-5B	-do-	2
Mirage 50	France	7
Mirage IIIEV	-do-	18
Mirage 5V	-do-	2
Mirage 5DV	-do-	1
Bombers		
Canberra	Britain	18
Counterinsurgency		
EMB-312	Brazil	18
OV-10E Broncos	United States	14
Reconnaissance		
Canberra PR-83	Britain	3
Transports		
C-47	United States	5
C-123	-do-	7
C-130H	-do-	6
G-222	Italy	6
Trainers		
EMB-312	Brazil	18
T-2D	United States	19
T-52	-do-	12
T-34	-do-	23
Attack helicopters		
SA-316	France	10
UH-1D	United States	12
UH-1H	-do-	4
Transport helicopters		
Bell 206	-do-	16
Bell 412	-do-	2
UH-1N	-do-	2
HB-350B	Brazil/France	5

Table 16. Major Armed Forces of Cooperation Equipment

Type and Description	Country of Origin	In Inventory
Armored personnel carriers		
UR-416	West Germany	25
Shorland	France	15
Fixed-wing aircraft		
Beechcraft Baron	United States	1
Cessna 4206	-do-	1
Cessna 337	-do-	2
Cessna 402C	-do-	1
King Air 90	-do-	1
King Air 200C	-do-	1
Queen Air 80	-do-	2
BN-2A	Britain	1
IAI-201	Israel	4
Helicopters		
A-109	Italy	4
Bell 206	United States	15
Bell 214ST	-do-	2
Coastal patrol craft		
Type A	Italy/Venezuela	28
Bertram type	United States	12
Monark type	-do-	12
River patrol craft		
Lago class	-do-	10
Monark type	-do-	15

Bibliography

Chapter 1

Alexander, Robert J. *Rómulo Betancourt and the Transformation of Venezuela.* New Brunswick, New Jersey: Transaction Books, 1982.

______. *The Venezuelan Democratic Revolution.* New York: Rutgers University Press, 1964.

Allen, Loring. *Venezuelan Economic Development: A Politico-Economic Analysis.* Greenwich, Connecticut: Jai Press, 1977.

Ameringer, Charles. "Leonardo Ruiz Pineda: Leader of Venezuelan Resistance, 1949–1952," *Journal of Inter-American Studies and World Affairs,* 21, No. 2, 1979, 209–32.

Arroyo Talavera, Eduardo. *Elections and Negotiation: The Limits of Democracy in Venezuela.* New York: Garland, 1986.

Baloyra, Enrique A. "Oil Policies and Budgets in Venezuela, 1938–1968," *Latin American Research Review,* 9, No. 2, 1974, 28–72.

Baloyra, Enrique A., and John D. Martz. *Political Attitudes in Venezuela: Societal Cleavages and Political Opinion.* Austin: University of Texas Press, 1979.

Bello López, Andrés. *Resumen de la historia de Venezuela.* Caracas: La Casa de Bello, 1978.

Betancourt, Rómulo. *La revolución democrática en Venezuela, 1959–1964.* (4 vols.) Caracas: Imprenta Nacional, 1968.

______. *Venezuela: Oil and Politics.* Boston: Houghton Mifflin, 1979.

______. *Venezuela's Oil.* (Trans., Donald Peck.) London: Allen and Unwin, 1978.

Bigler, Gene, and Franklin Tugwell. "Banking on Oil in Venezuela." Pages 152–89 in Andrew Maguire and Janet Welsh Brown (eds.), *Bordering on Trouble: Resources and Politics in Latin America.* Bethesda, Maryland: Adler and Adler, 1986.

Bitar, Sergio. *Venezuela: The Industrial Challenge.* (Trans., Michael Shifter and Dorsey Vera.) Philadelphia: Institute for the Study of Human Issues, 1987.

Blank, David Eugene. "Oil and Democracy in Venezuela," *Current History,* 78, No. 454, February 1980, 71–75, 84–85.

______. *Politics in Venezuela: A Country Study.* Boston: Little, Brown, 1973.

______. "Sowing the Oil," *Wilson Quarterly,* 8, No. 4, 1984, 63–78.

Blutstein, Howard I. *Venezuela: Politics in a Petroleum Republic.* New York: Praeger, 1984.

Bond, Robert D. (ed.). *Contemporary Venezuela and Its Role in International Affairs.* New York: New York University Press, 1977.

———. "Where Democracy Lives," *Wilson Quarterly,* 8, No. 4, 1984, 48-62.

Bonilla, Frank. *The Politics of Change in Venezuela, 2: The Failure of Elites.* Cambridge: MIT Press, 1970.

Bonilla, Frank, and José A. Silva Michelena (eds.). *The Politics of Change in Venezuela, 1: A Strategy for Research on Social Policy.* Cambridge: MIT Press, 1967.

Braveboy-Wagner, Jacqueline Ann. *The Venezuela-Guyana Border Dispute: Britain's Colonial Legacy in Latin America.* Boulder, Colorado: Westview Press, 1984.

Bridges, Tyler. "Where Did Venezuela's Money Go? Down the Toilet," *Washington Monthly,* 18, No. 11, 1986, 21-27.

Burggraaff, Winfield J. *The Venezuelan Armed Forces in Politics, 1935-1959.* Columbia: University of Missouri Press, 1972.

Carlisle, Douglas H. *Venezuelan Foreign Policy: Its Organization and Beginning.* Washington: University Press of America, 1979.

Carreras, Charles. *United States Economic Penetration of Venezuela and Its Effects on Diplomacy, 1895-1906.* New York: Garland, 1987.

Chester, Edward W. *United States Oil Policy and Diplomacy: A Twentieth-Century Overview.* Westport, Connecticut: Greenwood Press, 1983.

Clinton, Daniel Joseph. *Gómez: Tyrant of the Andes.* New York: Greenwood Press, 1969.

Coronel, Gustavo. *The Nationalization of the Venezuelan Oil Industry from Technocratic Success to Political Failure.* Lexington Books, Massachusetts: Lexington, 1983.

Crist, Raymond E. "Development and Agrarian Land Reform in Venezuela's Pioneer Zone: Social Progress along the Llano-Andes Border in a Half Century of Political Advance," *American Journal of Economics and Sociology,* 43, No. 2, 1984, 149-58.

Cunninghame, Graham, and Robert Bontine. *José Antonio Páez.* Port Washington, New York: Kennikat Press, 1970.

Davis, Charles L. *Working-Class Mobilization and Political Control: Venezuela and Mexico.* Lexington: University of Kentucky Press, 1989.

Ellner, Steven. "Factionalism in the Venezuelan Communist Movement, 1937-1948," *Science and Society,* 45, No. 1, 1981, 52-70.

———. "The MAS Party in Venezuela," *Latin American Perspectives,* 13, No. 2, 1986, 81-107.

———. "Political Party Dynamics in Venezuela and the Outbreak of Guerrilla Warfare,'' *Inter-American Economic Affairs,* 34, No. 2, 1980, 3-24.

______. ''The Venezuelan Left in the Era of the Popular Front, 1936-45,'' *Journal of Latin American Studies* [London], 11, No. 1, 1979, 169-84.

______. ''Venezuelans Reflect on the Meaning of the *23 de enero,*'' *Latin American Research Review,* 20, No. 1, 1985, 244-56.

______. *Venezuela's Movimiento al Socialismo: From Guerrilla Defeat to Innovative Politics.* Durham, North Carolina: Duke University Press, 1988.

Ewell, Judith. *The Indictment of a Dictator: The Extradition and Trial of Marcos Pérez Jiménez.* College Station: Texas A&M University Press, 1981.

______. *Venezuela: A Century of Change.* Stanford: Stanford University Press, 1984.

Fagan, Stuart. ''The Venezuelan Labor Movement: A Study in Political Unionism.'' (Ph.D. dissertation.) Berkeley: University of California, 1974.

Ferry, Robert J. *The Colonial Elite of Early Caracas: Formation and Crisis, 1567-1767.* Berkeley: University of California Press, 1989.

Gall, Norman. ''The Challenge of Venezuelan Oil,'' *Foreign Policy,* No. 18, Spring 1975, 44-67.

Gil Fortoul, José. *Historia Constitucional de Venezuela.* (3 vols.) (5th ed.) Caracas: Librería Piñango, 1967.

Gilmore, Robert L. *Caudillism and Militarism in Venezuela, 1810-1910.* Athens: Ohio University Press, 1964.

Gil Yepes, José Antonio. *The Challenge of Venezuelan Democracy.* (Trans., Evelyn Harrison I., Lolo Gil de Yanes, and Danielle Salti.) New Brunswick, New Jersey: Transaction Books, 1981.

Grayson, George W. ''Venezuela and the Puerto Ordaz Agreement,'' *Inter-American Economic Affairs,* 38, No. 3, 1984, 49-73.

Hassan, Mostafa Fathy. *Economic Growth and Employment Problems in Venezuela: An Analysis of an Oil-Based Economy.* New York: Praeger, 1975.

Heaton, Louis E. *The Agricultural Development of Venezuela.* (Praeger Special Studies in International Economics and Development.) New York: Praeger, 1969.

Hellinger, Daniel. ''Populism and Nationalism in Venezuela: New Perspectives on Acción Democrática,'' *Latin American Perspectives,* 11, No. 4, 1984, 33-59.

Hendrickson, Embert J. ''Gunboats, Dependency, and Oil: Issues in United States-Venezuelan Relations,'' *Latin American Research Review,* 20, No. 2, 1985, 262-67.

Herman, Donald L. *Christian Democracy in Venezuela.* Chapel Hill: University of North Carolina Press, 1980.

Herman, Donald L. (ed.). *Democracy in Latin America: Colombia and Venezuela.* New York: Praeger, 1988.

Herring, Hubert. *A History of Latin America from the Beginnings to the Present.* (3d ed.) New York: Knopf, 1968.

Hood, Miriam. *Gunboat Diplomacy, 1895-1905: Great Power Pressure in Venezuela.* Boston: Allen and Unwin, 1983.

Hussey, Roland Dennis. *The Caracas Company, 1728-1784: A Study in the History of Spanish Monopolistic Trade.* New York: Arno Press, 1977.

Karl, Terry Lynn. "Petroleum and Political Pacts: The Transition to Democracy in Venezuela," *Latin American Research Review,* 22, No. 1, 1987, 63-94.

Levine, Daniel H. *Conflict and Political Change in Venezuela.* Princeton: Princeton University Press, 1973.

______. *Religion and Politics in Latin America: The Catholic Church in Venezuela and Colombia.* Princeton: Princeton University Press, 1981.

______. "The Transition to Democracy: Are There Lessons from Venezuela?" *Bulletin of Latin American Research* [London], 4, No. 2, 1985, 47-61.

______. "Venezuela since 1958: The Consolidation of Democratic Politics." Pages 82-109 in Juan J. Linz and Alfred Stepan (eds.), *The Breakdown of Democratic Regimes: Latin America.* Baltimore: Johns Hopkins University Press, 1978.

Lieuwen, Edwin. *Petroleum in Venezuela: A History.* Berkeley: University of California Press, 1954. Reprint. New York: Russell and Russell, 1967.

______. *Venezuela.* New York: Oxford University Press, 1964.

Linz, Juan J., and Alfred Stepan (eds.). *The Breakdown of Democratic Regimes: Latin America.* Baltimore: John Hopkins University Press, 1978.

Lombardi, John V. *Venezuela: The Search for Order, the Dream of Progress.* New York: Oxford University Press, 1982.

Lombardi, John V., German Carrera Damas, and Roberta E. Adams. *Venezuelan History: A Comprehensive Working Bibliography.* Boston: Hall, 1977.

Looney, Robert E. "Factors Underlying Venezuelan Defense Expenditures, 1950-83: A Research Note," *Arms Control* [London], 7, No. 1, 1986, 74-101.

______. *The Political Economy of Latin American Defense Expenditures: Case Studies of Venezuela and Argentina.* Lexington, Massachusetts: Lexington Books, 1986.

______. "Venezuela's Economic Crisis: Origins and Successes in Stabilization," *Journal of Social, Political, and Economic Studies,* 11, No. 3, 1986, 327–37.

Maguire, Andrew, and Janet Welsh Bond (eds.). *Bordering on Trouble: Resources and Politics in Latin America.* Bethesda, Maryland: Adler and Adler, 1986.

McBeth, Brian Stuart. *Juan Vicente Gómez and the Oil Companies in Venezuela, 1908–1935.* Cambridge: Cambridge University Press, 1983.

McCoy, Jennifer L. "Democratic Dependent Development and State-Labor Relations in Venezuela." (Ph.D. dissertation.) Minneapolis: University of Minnesota, 1985.

______. "Labor and the State in a Party-Mediated Democracy: Institutional Change in Venezuela," *Latin American Research Review,* 24, No. 2, 1989, 35–67.

______. "The Politics of Adjustment: Labor and the Venezuelan Debt Crisis," *Journal of Inter-American Studies and World Affairs,* 28, No. 4, 1986–87, 103–38.

McKinley, P. Michael. *Pre-Revolutionary Caracas: Politics, Economy, and Society, 1777–1811.* New York: Cambridge University Press, 1985.

Marsland, William David. *Venezuela Through Its History.* Westport, Connecticut: Greenwood Press, 1976.

Martz, John D. *Acción Democrática: Evolution of a Modern Political Party in Venezuela.* Princeton: Princeton University Press, 1966.

______. "The Crisis of Venezuelan Democracy," *Current History,* 83, No. 490, February 1984, 73–77, 89.

______. "Venezuela's 'Generation of '28': The Genesis of Political Democracy," *Journal of Inter-American Studies and World Affairs,* 6, No. 1, January 1964, 17–33.

Martz, John D., and David J. Myers (eds.). *Venezuela: The Democratic Experience.* New York: Praeger, 1977.

______. *Venezuela: The Democratic Experience.* (Rev. ed.) New York: Praeger, 1986.

Martz, John D., David J. Myers, and Enrique A. Baloyra. *Electoral Mobilization and Public Opinion: The Venezuelan Campaign of 1973.* Chapel Hill: University of North Carolina Press, 1976.

Masur, Gerhard. *Simón Bolívar.* Albuquerque: University of New Mexico Press, 1969.

Moore, John Robert. *The Impact of Foreign Direct Investment on an Underdeveloped Economy: The Venezuelan Case.* New York: Arno Press, 1976.

Myers, David J. "Venezuela's MAS," *Problems of Communism,* 29, No. 5, 1980, 16–27.

Naím, Moisés, and Ramón Piñango (eds.). *El caso venezolano: Una ilusión de armonía.* Caracas: Ediciones IESA, 1985.

O'Leary, Daniel Florencio. *Bolívar and the War of Independence.* (Trans. and ed., Robert F. McNerney, Jr.) Austin: University of Texas Press, 1970.

Oropeza, Luis J. *Tutelary Pluralism: A Critical Approach to Venezuelan Democracy.* Cambridge: Harvard University Center for International Affairs, 1983.

Oviedo y Banos, José de. *The Conquest and Settlement of Venezuela.* (Trans., Jeannette Johnson Varner.) Berkeley: University of California Press, 1987.

Peeler, John A. *Latin American Democracies: Colombia, Costa Rica, Venezuela.* Chapel Hill: University of North Carolina Press, 1985.

Penniman, Howard R. (ed.). *Venezuela at the Polls: The National Elections of 1978.* Washington: American Enterprise Institute for Public Policy Research, 1980.

Pérez Saínz, Juan Pablo, and Paul Zarembka. "Accumulation and the State in Venezuelan Industrialization," *Latin American Perspectives,* 6, No. 3, 1979, 5–29.

Petras, James F., Morris Morley, and Steven Smith. *The Nationalization of Venezuelan Oil.* New York: Praeger, 1977.

Powell, John Duncan. *Political Mobilization of the Venezuelan Peasant.* Cambridge: Harvard University Press, 1971.

Rabe, Stephen G. *The Road to OPEC: United States Relations with Venezuela, 1919–1976.* Austin: University of Texas Press, 1982.

Randall, Laura. *The Political Economy of Venezuelan Oil.* New York: Praeger, 1987.

Ray, Talton F. *The Politics of the Barrios of Venezuela.* Berkeley: University of California Press, 1969.

Roseberry, William. *Coffee and Capitalism in the Venezuelan Andes.* Austin: University of Texas Press, 1983.

Rudolph, Donna Keyse, and G.A. Rudolph. *Historical Dictionary of Venezuela.* Metuchen, New Jersey: Scarecrow Press, 1971.

Salazar-Carrillo, Jorge. "Industrialization and Development in Venezuela," *Latin American Research Review,* 21, No. 3, 1986, 257–66.

———. *Oil in the Economic Development of Venezuela.* New York: Praeger, 1976.

Salcedo Bastardo, J.L. *Historia Fundamental de Venezuela.* (4th ed.) Caracas: Universidad Central de Venezuela, 1972.

Schuyler, George W. *Hunger in a Land of Plenty.* Cambridge: Schenkman, 1980.

Silva Michelena, José A. *The Politics of Change in Venezuela, 3: The*

Illusion of Democracy in Dependent Nations. Cambridge: MIT Press, 1971.

Sonntag, Heinz R., and Rafael de la Cruz. "The State and Industrialization in Venezuela," *Latin American Perspectives,* 12, No. 4, 1985, 75–104.

Stewart, William Stanley. *Change and Bureaucracy: Public Administration in Venezuela.* Chapel Hill: University of North Carolina Press, 1978.

Sullivan, William M. *Dissertations and Theses on Venezuelan Topics, 1900–1985.* Metuchen, New Jersey: Scarecrow Press, 1988.

Sullivan, William M., and Brian S. McBeth. *Petroleum in Venezuela: A Bibliography.* Boston: Hall, 1985.

Taylor, Philip Bates, Jr. *The Venezuelan Golpe de Estado of 1958: The Fall of Marcos Pérez Jiménez.* Washington: Institute for the Comparative Study of Political Systems, 1968.

Taylor, Philip Bates, Jr. (ed). *Venezuela: 1969, Analysis of Progress.* Washington: Johns Hopkins University School of Advanced International Studies, 1971.

Treverton, Gregory F. "Venezuela's New Role in World Affairs," *World Today* [London], 32, No. 8, August 1976, 308–16.

Tugwell, Franklin. *The Politics of Oil in Venezuela.* Stanford: Stanford University Press, 1975.

Vallenilla, Luis. *Oil, the Making of a New Economic Order: Venezuelan Oil and OPEC.* New York: McGraw Hill, 1975.

Vallenilla Lanz, Laureano. *Cesarismo democrático: estudios sobre las bases sociológicas de la constitución efectiva de Venezuela.* Caracas: Fondo Editorial Lola de Fuenmayor, Centro de Investigaciones Historicas, Universidad Santa María, 1983.

Wagner, Erika. *The Prehistory and Ethnohistory of the Carache Area in Western Venezuela.* (Publications in Anthropology, No. 71.) New Haven: Yale University Press, 1967.

Watson, Gayle Hudgens. *Colombia, Ecuador, and Venezuela: An Annotated Guide to Reference Materials in the Humanities and Social Studies.* Metuchen, New Jersey: Scarecrow Press, 1971.

Watters, Mary. *A History of the Church in Venezuela, 1810–1930.* Chapel Hill: University of North Carolina Press, 1933.

Wiarda, Howard J., and Harvey F. Kline (eds.). *Latin American Politics and Development.* (2d ed.) Boulder, Colorado: Westview Press, 1985.

Wiarda, Iêda Siqueira. "Venezuela: The Politics of Democratic Developmentalism." Pages 293–316 in Howard J. Wiarda and Harvey F. Kline (eds.), *Latin American Politics and Development.* (2d ed.) Boulder, Colorado: Westview Press, 1985.

Wise, George S. *Caudillo: A Portrait of Antonio Guzmán Blanco.* Westport, Connecticut: Greenwood Press, 1970.

Wright, Winthrop R. "Race, Nationality, and Immigration in Venezuelan Thought, 1890–1937," *Canadian Review of Studies in Nationalism* [Charlottetown], 6, No. 1, 1979, 1–12.

Chapter 2

Alonso, Isidoro. *La Iglesia en Venezuela y Ecuador.* Fribourg, Switzerland: Federación Internacional de los Institutos Católicos de Investigaciones Sociales y Socio-religiosas, 1961.

Appleyard, Donald. *Planning a Pluralist City: Conflicting Realities in Ciudad Guayana.* Cambridge: MIT Press, 1976.

Aranda, Sergio. *Las clases sociales y el estado en Venezuela.* Altamira Sur, Caracas: Editorial Pomaire, 1983.

Arellano Moreno, Antonio. *Orígenes de la Economía Venezolana.* (2d ed.) Caracas: Edime, 1963.

Arnove, Robert F. *Student Alienation: A Venezuelan Study.* New York: Praeger, 1971.

Banks, Arthur S. "Venezuela." Pages 683–85 in Arthur S. Banks (ed.), *Political Handbook of the World, 1989.* Binghamton, New York: CSA, 1989.

Bethel, Leslie (ed.). *The Cambridge History of Latin America,* 3. Cambridge: Cambridge University Press, 1985.

Blank, David Eugene. *Venezuela: Politics in a Petroleum Republic.* New York: Praeger, 1984.

Brito Figueroa, Federico. *La estructura económica de Venezuela colonial.* Caracas: Universidad Central de Venezuela, Ediciones de la Biblioteca, 1978.

Burroughs, G.E.R. *Education in Venezuela.* Hamden, Connecticut: Archon Books, 1974.

Butland, Gilbert. *Latin America, A Regional Geography.* New York: Wiley and Sons, 1972.

Carías, Rafael. *¿Quiénes somos los venezolanos?: Antropología cultural del venezolano.* Los Teques: Editorial ISSFE, 1982.

Casas Armengol, M. "Venezuela: System of Education." Pages 5425–31 in Torsten Husen and T. Neville Postlethewaite (eds.), *The International Encyclopedia of Education.* Oxford: Pergamon Press, 1985.

Chagnon, Napoleon A. "Yanomano, the True People," *National Geographic,* 150, No. 2, August 1976, 210–23.

Clayton, Lawrence A. *The Bolivarian Nations of Latin America.* Arlington Heights, Illinois: Forum Press, 1984.

Coromoto Segovia, Yanet. "La Cultura Guajira: Integración y Resistencia en Maracaibo," *Boletín Antropológico* [Mérida, Venezuela], No. 11, August-December 1986, 61-67.

Díaz Legórburu, Raúl. *Venezuela: The Basic Features.* Washington: Embassy of Venezuela, n.d.

Edmonston, Barry. "Fertility Decline and Socioeconomic Change in Venezuela," *Journal of Inter-American Studies and World Affairs,* 19, No. 2, August 1977, 369-92.

Ellner, Steven. "Educational Policy." Pages 296-328 in John D. Martz and David J. Myers (eds.), *Venezuela: The Democratic Experience.* (Rev. ed.) New York: Praeger, 1986.

Embassy of Venezuela. *Universities in Venezuela.* Washington: n.d.

The Encyclopedia of Education. (Ed., Lee C. Deighton.) New York: Macmillan, 1971.

Febres, Carlos Eduardo. "Religión y Comportamiento Político de la Clase Obrera en Caracas," *Revista de la Facultad de Ciencias Jurídicas y Políticas* [Caracas], 61, 1981, 247-91.

Federal Republic of Germany. Statistisches Bundesamt. *Länderbericht Venezuela, 1987.* (Statistik des Auslandes Series.) Wiesbaden: 1987.

Fitzgibbon, Russell H., and Julio A Fernandez. *Latin America: Political Culture and Development.* Englewood Cliffs, New Jersey: Prentice Hall, 1981.

Flórez Nieto, Carmen Elisa. *The Existence of a Latin American Mortality Pattern.* Bogotá, Colombia: Universidad de los Andes, 1985.

Frances, Antonio. *Venezuela posible.* Caracas: CORIMON, IESA, 1990.

Friedmann, John. *Venezuela: From Doctrine to Dialogue.* Syracuse: Syracuse University Press, 1965.

Fuchs, Helmuth. *Bibliografía básica de etnología de Venezuela.* Sevilla, Spain: Universidad de Sevilla, 1964.

García Ponce, Antonio. *Crisis oligoriquía y latifundio.* Barquisimeto, Venezuela: Fondo Editorial Buria, 1986.

Gómez, Luis, and Margarita López M. *Democratización y modernización del estado en Venezuela: Los actores sociales y políticos.* Caracas: CENDES, 1987.

"Good Signs in Venezuela?" *Miami Herald,* July 3, 1987, 3.

Goodwin, Paul B., Jr. *Latin America.* Guilford, Connecticut: Dushkin Group, 1988.

Grove, Noel. "Venezuela's Crisis of Wealth," *National Geographic,* 150, No. 2, August 1976, 174-208.

Herman, Donald L. "Agriculture." Pages 329-63 in John D. Martz and David J. Myers (eds.), *Venezuela: The Democratic Experience.* (Rev. ed.) New York: Praeger, 1986.

The International Encyclopedia of Education. (Eds., Torsten Husen and T. Neville Postlethewaite.) Oxford: Pergammon Press, 1985.

The International Encyclopedia of Higher Education, 9. (Ed., Asa S. Knowles.) San Francisco: Jossey-Bass, 1978.

Karst, Kenneth L., Murray L. Schwartz, and Audrey J. Schwartz. *The Evolution of Law in the Barrios of Caracas*. Los Angeles: Latin American Center, University of California, 1973.

Levine, Daniel H. "Church Elites in Venezuela and Colombia: Context, Background, and Beliefs," *Latin America Research Review,* 14, No. 2, Spring 1979, 51–79.

______. "Democracy and the Church in Venezuela," *Journal of Inter-American Studies and World Affairs,* 19, No. 1, February 1976, 3–22.

______. *Religion and Politics in Latin America: The Catholic Church in Venezuela and Colombia*. Princeton: Princeton University Press, 1981.

______. "Urbanization, Migrants, and Politics in Venezuela," *Journal of Inter-American Studies and World Affairs,* 18, No. 2, August 1975, 358–72.

Lombardi, John V. *Venezuela: The Search for Order, the Dream of Progress*. New York: Oxford University Press, 1982.

López-Orihuela, Alcides. *El pacto y la democracia sociales*. Caracas: Editorial Greco, 1986.

Lynch, John. "The Origins of Spanish American Independence." Pages 30–45 in Leslie Bethell (ed.), *The Cambridge History of Latin America,* 3. Cambridge: Cambridge University Press, 1985.

McMillan, Douglass F. "Venezuelan University Students as a Force in National Politics." (Ph.D dissertation.) Albuquerque: University of New Mexico, 1970.

Margolies, Luisa (ed.). *The Venezuelan Peasant in Country and City*. Caracas: EDIVA, 1979.

Martz, John D., and David J. Myers (eds.). *Venezuela: The Democratic Experience*. (Rev. ed.) New York: Praeger, 1986.

Méndez Castellano, Hernán. *Aproximación a la salud de la Venezuela del siglo XXI*. Caracas: Departamento de Relaciones Públicas de Lagoven, 1985.

Montero, Maritza. *Ideología, alienación e identidad nacional: Una aproximación psicosocial al ser venezolano*. Caracas: Universidad Central de Venezuela, Ediciones de la Biblioteca, 1984.

Pacheco Hellal, Edilberto. *El aborto en Venezuela*. Caracas: Fondo Editorial Carlos Aponte, 1986.

Peattie, Lisa Redfield. *The View from the Barrio*. Ann Arbor: University of Michigan Press, 1968.

Perera, Ambrosio. *Historia de la medicina en Venezuela.* Caracas: Imprenta Nacional, 1951.

Pollak-Eltz, Angelina. *Regards sur les cultures d'origine africaine au Venezuela.* Montreal: University of Montreal, 1977.

Powell, John Duncan. *Political Mobilization of the Venezuelan Peasant.* Cambridge: Harvard University Press, 1971.

Ramón Vaello, Yolanda. *La Mujer en La Vida Nacional y en la Prensa.* Caracas: Editorial Arte, 1985.

Ray, Talton F. *The Politics of the Barrios of Venezuela.* Berkeley: University of California Press, 1969.

Rey, Juan Carlos. "El futuro de la democracia en Venezuela." Pages 217–26 in *Venezuela hacia el año 2000.* Caracas: Editorial Nueva Sociedad, 1987.

Rivas Toro, José Gregorio. *Origen de los problemas socio-económicos de Venezuela y América Latina.* Valencia: Vadell Hnos Editores, 1985.

Robinson, Harry. *Latin America.* London: Macdonald and Evans, 1970.

Ruscoe, Gordon C. "Venezuela." Pages 437–42 in Lee C. Deighton (ed.), *The Encyclopedia of Education.* New York: Macmillan, 1970.

Seijas, Haydée. "Metodología, operación, y resultados globales del Censo Indígena, 1982." (Paper presented at the 33d Annual Convention of the Venezuelan Association for the Advancement of Science, October 1983.) Caracas: October 1983.

Tovar, Ramón A. *La Población de Venezuela.* Caracas: Instituto de Investigaciones, 1968.

Tugwell, Franklin. *The Politics of Oil in Venezuela.* Stanford: Stanford University Press, 1975.

United States. Central Intelligence Agency. *The World Factbook, 1989.* Washington: GPO, 1989.

______. Department of Health and Human Services. Social Security Administration. Office of Research, Statistics, and International Policy. *Social Security Programs Throughout the World, 1985.* (Research Report No. 60.) Washington: GPO, 1985.

______. Department of State. *Background Notes: Venezuela.* Washington: April 1987.

Uslar Pietri, Arturo. *Sumario de Economía Venezolana.* Caracas: Fundación Mendoza, 1958.

Venezuela. Ministerio de Sanidad y Asistencia Social. *Anuario de Epidemiología y Estadística del Ministerio de Sanidad y Asistencia Social.* Caracas: 1973.

______. Ministerio de Sanidad y Asistencia Social. *Anuario de*

Epidemiología y Estadística del Ministerio de Sanidad y Asistencia Social. Caracas: 1981.

______. Oficina Central de Estadística e Informática. *Censo indígena de Venezuela.* Caracas: 1982.

Vila, Marco-Aurelio. *Geografía de Venezuela.* Caracas: Fundación Eugenio Mendoza, 1962.

Villamizar, Thania. "Proceso de represión a las prácticas mágico-religiosas en Mérida," *Boletín Antropológico* [Mérida, Venezuela], No. 11, August-September 1986, 28-33.

Waggoner, George R. "Venezuela, Republic of." Pages 4327-33 in Asa S. Knowles (ed.), *The International Encyclopedia of Higher Education,* 9. San Francisco: Jossey-Bass, 1978.

Watson, Lawrence Craig. *Guajiro Personality and Urbanization.* Los Angeles: Latin American Center, University of California, 1968.

Watters, Mary. *A History of the Church in Venezuela, 1810-1930.* New York: AMS Press, 1971.

Chapter 3

Allen, Loring. *Venezuelan Economic Development: A Politico-Economic Analysis.* Greenwich, Connecticut: Jai Press, 1977.

Banco Central de Venezuela. *Boletín Mensual* [Caracas], No. 546, July 1989.

______. *Declaración de Fin de Año del Presidente del Banco Central de Venezuela.* Caracas: 1989.

Bigler, Gene E., and Enrique Viloria V. "State Enterprises and the Decentralized Public Administration." Pages 183-217 in John D. Martz and David J. Myers (eds.), *Venezuela: The Democratic Experience.* (Rev. ed.) New York: Praeger, 1986.

Bitar, Sergio, and Eduardo Troncoso. "La Industrialización de Venezuela: 1950-1980," *El Trimestre Económico* [Mexico City], 49, No. 194, April-June 1982, 265-94.

Blank, David Eugene. "Petroleum: The Community and Regional Perspectives." Pages 270-95 in John D. Martz and David J. Myers (eds.), *Venezuela: The Democratic Experience.* (Rev. ed.) New York: Praeger, 1986.

______. "Sowing the Oil," *Wilson Quarterly,* 8, Autumn 1984, 63-78.

______. *Venezuela. Politics in a Petroleum Republic.* New York: Praeger, 1984.

Bourguignon, Frances. "Oil and Income Distribution in Venezuela, 1968-1976." Pages 187-200 in Jacques de Bandt, Peter Mandi, and Dudley Seers (eds.), *European Studies in Development*. New York: St. Martins Press, 1980.

Charters, Ann. "Waiting to Bid Big," *Latin Finance*, No. 16, April 1990, 37-41.

Chelminski, Vladimir. "The Venezuelan Experience: How Misguided Policies Paralyzed a Prosperous Economy," *Journal of Economic Growth*, 3, No. 4, Summer 1989, 28-36.

Childres, Victor E. *Housing Venezuela's Urban Population*. (Universities Field Staff International, UFSI Reports, South America, No. 31.) Hanover, New Hampshire: 1983.

Crist, Raymond E. "Development and Agrarian Land Reform in Venezuela's Pioneer Zone: Social Progress along the Llanos-Andes Border in a Half Century of Political Advance," *American Journal of Economics and Sociology*, 43, No. 2, 1984, 149-58.

Crockford, G.N. *Insuring Foreign Risks: A Guide to Regulation Worldwide*. Wiltshire, United Kingdom: Kluwer, 1987.

de Bandt, Jacques, Peter Mandi, and Dudley Seers (eds.). *European Studies in Development*. New York: St. Martins Press, 1980.

de Krivoy, Ruth. "Venezuela Ante el Proceso de Integración Andina," *Integración Latinoamericana* [Buenos Aires], 12, No. 127, September 1987, 20-48.

Echevarra, Oscar A. *Opportunities from Debt: A Primer on Venezuelan Investments and Debt Equity Swaps*. Caracas: EISCA, 1988.

______. "Venezuela's Debt Menu," *Latin Finance*, No. 17, May 1990, 19-21.

Economist Intelligence Unit. *Country Profile: Venezuela, Suriname, Netherlands Antilles, 1989-90*. London: 1990.

______. *Country Profile: Venezuela, Suriname, Netherlands Antilles, 1990-91*. London: 1991.

Ellner, Steven. "Venezuela: No Exception," *NACLA Report on the Americas*, 23, No. 1, May 1989, 8-10.

Ewell, Judith. *Venezuela: A Century of Change*. Stanford: Stanford University Press, 1984.

García-Zamor, Jean Claude, and Stewart E. Sutin (eds.). *Financing Development in Latin America*. New York: Praeger, 1980.

Heaton, Louis E. *The Agricultural Development of Venezuela*. (Praeger Special Studies in International Economics and Development.) New York: Praeger, 1969.

Herman, Donald L. "Agriculture." Pages 329-63 in John D. Martz and David J. Myers (eds.), *Venezuela: The Democratic Experience*. (Rev. ed.) New York: Praeger, 1986.

Howell, Thomas R., William A. Noellert, Jesse G. Kreier, and Alan W. Wolff. *Steel and the State: Government Intervention and Steel's Structural Crisis*. Boulder, Colorado: Westview Press, 1988.

Hughes, Thomas L. "Venezuela: Debt-Equity Programme," *International Financial Law Review* [London], 8, No. 9, September 1989, 46–47.

Inter-American Development Bank. *Annual Report.* Washington: 1987.

______. *Annual Report.* Washington: 1988.

______. *Annual Report.* Washington: 1989.

______. *Economic and Social Progress in Latin America, 1984.* Washington: 1985.

International Labour Organization. *The Federación Campesina de Venezuela.* Geneva: 1982.

International Monetary Fund. *Annual Report on Exchange Agreements and Exchange Restrictions.* Washington: 1989.

______. *Direction of Trade Statistics Yearbook, 1989.* Washington: 1989.

International Petroleum Encyclopedia, 1989. Tulsa, Oklahoma: Pennwell, 1989.

Lombardi, John V. "The Patterns of Venezuela's Past." Pages 3–31 in John D. Martz and David J. Myers (eds.) *Venezuela: The Democratic Experience.* (Rev. ed.) New York: Praeger, 1986.

MacDonald, Scott B. "Financial Reform in Venezuela," *Supervisions,* March 1990.

McLeod, Darryl. "Latin American Capital Flight in Perspective." (Paper presented at Conference of Latin American Studies Association Congress, December 1989.) Bronx, New York: Fordham University, December 1989.

Marín Quijada, Enrique. "Limitations of Legislation in Improving Working Conditions: The Venezuelan Experience," *International Labour Review* [Geneva], 118, No. 1, January–February 1979, 113–22.

Martínez-Natera, Piar. *Geografía Económica de Venezuela.* Caracas: Ediciones CO–BO, 1983.

Martz, John D. "Petroleum: The National and International Perspectives." Pages 243–69 in John D. Martz and David J. Myers (eds.), *Venezuela: The Democratic Experience.* (Rev. ed.) New York: Praeger, 1986.

Martz, John D., and David J. Myers. "The Politics of Economic Development." Pages 72–108 in John D. Martz and David J. Myers (eds.), *Venezuela: The Democratic Experience.* (Rev. ed.) New York: Praeger, 1986.

Martz, John D., and David J. Myers (eds.). *Venezuela: The Democratic Experience.* (Rev. ed.) New York: Praeger, 1986.

Petras, James F., Morris Morley, and Steven Smith. *The Nationalization of Venezuelan Oil.* New York: Praeger, 1977.

Price Waterhouse. *Doing Business in Venezuela.* New York: 1985.

Rakowski, Cathy A. "Women in Nontraditional Industry: The Case of Steel in Ciudad Guayana, Venezuela." (Research paper.) (WID Working Papers Series, No. 104.) East Lansing: Michigan State University, November 1985.

Ramírez Guerrero, Jaime. *Programas de Formación Profesional para el Sector Informal Urbano en Colombia y Venezuela.* Montevideo, Uruguay: International Labour Organization, 1988.

Randall, Laura. *The Political Economy of Venezuelan Oil.* New York: Praeger, 1987.

Riva, Joseph P., Jr. *The Petroleum Production Potential of South America.* (Congressional Research Service Report for Congress Series, No. 90-270 SPR.) Washington: Science Policy Research Division, Congressional Research Service, Library of Congress, May 31, 1990.

______. *Venezuelan Petroleum: A Source of Increasing U.S. Imports?* (Congressional Research Service Report for Congress Series, No. 90-70 SPR.) Washington: Science Policy Research Division, Congressional Research Service, Library of Congress, February 2, 1990.

Salazar-Carrillo, Jorge. "Industrialization and Development in Venezuela." (Discussion Papers in Economics, No. 57.) Miami: Department of Economics, Florida International University, November 1986.

Salgado, Rene. "Economic Pressure Groups and Policy Making in Venezuela: The Case of FEDECAMARAS Reconsidered," *Latin American Research Review,* 22, No. 3, 1987, 91-106.

"South Survey: Venezuela," *South* [London], August 1989, 39-47.

Statistical Bulletin of the OAS, 8, Nos. 3-4, July/December 1986.

Sutin, Stewart E. "The Role of Financieras in Development." Pages 194-97 in Jean Claude Garcia-Zamor and Stewart E. Sutin (eds.), *Financing Development in Latin America.* New York: Praeger, 1980.

Tugwell, Franklin. *The Politics of Oil in Venezuela.* Stanford: Stanford University Press, 1975.

United Nations. Economic Commission for Latin America and the Caribbean. *Statistical Yearbook for Latin America and the Caribbean, 1988.* New York: 1989.

______. Food and Agriculture Organization. *FAO Production Yearbook, 1987,* 41. Rome: 1988.

United States. Department of Agriculture. Economic Research Service, Agriculture and Trade Analysis Division. *World Agricultural Trends and Indicators, 1970-1988.* (Statistical Bulletin No. 781.) Washington: 1989.

______. Department of Agriculture. Foreign Agricultural Service. *Venezuela: 1989 Agricultural Situation Report.* Washington: 1989.

______. Department of Commerce. "A Guide to Telecommunications Markets in Latin America." (Research paper.) Washington: March 1989.

______. Department of Commerce. *Foreign Economic Trends and Their Implications for the United States: Venezuela.* Washington: GPO, 1989.

______. Department of Commerce. *Foreign Economic Trends and Their Implications for the United States: Venezuela.* Washington: GPO, 1990.

______. Department of Labor. *Foreign Labor Trends: Venezuela, 1988-89.* Washington: GPO, 1989.

Urdaneta, Lourdes. *Participación Económica de la Mujer y la Distribución del Ingreso,* 13. (Colección de Estudios Económicos.) Caracas: Government of Venezuela, 1986.

Venezuela. *La Cooperación Internacional de Venezuela: Solidaridad en Acción.* Caracas: 1982.

______. *Indicadores de la Fuerza de Trabajo 1988.* Caracas: 1989.

______. Ministerio de Energía y Minas. *Energy in Venezuela* [Caracas], No. 26, July-August 1989.

______. Oficina Central de Estadística e Informática. *Anuario Estadístico de Venezuela, 1988.* Caracas: 1989.

______. Oficina Central de Estadística e Informática. *Coyuntura Económica,* 14. Caracas: 1989.

Vezga de Nahon, Milagros, and Luis Bruzco Ortega. "La Concentración Bancaria en Venezuela," *Revista del Banco Central de Venezuela* [Caracas], 1, No. 2, April-June 1986, 117-64.

Wadsted, Otto G. "Industrialization Programs, Factor Proportion, and Employment Brazil's Northeast and Venezuela's Guayana." (Research paper.) Cambridge: Institute for International Development, Harvard University, August 1984.

Winrock International. *Agricultural Development Indicators.* Morrilton, Arkansas: 1987.

World Bank. International Finance Corporation. *Emerging Stock Markets Factbook, 1989.* Washington: 1989.

______. International Finance Corporation. Capital Markets Division. *Latin American Experience in Developing Capital Markets.* (Conference Proceedings, Quito and Guayaquil, Ecuador, April 20-25, 1981.) Washington: 1981.

______. *Trends in Developing Economies, 1989.* Baltimore: Johns Hopkins University Press, 1989.

______. *World Debt Tables, 1989-90.* Washington: 1990.

______. *World Development Report, 1989.* New York: Oxford University Press, 1989.

Zambrano Sequín, Luis. "Consideraciones Críticas en Torno a la Política de Desarrollo Regional en Venezuela," *Pensamiento Iberoamericano* [Madrid], No. 10, July-December 1986, 225-41.

(Various issues of the following publications were also used in the preparation of this chapter: *Christian Science Monitor;* Economist Intelligence Unit, *Country Report: Venezuela, Suriname, Netherlands Antilles* [London]; *Financial Times* [London]; *Latin Finance; Miami Herald; New York Times; Nuevo Heraldo; Número* [Caracas]; *Times of the Americas; Universal* [Caracas]; *Wall Street Journal;* and *Washington Post.*)

Chapter 4

Alexander, Robert J. *The Communist Party of Venezuela.* Stanford: Hoover Institution Press, 1969.

______. *Rómulo Betancourt and the Transformation of Venezuela.* New Brunswick, New Jersey: Transaction Books, 1982.

Alonso, Isidoro. *La Iglesia en Venezuela y Ecuador.* Fribourg, Switzerland: Federación Internacional de los Institutos Católicos de Investigaciones Sociales y Socio-religiosas, 1961.

Appleyard, Donald. *Planning a Pluralist City: Conflicting Realities in Ciudad Guayana.* Cambridge: MIT Press, 1976.

Arellano Moreno, Antonio. *Orígines de la Economía Venezolana.* (2d ed.) Caracas: Edime, 1963.

Arnove, Robert F. *Student Alienation: A Venezuelan Study.* New York: Praeger, 1971.

Baloyra, Enrique A., and John D. Martz. *Political Attitudes in Venezuela: Societal Cleavages and Political Opinion.* Austin: University of Texas Press, 1979.

Blank, David Eugene. *Politics in Venezuela.* Boston: Little, Brown, 1973.

______. *Venezuela: Politics in a Petroleum Republic.* New York: Praeger, 1984.

Burggraaff, Winfield J. *The Venezuelan Armed Forces in Politics, 1935-1959.* Columbia: University of Missouri Press, 1972.

Chagnon, Napoleon A. "Yanomano, the True People," *National Geographic,* 150, No. 2, August 1976, 210-23.

Clayton, Lawrence A. *The Bolivarian Nations of Latin America.* Arlington Heights, Illinois: Forum Press, 1984.

Coronel, Gustavo. *The Nationalization of the Venezuelan Oil Industry from Technocratic Success to Political Failure.* Lexington, Massachusetts: Lexington Books, 1983.

Díaz Legórburu, Raúl. *Venezuela: The Basic Features.* Washington: Embassy of Venezuela, n.d.

Ellner, Steven. "Educational Policy." Pages 296–328 in John D. Martz and David J. Myers (eds.), *Venezuela: The Democratic Experience.* (Rev. ed.) New York: Praeger, 1986.

______. *Venezuela's Movimiento al Socialismo: From Guerrilla Defeat to Innovative Politics.* Durham, North Carolina: Duke University Press, 1988.

Embassy of Venezuela. *Universities in Venezuela.* Washington: n.d.

Febres, Carlos Eduardo. "Religión y Comportamiento Político de la Clase Obrera en Caracas," *Revista de la Facultad de Ciencias Jurídicas y Políticas* [Caracas], 61, 1981, 247–91.

Friedman, John. *Venezuela: From Doctrine to Dialogue.* Syracuse: Syracuse University Press, 1965.

Grove, Noel. "Venezuela's Crisis of Wealth," *National Geographic,* 150, No. 2, August 1976, 174–208.

Herman, Donald L. "Agriculture." Pages 329–63 in John D. Martz and David J. Myers (eds.), *Venezuela: The Democratic Experience.* (Rev. ed.) New York: Praeger, 1986.

______. *Christian Democracy in Venezuela.* Chapel Hill: University of North Carolina Press, 1980.

Karst, Kenneth L., Murray L. Schwartz, and Audrey J. Schwartz. *The Evolution of Law in the Barrios of Caracas.* Los Angeles: Latin American Center, University of California, 1973.

Kurian, George Thomas. *Encyclopedia of the Third World,* 3. (3d ed.) New York: Facts on File, 1987.

Levine, Daniel H. *Religion and Politics in Latin America: The Catholic Church in Venezuela and Colombia.* Princeton: Princeton University Press, 1981.

Lieuwen, Edwin. *Petroleum in Venezuela: A History.* Berkeley: University of California Press, 1954. Reprint. New York: Russell and Russell, 1967.

Lombardi, John V. *Venezuela: The Search for Order, the Dream of Progress.* New York: Oxford University Press, 1982.

McDonald, Ronald H., and J. Mark Ruhl (eds.). *Party Politics and Elections in Latin America.* Boulder, Colorado: Westview Press, 1989.

McMillan, Douglass F. "Venezuelan University Students as a Force in National Politics." (Ph.D. dissertation.) Albuquerque: University of New Mexico, 1970.

Magallanes, Manuel Vicente. *Los Partidos Políticos en la Evolución Histórica Venezolana.* Caracas: Ediciones Centauro, 1983.

Margolies, Luisa (ed.). *The Venezuelan Peasant in Country and City.* Caracas: EDIVA, 1979.

Martz, John D. *Acción Democrática: Evolution of a Modern Political Party in Venezuela.* Princeton: Princeton University Press, 1966.

______. "Venezuela's 'Generation of '28': The Genesis of Political Democracy," *Journal of Inter-American Studies and World Affairs,* 6, No. 1, January 1964, 17–33.

Martz, John D., and Enrique A. Baloyra. *Electoral Mobilization and Public Opinion: The Venezuelan Campaign of 1973.* Chapel Hill: University of North Carolina Press, 1976.

Martz, John D., and Peter B. Harkins. "Urban Electoral Behavior in Latin America: The Case of Metropolitan Caracas," *Comparative Politics,* 53, 1973, 523–49.

Martz, John D., and David J. Myers (eds.). *Venezuela: The Democratic Experience.* (Rev. ed.) New York: Praeger, 1986.

Myers, David J. "Urban Voting, Structural Cleavages, and Party System Evolution: The Case of Venezuela," *Comparative Politics,* 8, 1975, 119–51.

______. *Venezuela's Pursuit of Caribbean Basin Interests: Implications for United States National Security.* (Rand Publications Series.) Santa Monica: Rand, 1985.

O'Connor, Robert E. "The Media and the Campaign." Pages 171–90 in Howard R. Penniman (ed.), *Venezuela at the Polls: The National Elections of 1978.* Washington: American Enterprise Institute for Public Policy Research, 1980.

Penniman, Howard R. (ed). *Venezuela at the Polls: The National Elections of 1978.* Washington: American Enterprise Institute for Public Policy Research, 1980.

Powell, John Duncan. *Political Mobilization of the Venezuelan Peasant.* Cambridge: Harvard University Press, 1971.

Ray, Talton F. *The Politics of the Barrios of Venezuela.* Berkeley: University of California Press, 1969.

Tovar, Ramón A. *La Población de Venezuela.* Caracas: Instituto de Investigaciones, 1968.

Tugwell, Franklin. *The Politics of Oil in Venezuela.* Stanford: Stanford University Press, 1975.

United States. Department of State. *Background Notes: Venezuela.* Washington: April 1987.

Uslar Pietri, Arturo. *Sumario de la Economía Venezolana.* Caracas: Fundación Mendoza, 1958.

Vallenilla, Luis. *Oil, the Making of a New Economic Order: Venezuelan Oil and OPEC.* New York: McGraw Hill, 1975.

Zchock, Dieter K., et al. "The Education-Work Transition of Venezuelan University Students," *Journal of Inter-American Studies and World Affairs,* 16, February 1974, 96–118.

(Various issues of the following publication were also used in the preparation of this chapter: Foreign Broadcast Information Service, *Daily Report: Latin America.*)

Chapter 5

Anderson, Robert Bruce. "Civilian Control of Professionalizing Militaries: Implications of the Venezuelan Case." (Ph.D. dissertation.) (University Microfilms Doctoral Dissertation Series, No. AAC8520819.) Denver, Colorado: University of Denver, June 1985.

Braveboy-Wagner, Jacqueline Anne. *The Venezuela-Guyana Border Dispute: Britain's Colonial Legacy in Latin America.* Boulder, Colorado: Westview Press, 1984.

Burggraaff, Winfield J. *The Venezuelan Armed Forces in Politics, 1935-1959.* Columbia: University of Missouri Press, 1972.

Caffrey, Dennis F. "The Inter-American Military System: Rhetoric vs. Reality." Pages 41-59 in Georges Fauriol (ed.), *Security in the Americas.* Washington: National Defense University Press, 1989.

Child, Jack. "Geopolitical Conflicts in South America." Pages 309-27 in Georges Fauriol (ed.), *Security in the Americas.* Washington: National Defense University Press, 1989.

English, Adrian J. *Armed Forces of Latin America: Their Histories, Development, Present Strength, and Military Potential.* London: Jane's, 1984.

Fauriol, Georges (ed.). *Security in the Americas.* Washington: National Defense University Press, 1989.

Gil Yepes, José Antonio. "Political Articulation of the Military Sector in Venezuelan Democracy." Pages 148-82 in John D. Martz and David J. Myers (eds.), *Venezuela: The Democratic Experience.* (Rev. ed.) New York: Praeger, 1986.

Hazleton, William A. "Colombian and Venezuelan Foreign Policy: Regional Powers in the Caribbean Basin." Pages 245-75 in Donald L. Herman (ed.), *Democracy in Latin America: Colombia and Venezuela.* New York: Praeger, 1988.

Herman, Donald L. *Democracy in Latin America: Colombia and Venezuela.* New York: Praeger, 1988.

Looney, Robert E. *The Political Economy of Latin American Defense Expenditures: Case Studies of Venezuela and Argentina.* Lexington, Massachusetts: Lexington Books, 1986.

Martz, John D. "National Security and Politics: The Colombian-Venezuelan Border," *Journal of Inter-American Studies and World Affairs,* 30, No. 4, Winter 1988-89, 117-38.

Meléndez Meléndez, Lila. *¿Qué es el Servicio Militar Femenino y en qué Consiste la Instrucción Premilitar?* Caracas: Miguel Ángel García e hijo, 1984.

The Military Balance, 1990–1991. London: International Institute for Strategic Studies, 1990.

Millan, Victor, and Michael A. Morris. *Conflicts in Latin America: Democratic Alternatives in the 1990s.* (Conflict Studies Series, No. 230.) London: Research Institute for the Study of Conflict and Terrorism, April 1990.

Müller Rojas, Albert. "Equipamiento Militar, Política de Defensa y Política Exterior: El Caso Venezolano," *Política Internacional* [Caracas], No. 2, April–June 1986, 22–33.

Myers, David J. *Venezuela's Pursuit of Caribbean Basin Interests: Implications for United States National Security.* Santa Monica, California: Rand, January 1985.

Premo, Daniel L. "Coping with Insurgency: The Politics of Pacification in Colombia and Venezuela." Pages 219–44 in Donald L. Herman (ed.), *Democracy in Latin America: Colombia and Venezuela.* New York: Praeger, 1988.

Riva, Joseph P., Jr. *Venezuelan Petroleum: A Source of Increasing U.S. Imports?* (Congressional Research Service Report for Congress Series, No. 90–70 SPR.) Washington: Science Policy Research Division, Congressional Research Service, Library of Congress, February 2, 1990.

Rouquié, Alain. *The Military and the State in Latin America.* Berkeley: University of California Press, 1987.

Schaposnik, Eduardo C. *La Democratización de las Fuerzas Armadas Venezolanas.* Caracas: Instituto de Investigaciones Sociales, 1985.

United States. Congress. 97th, 2d Session. Senate. Committee on Foreign Relations. *Proposed Sale of F–16s to Venezuela.* Washington: GPO, 1982.

Varas, Augusto. *Militarization and the International Arms Race in Latin America.* (Foreign Relations of the Third World Series.) Boulder, Colorado: Westview Press, 1985.

Venezuela. Ministerio de la Defensa. *Leyes y Reglamentos.* (2 vols.) Caracas: 1983.

______. Ministerio de la Defensa. *Memoria y Cuenta, 1986.* Caracas: 1987.

______. Ministerio de la Defensa. *Memoria y Cuenta, 1987.* Caracas: 1988.

______. Ministerio de la Defensa. *Memoria y Cuenta, 1988.* Caracas: 1989.

(Various issues of the following publications were also used in the preparation of this chapter: *Business Latin America; Bulletin of the Atomic Scientists; Christian Science Monitor; Defence* [London]; *Defense and Foreign Affairs Weekly; Europa World Year Book* [London]; *Facts on File;* Foreign Broadcast Information Service, *Daily Report: Latin America; Fuerzas Armadas de Venezuela* [Caracas]; *Insight; International Narcotics Control Strategy Report; Jane's Defence Weekly* [London]; *Keesing's Contemporary Archives* [London]; *Keesing's Record of World Events* [London]; *Latin American Weekly Report* [London]; *Latin American Monitor; Política Internacional* [Caracas]; *Proceedings; Problems of Communism; Tecnología Militar* [Madrid]; *Times of the Americas; El Universal* [Caracas]; *Washington Post;* and *World Military Expenditures and Arms Transfers.*)

Glossary

Andean Common Market (Ancom)—A free-trade association formed in 1969 by Bolivia, Chile, Colombia, Ecuador, and Peru. Venezuela joined the organization in 1973. Chile withdrew in 1977. Also known as the Andean Pact or the Andean Group (Grupo Andino).

bolívar (B)—Venezuela's monetary unit, divided into 100 céntimos. The bolívar traded at a fixed rate of B4.29 = US$1 from 1976 to 1983, but was devalued officially several times between 1983 and 1989. The 1989 devaluation established a floating rate at B36 = US$1; by late 1990, the rate had reached B43 = US$1.

Caribbean Basin—Broad geopolitical region encompassing all nations and dependencies in or bordering on the Caribbean Sea, thus including the Caribbean islands, northern South America, Central America, Mexico, and the United States.

Contadora Group—The "core-four" nations—Colombia, Mexico, Panama, and Venezuela—that in a January 1983 meeting on Contadora Island (off the Pacific coast of Panama) launched a diplomatic initiative to prevent through negotiations a regional conflagration among the Central American states of Guatemala, El Salvador, Honduras, Nicaragua, and Costa Rica. In September 1984, the negotiating process produced a draft treaty, the Contadora Acta, which was judged acceptable by the government of Nicaragua but rejected by the other four Central American states concerned. The governments of Peru, Uruguay, Argentina, and Brazil formed the Contadora Support Group in 1985 in an effort to revitalize the faltering talks. The process was suspended unofficially in June 1986 when the Central American governments refused to sign a revised Acta. The Contradora process was effectively superseded by direct negotiations among the Central American states.

encomienda—A system whereby the Spanish crown granted rights over Indian labor and tribute to individual colonists (*encomenderos*), who in turn undertook to maintain order and to propagate Christianity among the Indians. It ended officially in 1687.

fiscal year (FY)—Calendar year.

General Agreement on Tariffs and Trade (GATT)—An international organization established in 1948 and headquartered in Geneva that serves as a forum for international trade negotiations.

GATT members pledge to further multilateral trade by reducing import tariffs, quotas, and preferential trade agreements and promise to extend to each other any favorable trading terms offered in subsequent agreements with third parties.

Gran Colombia (Republic of)—Declared independent of Spain in 1821. Consisted of present-day Venezuela, Colombia, Ecuador, and Panama. Venezuela seceded from it in 1829.

gross domestic product (GDP)—A measure of the total value of goods and services produced by the domestic economy during a given period; usually one year. Obtained by adding the value contributed by each sector of the economy in the form of profits, compensation to employees, and depreciation (consumption of capital). The income arising from investments and possessions owned abroad is not included. Hence, the term *domestic* is used to distinguish GDP from gross national product (*q.v.*).

gross national product (GNP)—Total market value of all final goods and services produced by an economy during a year. Obtained by adding gross domestic product (*q.v.*) and the income received from abroad by residents less payments remitted abroad to nonresidents.

International Monetary Fund (IMF)—Established along with the World Bank (*q.v.*) in 1945, the IMF is a specialized agency affiliated with the United Nations that takes responsibility for stabilizing international exchange rates and payments. The main business of the IMF is the provision of loans to its members when they experience balance of payments difficulties. These loans often carry conditions that require substantial internal economic adjustments by the recipients.

liberation theology—An activist movement led by Roman Catholic clergy who trace their inspiration to Vatican Council II (1965), where some church procedures were liberalized, and the Second Latin American Bishops' Conference in Medellín, Colombia (1968), which endorsed greater direct efforts to improve the lot of the poor.

llanos—Plains region that runs in a broad band across central Venezuela. Residents referred to as *llaneros*.

pardo(s)—Person(s) of mixed racial origin, including any combination of European, Indian, and African antecedents.

rancho(s)—An urban shelter, or shanty, constructed of makeshift materials, generally by the occupant.

trienio—A three-year period, usually refers to the 1945–48 democratic government.

World Bank—The informal name used to designate a group of three affiliated international institutions: the International Bank for Reconstruction and Development (IBRD), the International Development Association (IDA), and the International Finance Corporation (IFC). The IBRD, established in 1945, has the primary purpose of providing loans to developing countries for productive projects. The IDA, a legally separate loan fund administered by the staff of the IBRD, was set up in 1960 to furnish credits to the poorest of developing countries on much easier terms than those of conventional IBRD loans. The IFC, founded in 1956, supplements the activities of the IBRD through loans and assistance designed specifically to encourage the growth of productive private enterprises in less-developed countries. The president and certain senior officers of the IBRD hold the same positions in the IFC. The three institutions are owned by the governments of the countries that subscribe their capital. To participate in the World Bank group, member states must first belong to the International Monetary Fund (*q.v.*).

Index

Acción Democrática (AD). *See* Democratic Action
acquired immune deficiency syndrome (AIDS), 75
AD. *See* Democratic Action
Advanced Officers School, 202
agrarian reform (*see also* land reform), 164-65; under Caldera, 29; inadequacy of, 61, 155
Agrarian Reform Law (1960), 91
Agricultural and Livestock Development Bank (Bandagro), 116, 117
agricultural extension services, 71, 96
agricultural production: under Caldera, 29; decline in, 15, 81; expansion of, 82
agricultural products, 92-95; cash crops, 94-95; corn, 92; cotton, 94; export of, 41, 94; food crops, 92-94; fruits, 93-94; imports of, 92; legumes, 93; oilseeds, 94, 95; rice, 92-93, 96; sorghum, 92; sugarcane, 94; tobacco, 7; tubers, 93; vegetables, 93; wheat, 7
agriculture, 89-97; under colonial rule, 6-7; credit subsidies for, 126; export, 13, 89; financing for, 117; geographical distribution of, 45; under Gómez, 51; government policies toward, 89, 153; growth rate of, 90; under Guzmán, 13; impact of, on imports, 92; impact of urban migration on, 92; labor force in, 87, 89; land area suitable for, 91; land policies, 90-92; lobby, 160; under Lusinchi, 84; as percentage of gross domestic product, 89; technology in, 95-96
AIDS. *See* acquired immune deficiency syndrome
air force, 192, 200-201; aircraft of, 200-201; bombing of Caracas by, 22-23; granted autonomy, 180; insignia, 202, 203, 204, 205; internal security duty, 207; organization of, 201; under Pérez, 181; personnel in, 201; ranks of, 202; training in, 201; uniforms, 202
airline, national, 33
airports, 122
air transportation, 122
Ajaguan people, 48
Alcasa, 106
Alfonso XII, 188
aluminum, 81, 113; export of, 125; production of, 143
aluminum industry, xxii, 81, 112; foreign-exchange earnings from, 105; investment in, 130; production, 106
Alunasa, 106
Alusuisse, 106
Amazonas territory, 137
Amazon River, 46
Ancom. *See* Andean Common Market
Andean Common Market (Ancom), 28, 170; entrance into, 29-30, 126; imports from, 124-25
Andean countries: financial aid to, 31
Andean Development Corporation, 126
Andean Reserve Fund, 130
Andean Satellite Corporation (CONDOR), 123
Angel Falls, 45
Ankoko Island, 190
ANSA. *See* Italian News Agency
Anzoátegui: petrochemical complex in, 103
AP. *See* Associated Press
Aragua, xxiv
Arawak people, 48
Argentina: relations with, 169, 171
Aristide, Jean-Bertrand, xxv
armed forces: administration of, 196-97; border control by, 156, 165; chain of command, 197; civic-action projects of, 193-94; conditions in, 24; conflict within, xxv-xxvi; co-optation of, 156; in coup d'état of 1948, 20; deployment of, 197; foreign training missions, 179; history of, 177-82; impact of oil on, 177; insignia of, 202-3, 204-5; influence of political parties on, xxii-xxiii; internal security under, xxiii; lobbying by, 182; missions of, 165, 183, 192-94; National Security Police as threat to, 181; opposition of, to Pérez, 22; participation by, in United Nations peacekeeping mission, 170; under Pérez, 181; political influence of, 165; political involvement

of, 155-56, 182; political pressures on, 192; presidential control of, 141; professionalization of, 179; ranks of, 202; regions of, 197; responsibilities of, 193; role of, 179, 193; role of women in, 194-95; service in, 24; social welfare under, 179; uniforms of, 202; uprisings, 26
Armed Forces of Cooperation (FAC) (National Guard), 147, 189, 201-2; chain of command in, 201-2; efforts of, against drug trafficking, 194, 206; internal security duty, 207, 208; matériel of, 202; missions of, 194, 210; organization of, 201; personnel in, 201; training of, 202
Armed Forces of National Liberation (FALN), 26, 161
army, 9, 198-99; under Castro, 178-79; chain of command, 178-79; deployment, 198-99; disbanded, 178; foreign training of, 14; general staff of, 178-79; under Gómez, 179; innovations in, 178-79; insignia, 202, 203, 204, 205; matériel, 199; organization of, 198-99; personnel, 198; as political support, 14; prestige, 198; ranks, 202; reestablished, 178; training, 199; uniforms, 202
Associated Press (AP), 166
associations, professional, 159, 165; political power of, 159-60
Audiencia de Santa Fe de Bogotá , 6
Audiencia de Santo Domingo, 6
Audiencia de Venezuela, 8
Authentic Renovating Organization, 163
automobile industry, 112; output of, 112-13
automobiles, 121
autonomous entities, 85; under industrial development, 33
Ayaman people, 48

balance of payments, 127-28; deficit, 127; fluctuations in, 127; in the 1980s, 127; problems with, 36; under restructuring, 125
Banap. *See* National Savings and Loan Bank
Banco Central de Venezuela (BCV). *See* Central Bank of Venezuela
Banco de Desarrollo Agropecuario (Bandagro). *See* Agricultural and Livestock Development Bank
Banco de Venezuela, 116
Banco Industrial de Venezuela (BIV). *See* Industrial Bank of Venezuela
Banco Italo-Venezolano, 116
Banco Latino, 116
Banco Mercantil, 116
Banco Nacional de Ahorro y Préstamo (Banap). *See* National Savings and Loan Bank
Banco Occidental de Descuento, 116-17
Banco Provincial, 116
Banco República, 116
Bandagro. *See* Agricultural and Livestock Development Bank
Bandera Roja (BR). *See* Red Flag
bank, central, 17
Bank Advisory Committee, 129
Bankers' Association, 160
banking lobby, 160
banks: agricultural, 17; foreign, 116; industrial, 17; mortgage, 117-18; public-sector, 116
banks, commercial, 96; debt to, 129; lending policies, 116; loans from, 34-35; number of, 116
banks, development, 17, 96; funding, 117; number of, 117; specialized services of, 117
Barinas Province, 6
Barinas state, 92
Barquisimeto: concentration of population in, 52; population of, 53; schools in, 74
Barrios, Gonzalo, 28
Battle of Carabobo, 11
Bauxita de Venezuela (Bauxiven), 105
bauxite, xxii; production, 105-6; reserves, 105
Bauxiven. *See* Bauxita de Venezuela
BCV. *See* Central Bank of Venezuela
BDN. *See* Democratic National Bloc
beef: export of, 50
Belgian Aleurope Aluminum Company, 106
Betancourt, Rómulo, 16, 17, 23, 136, 162, 180; attempted coup against, 156; co-optation of military by, 183; election of, 138; exiled, 20, 163; as president, 19, 167, 182
Betancourt administration, 24, 141; cabinet in, 142; economy under, 27; foreign

policies of, 26, 169–70; junta under, 19; opposition to, 182; protests against, 26; students' role in, 161
Betancourt Doctrine, 27, 29, 169
Betancur Cuartas, Belisario, 185
Bethlehem Steel, 106
Bitúmenes del Orinoco. *See* Orinoco Asphalt
BIV. *See* Industrial Bank of Venezuela
blacks, 49; in independence movement, 50; as percentage of population, 63; social status of, 64
Bloque Democrático Nacional (BDN). *See* Democratic National Bloc
Bolivarian Movement, xxvii-xxviii
Bolívar Palacios, Simón, xxi, 3, 9–10, 50, 61, 166; background of, 10; exiled, 10; as liberator, 135, 139, 168, 178; as president, 10, 11; public education goals of, 70–71
Bolívar state; gold in, 110; resettlement in, 56
Bolivia, 11; economic policies, 127; imports from, 125
Bonaparte, Joseph, 9
Bonaparte, Napoléon, 9
borders: disputes over, 189–91; illegal activities along, 170, 192; military control of, 156, 193
Boves, José Tomás, 10
BR. *See* Red Flag
Brady, Nicolas, 129
Brady Plan, 129–30
Brazil: imports from, 124; interest of, in Essequibo dispute, 190–91; relations with, 191-92
Brazo Casiquiare, 46
Britain: imports from, 124; investment by, 128
broadcasting, 166
budget deficit, 36
Budget Office, 85
bureaucracy, 142; corruption in, xxv, 142, 148, 149; development of, 13, 15; expansion of, 83, 142; labor force in, 87; political role of, 158–59; problems caused by, xxi; reform of, 148, 158; scandals in, 158
Burelli Rivas, Miguel Angel, 29
Burnham, Forbes, 191
business: associations, 165; newspapers of, 166
bus services, 121
cacao (*see also* cocoa): cultivation of, 94
CADAFE. *See* National Electricity Company
Caldera administration, 29, 149; foreign policy under, 169; pacification program of, 30; reform under, xxii, 29, 148
Caldera Rodríguez, Rafael, 16, 19, 136, 162; in 1952 elections, 21; in 1958 elections, 23; in 1968 elections, 29; popularity of, xxvii
Calderón Berti, Humberto, 37
Cali Cartel, xxiv
Cámara Venezolana de la Industria de Radiodifusión. *See* Venezuelan Chamber of the Broadcasting Industry
Cametro. *See* Caracas Metro
Canada: exports to, 126; imports from, 124; trade with, 100
Canary Islanders, 7
CANTV. *See* Compañía Nacional de Teléfonos de Venezuela
capital: account, 128; accumulation, 24; investment, 85; markets, 118; outflow, 36, 127, 128, 129
Caprile family, 166
Capuchin missionaries, 6, 69
Caquetío people, 48
Carabobo: petrochemical complex in, 103; protests in, xxiv
Carabobo University, 74
Caracas, 45; AIDS in, 75; barrios of, 56–58; bombed by Venezuelan air force, 22–23; development of, 13; growth of, 8, 13, 56; illegal immigrants in, 55; importance of, 136, 166; manufacturing in, 112; migration to, 51, 55; military region, 197; newspapers in, 166; percentage of population living in, 52; population of, 41, 53; protests in, xxiv, 159; rainfall in, 46; *ranchos* in, 26; schools in, 71
Caracas *cabildo,* 9
Caracas Chamber of Industry, 160
Caracas Company, 3, 7–8; disputes of, with cocoa growers, 8
Caracas junta, 9
Caracas Metro (Cametro), 56, 121
Caracas Province, 6
Caracas Stock Exchange (*see also* stock market), 118
Carbones de Zulia (Carbozulia), 110
Carbozulia. *See* Carbones de Zulia
Caribbean: financial aid to, 30, 31;

imports from, xxv; oil exports to, 101, 172; slave labor in, 5
Caribbean Basin: influence in, 184; regional power in, 183, 184
Caribbean Community and Common Market (Caricom), xxviii
Caribbean Development Bank, 30, 130
Caribbean Sea, 190, 191
Caricom. *See* Caribbean Community and Common Market
Caruachi hydroelectric complex, 104
Castro, Cipriano, 14
Castro administration (1899-1908), 14; military innovations under, 178
Castro Ruz, Fidel, 25, 169, 185; disintegration of regime of, xxiii; efforts of, to export revolution, 28, 187; as threat, 186
Catholic Church. *See* Roman Catholic Church
Caucasians: as percentage of population, 63
caudillismo, 3, 135-36, 177; end of, 179; militia system in, 178; political system in, 41
caudillos, 41, 139; personal armies of, 178
CAVIM. *See* Venezuelan Military Industries Company
Central America: financial aid to, 30, 31; oil exports to, 101; political support for, 172
Central American Bank for Integration, 131
Central Bank of Venezuela (BCV), 36-37, 85, 99; interest rate policies of, 117; modernization under, 115-116; privatization of, 117
Central Office of Coordination and Planning (Cordiplan), 83; creation of, 148; goals of, 148, 153, 158; minister of, 142; modernization under, 115-16; reform under, 149; responsibilities of, 85
Central Office of Personnel, 148
Central University of Venezuela, 16, 74; closed by Pérez administration, 21; leftist activities in, 28, 161, 162
Chamber of Deputies (*see also* Congress), 18, 143, 154, 163; seat distribution system in, 152; women in, 67
Chamber of the Petroleum Industry, 160
Chamorro, Violeta Barrios de, 170
Champlin, 101
charitable organizations, 77
Charles IV, 9
Chávez Frías, Hugo, xxv, xxvi
children: abandonment of, 62; day care for, 67; support of, 58
Chile: economic policies, 127; trade agreements with, xxviii; training of Venezuelan army by, 14
chocolate, 7
cigarette industry, 94
Círculo de las Fuerzas Armadas. *See* Officers Club
Citgo, 101, 130
Ciudad Bolívar: military region, 197; protests in, xxiv
Ciudad Guayana, 191; concentration of population in, 52; creation of, 56; industrial development in, 33-34, 97; manufacturing in, 112; population of, 34
civil liberties, 25
civil servants: professionalization of, 148-49; training for, 148
civil war, 9
class system (*see also under individual classes*): effect of independence on, 41-42; effect of oil on, 41-42
climate, 45-46; rainy season, 45-46; temperature zones, 46
coal: deposits, 110; export of, 81; markets for, 110; production, 110
coal industry, 36
cocaine: exports, xxiv; transshipment of, 203, 206
cocoa (*see also* cacao), 94; boom, 3; under *encomienda* system, 82; export of, 125; growers, 8, 41; impact of, 7, 82; as principal export, 3, 7, 12; production, 41; rebellion (1749), 8
coffee, 94; boom, 15, 82; exports, 94, 125; growers, 41; impact of, on society, 50, 82; as principal export, 3, 12, 50; production, 13, 41
Coffee Stabilization Fund, 130
Colombia (*see also* New Granada): border with, 66, 125, 147; border disputes with, 188; in Contadora Group, 170, 184-85; drug trafficking in, 203; economic cooperation with, xxv; guerrilla strikes from, 189; illegal immigrants from, 54, 170; imports from, 125; internal security problems of, 188; meeting of presidents of, 169, 70; relations with, 169-70, 187-89; security

cooperation with, 188; territory disputes with, 169, 188
Colombian-Caribbean Highway, 121
colonial rule, 6-8; administration, 6; agriculture under, 6-7; army under, 177; militia system under, 177-78; provinces under, 6
colonial society: hierarchy in, 7; impact of cocoa on, 7
Columbus, Christopher, 3; explorations of, 4
Comité de Organización Política Electoral Independiente (COPEI). *See* Social Christian Party
Command and Staff School, 201
commerce: financing for, 117; labor force in, 87; lobby, 160
Commission on Public Administration, 148; reform plan of, 148
Committee of Autonomous Unions, 161
communications (*see also* telecommunications): infrastructure development, 13
Communication Satellite Corporation (COMSAT), 123
communism: containment of, 186; threat of expansion of, 187
communists (*see also* Venezuelan Communist Party), 20
Compañía Anónima de Administración y Fomento Eléctrico (CADAFE). *See* National Electricity Company
Compañía Anónima Metro de Caracas (Cametro). *See* Caracas Metro
Compañía Anónima Venezolana de Industrias Militares (CAVIM). *See* Venezuelan Military Industries Company
Compañía Nacional de Teléfonos de Venezuela (CANTV), 122-23
COMSAT. *See* Communication Satellite Corporation
CONDOR. *See* Andean Satellite Corporation
Confederación de Trabajadores de Venezuela (CTV). *See* Confederation of Venezuelan Workers
Confederation of Venezuelan Workers (CTV), xxvii, 36, 87, 160
Congress (*see also under individual houses*), 18, 118; appointment of judges by, 147; apportionment of seats in, 19; authority of, 144; committees in, 144; immunity in, 144; legislation in, 144-45; organization of, 144; political significance of, 144
Congress at Angostura (1819), 10
conquest, 5
conscription, 194, 195; deferment from, 194; registration for, 194
conscripts, 194; women as, 194-95
Consejo Supremo Electoral (CSE). *See* Supreme Electoral Council
Consejo Venezolano para los Niños (CVN). *See* Venezuelan Children's Council
Consensus of Lima (1973), 30
Conservatives, 12
Constituent Assembly, 20
constitution: changes of, 139; of 1811, 9; of 1830, 12; of 1952, 21; of 1857, 13; of 1936, 17, 21; of 1947, 20, 21, 151; of 1952, 21
constitution of 1961, 136; civil liberties under, 25, 137, 139, 141; civil obligations under, 140; elections under, 138; legislature under, 25; local government under, 149-50; president under, 25, 138; religious freedom under, 68; revisions of, 140; social justice goals of, 60
Constitution of the Republic of Gran Colombia, 11
construction industry, 114; government role in, 114; illegal immigrants working in, 55; labor force in, 114; as percentage of gross domestic product, 114; state-owned enterprises in, 114
Contadora Group, 170, 172, 184-85
Contadora process, 185-86; goals of, 185; problems in, 185-86
contraceptives, 52
COPEI. *See* Social Christian Party
Cordiplan. *See* Central Office of Coordination and Planning
Coro: slave trade in, 5
Corporación Venezolana de Fomento (CVF). *See* Venezuelan Development Corporation
Corporación Venezolana de Guayana (CVG). *See* Venezuelan Corporation of Guayana
Corporación Venezolana de Petróleos (CVP). *See* Venezuelan Petroleum Corporation
Corpoven, 99
Correo Nacional, 165
corruption, 35, 38, 77, 81, 136; under

Gómez, 179; of judges, 206; under Pérez, xxv, xxvii; under Pérez Jiménez, 68, 82, 128; in petroleum industry, 102; in prisons, 211
Costa Rica, 185
cotton: under *encomienda* system, 82; as export crop, 50
Council of Ministers, 142
coups d'état, 155; of 1945, 18-19, 160, 180; of 1948, 20, 68, 181; of 1980, 14
coups d'état, attempted, 136, 156; against Betancourt, 182; against Pérez, xxii-xxiii, xxv; possibility of, xxvi, 28
credit cards, 117
Crespo, Joaquín, 14
Crespo administration (1892-98), 14
criminal justice system, 209-10; extradition in, 210; influences on, 209; offenses, 210; penalties, 210; problems in, 209; public defenders program, 209
criollos, 7, 49; in independence movement, 49, 139; social status of, 64
CSE. *See* Supreme Electoral Council
CTV. *See* Confederation of Venezuelan Workers
Cuba, xxiii; expelled from Organization of American States, 26; exports to, 126; influence on, 184; relations with, xxv, 26, 28, 169; as threat, 186, 192
Cuban Revolution, 25-26
Cumanagoto people, 48
Cumaná Province, 6
currency: devaluation, xxiii, 84, 86, 126, 155; fluctuation of, xxviii
Currency Exchange Office (Recadi): scandals in, 86
current account: deficit, 127; merchandise trade in, 127; services in, 127; transfers in, 127
customs: military responsibilities in, 193
Cuyuni River, 190
CVF. *See* Venezuelan Development Corporation
CVG. *See* Venezuelan Corporation of Guayana
CVN. *See* Venezuelan Children's Council
CVP. *See* Venezuelan Petroleum Corporation

Daily Journal, 166
death penalty, 210
Declaration of Principles and Governing Program, 24
defense budget: as percentage of government budget, 196; stability of, 196; under *trienio,* 180
defense spending, 195-96; control over, 195; limitations on, 195-96; as percentage of gross domestic product, 196; tightening of, xxv
Delgado Chalbaud, Carlos, 19, 180; assassinated, 21, 181; military junta under, 20-21, 181
Delta Amacuro territory, 137
democracy: commitment to, 154, 168, 173, 177; established, xxi, 135; threats to, 136; transition to, 135
Democratic Action (AD), xxii, 25, 87, 163, 164; agrarian reform under, 164-65; co-optation of military by, 156; coup by, 18-19, 160; in elections, 21, 23, 28, 31, 35, 37, 150-51, 152, 154; foreign relations under, 172; formed, 18, 162; interparty cooperation of, 24; leaders exiled, 21; outlawed, 21; peasant leagues of, 61, 162, 164-65; platform of, 20; relations of, with church, 68; role of middle class in, 162; social justice goals of, 60, 153, 155, 180; in *trienio* junta, 19, 180; underground activities of, 21
"Democratic Caesarism," 14-15, 22
Democratic National Bloc (BDN), 162
Democratic Republican Union (URD), 20, 25, 162; interparty cooperation of, 24, 28; leaders exiled, 21; in 1952 elections, 21; in 1958 elections, 23; in 1968 elections, 29; in 1973 elections, 30, 31
Deposit Insurance Corporation, 116
diamonds, 110, 111
Diario 2001, 166
Diego de Losada, 6
diet, 75
Dirección de Seguridad e Inteligencia Policial (Disip). *See* Directorate of Intelligence and Prevention Services
Directorate of Frontiers, 193
Directorate of Intelligence and Prevention Services (Disip), 208
Disip. *See* Directorate of Intelligence and Prevention Services
districts, 150
doctors, 75
Dominican missionaries, 69

Dominican Republic: political support for, 172
drug trafficking, xxiv, 147, 170, 203; efforts against, 194; role of Venezuela in, 206

earthquake of 1812, 9
Eastern Europe: relations with, 29
Eastern University, 74
economic development, 72; business participation in policy making for, 160; government commitment to, 153, 173; under Medina, 18; promotion of, 186
economic growth: under Leoni, 28; impact of, 66; and new home starts, 114
economic infrastructure, 12; program for developing, 17-18
economic institutions, 81
economic modernization, 17
economic policies, 82, 84-86; exchange-rate policy, 86; fiscal policy, 84-85; monetary policy, 85-86; of Pérez, xxvi
economic reform, 92
economy: agricultural, 177; under Betancourt, 27; under Lusinchi, 84; political cooperation in, 24; role of, in foreign policy, 155; role of bureaucracy in, 158; role of petroleum in, 97
Ecuador, 11; economic policies, 127; imports from, 125
education (*see also* schools), 70-74; abroad, 74; adult, 74; basic, 74; under Caldera, 29; compulsory, 70; in elite class, 59; free, 70, 71; government programs in, 153; under Guzmán, 13; impact of, 67; influences on, 70, 72; in middle class, 60; natural science in, 72; under Pérez, 22; under Pérez Jiménez, 71; preschool, 72; private, 20; reforms, 155; role of church in, 69, 70, 71, 156; social sciences in, 72; system, 74; technical, 74; vocational, 72
education, public, 15; desire for, 70; established, 71; government regulation of, 20
Eisenhower, Dwight D., 22
El Callao gold mine, 110
El Cerro Bolívar iron mine, 108
El Diario de Caracas, 166
elections, local: abstentions in, 152-53; of council members, 150; frequency of, 151; of governors, 137, 150, 151; of mayors, 151; of 1948; of 1989, 150-51
elections, national, 151-52; constitutional provisions for, 138; frequency of, 151; legitimacy of, 152; of 1947, 20, 180; of 1952, 21, 181; of 1957, 22; of 1958, 23, 182; of 1963, 26, 27; of 1968, 28-29; of 1973, 30-31; of 1978, 35; of 1983, 37; of 1988, 152; outcomes of, 154; quotient system in, 152; regulation of, 138
electoral system, 151-53; ballots in, 151; participation in, 151; registration in, 151
electricity (*see also under hydroelectric*): capacity, 103-4; consumption, 103-4; generation, 103, 143, 169; thermal, 103
elite class, 58-59, 177; composition of, 41, 58-59; education in, 59, 72; ethnic makeup of, 59; mores of, 59; permeability of, 59; professions of, 59; religion of, 59; women in, 59
El Mundo, 166
El Nacional, 166
El Salvador, 185
El Tocuyo: slave trade in, 5
El Universal, 166
Emparán, Vicente, 9
encomienda system, 82
Escalante, Diógenes, 18
Echeverría Alvarez, Luis, 31
España, José María, 50
Essequibo region, 189; dispute over, 169, 190
Estrada, Pedro, 21
ethnic groups, 48-50, 63-66; ancestry of, 49; breakdown of, 63; in elite class, 59; in middle class, 59; perceptions of, 49; racial mixture among, 63, 64; relations among, 49
Europe: education in, 74; immigrants from, 53; iron exported to, 110; foreign investment under, 171-72; trade with, 100
European Economic Community: voluntary restraint agreement with, 108
exchange-rate: liberalization, 95; manipulation, 125; policies, 86, 123; system, 84, 86
exchange rates, multiple, 124
executive, 140-43; elections of, 140-41; qualifications for, 140; stability of, 154
exporters: tax rebates for, 126

exports, 125–26; agricultural, 3, 7, 12, 15, 41, 50, 94; agriculture as percentage of, 89; of gold, 111; income from, 77; of iron, 110; leather, 7; nontraditional, 125; petroleum, 97, 101; traditional, 50, 125; to the United States, 126
Extended Fund Facility, 131
Exxon, 98

FAC. *See* Armed Forces of Cooperation
Falcón, Juan C.: as president, 13
Falcón state, 48
Falklands/Malvinas conflict, 171
FALN. *See* Armed Forces of National Liberation
FAN. *See* National Armed Forces
farming. *See* agriculture
Federación de Cámaras y Asociaciones de Comercio y Producción (Fedecámaras). *See* Federation of Chambers and Associations of Commerce and Production
Federación Estudiantil de Venezuela (FEV). *See* Venezuelan Student Federation
federalism, 13, 139, 140
Federal Republic of Germany, 124; exports to, 126; investment by, 128
Federal War (1858–63), 13, 50
Federation of Chambers and Associations of Commerce and Production (Fedecámaras), 88, 160
FEI. *See* Independent Electoral Front
feminist movement, 67
Ferdinand VII, 9, 10, 11
Fernández, Lorenzo, 31
Ferrominera, 108
FEV. *See* Venezuelan Student Federation
Fiat, 112
financial aid: oil money used for, 30, 31; oil subsidies as, 184; from United States, 130
financial infrastructure, 115
financial restructuring, 116
financial sector: components of, 115; reform of, 85
First Republic, 9
fiscal accounts, 84–85
fishing, 96–97
FIV. *See* Venezuelan Investment Fund
FND. *See* National Democratic Front
Fondo de Inversiones de Venezuela (FIV). *See* Venezuelan Investment Fund
Fondo Nacional de Investigaciones Agropecuarios. *See* National Agricultural and Livestock Research Fund
food: imports, 92, 155; subsidies for, 25
food riots, 77, 84, 90, 123, 136–37, 154, 159, 206–7; casualties in, 62, 207; causes of, 130, 206–7
Ford, 112
Foreign Commerce Institute, 142
foreign debt, 38, 77, 128–30, 158; attempts to pay, 37, 99; debt-for-equity program, 130; interest payments on, 85; management efforts, 129; payments, 129; private, 129; public-sector, 35, 37; reduction, 129; rescheduling agreements, 129; size of, 36; from United States, 171
foreign exchange: authority, 85; generated by mining industry, 105; generated by steel industry, 108; system, 37
foreign investment, 111, 171–72
foreign loans, 13, 34–35, 36
foreign policy, 29–30; presidential authority over, 141; role of economy in, 155
foreign relations, 29, 167–73; economic relations, 124–32; under Pérez, xxv; principles of, 167
foreign trade, 124–27; contraband, 125; deficit, 124; policy, 126
Foreign Trade Institute, 126
forestry, 97, 131
forests, 92
Formula One, 163
France: imports from, 124; influence of, on education system, 72; military training in, 179
Franciscan missionaries, 6
Frente Electoral Independiente (FEI). *See* Independent Electoral Front
Frente Nacional Democrática (FND). *See* National Democratic Front
Frente Sandinista de Liberación Nacional. (FSLN). *See* Sandinista National Liberation Front
FSLN. *See* Sandinista National Liberation Front
Fuerzas Armadas de Cooperación (FAC). *See* Armed Forces of Cooperation
Fuerzas Armadas de Liberación Nacional

(FALN). *See* Armed Forces of National Liberation
Fuerzas Armadas Nacionales (FAN). *See* National Armed Forces

Gaceta de Caracas, 165
Gallegos, Rómulo, 162, 180; exiled, 20, 163; as president, 20, 163
gas, natural, xxii, 101-2; pipeline, 102; production, 36
GATT. *See* General Agreement on Tariffs and Trade
Gaviria, César, 170
GDP. *See* gross domestic product
General Agreement on Tariffs and Trade (GATT): adherence to, 126
Generalized System of Trade Preferences, 32
General Motors, 112
Generation of 1928, xxi, 16, 17, 136, 162, 163
geography, 42-48, 182; climate, 45-46; hydrography, 46-47; regions, 42; topography, 42-45
gold, xxii; exploration for, 5; exports, 111; foreign interests in, 111; illegal mining of, 191-92; production, 110-11; reserves, 110
Golfo de Guajira. *See* Golfo de Venezuela
Golfo de Venezuela, 169, 188
Gómez, Juan Vicente, 14, 50-51, 58, 179; background, 51; death of, 136; efforts to overthrow, 16
Gómez dictatorship (1908-35), 14; army under, 14, 179; corruption under, 179; discovery of oil under, xxi; dissidents exiled by, 162; education under, 71; secret police under, 14
government, local, 85, 137, 149-51; elections, 150; structure, 149
government, national: division of powers in, 139; economic development by, 140; goals of, 142; relations of, with church, 68; spending, 85
government, state: administrative structure of, 137-38; governors of, 137; legislative assemblies of, 137
governors: election of, 139, 142, 150
Graduate Institute of Public Administration (IESA), 148
Gran Colombia, 11, 135; division of, 12
Gran Sabana, 45
Grenada: United States intervention in, 184
gross domestic product (GDP): agriculture as percentage of, 89; construction as percentage of, 114; decline in, 36; financial aid as percentage of, 131; government spending as percentage of, 85; growth of, xxiii, xxviii; military spending as percentage of, 196; in 1980s, 81; in 1990s, xxiv, xxviii; oil-related, xxiii-xxiv, 97
Guajiro people, 48, 49; culture of, 49, 66; religion of, 68
Gual, Manuel, 50
Guárico State, 92, 93
Guasina Island concentration camp, 21
Guatemala, 185; oil exploration in, 100
Guayana Province, 6
guerrilla warfare, 26, 170
Guevara, Ernesto "Che," 30
Guiana highlands, 45, 97
Guri Dam, 103, 169
Guyana: oil exploration in, 100; relations with, 169, 189-91; territory disputes with, 169, 189-91
Guzmán Blanco, Antonio, 13
Guzmán administration (1870-88): corruption in, 13; established, 13; public education established under, 71

hacendados, 41
Haiti, xxv
health (*see also* population statistics), 74-76; causes of death, 75; diet, 75; endemic diseases, 75; government programs in, 153; military responsibilities in, 193-194; public, 75, 76; reforms, 155
health care, 16; availability of, 75-76; facilities, 75, 76, 77; under Pérez, 22; personnel, 75; subsidies for, 25
Herrera administration, 35-37; austerity measures under, 36-37; foreign affairs under, 188; spending under, 83-84
Herrera Campíns, Luis, 35, 167, 170
Herring, Hubert, 21
Honduras, 185
House of Welser, 5
housing (*see also ranchos*): subsidies for, 25

Hydrocarbons Reversion Law (1971), 29, 101
hydroelectric generation, xxii, 48, 103; expansion of, 104; potential, 103
hydroelectric industry, 33, 83
Hypothesis of Caraballeda, 188

IDB. *See* Inter-American Development Bank, 31
IESA. *See* Graduate Institute of Public Administration
IMF. *See* International Monetary Fund
immigration, 54-55; from Africa, 54; from Argentina, 54; from Chile, 54; from Colombia, 54, 169; from Europe, 53, 54, 160; illegal, 55, 169, 189; from the Middle East, 54; military responsibilities in, 193; from Spain, 49, 53, 54; from Uruguay, 54; of workers, 54, 55; after World War II, 53-54
import: liberalization, 125; licensing restrictions, 125; policy, 125; protection, 84
imports, 126; of food, 51, 92; impact of oil on, 124; increase in, 15, 51; total, 124
INA. *See* National Agrarian Institute
income: of blue-collar laborers, 87; distribution, 33, 87, 118; during oil boom, xxi; per capita, 136; tax laws, 18; of white-collar laborers, 87
independence, 3; declared, 9, 135; effect of, 41-42, 82
independence, war of: battles in, 8, 9, 10, 11; legacy of, 138-39; militias in, 178
independence movement: blacks in, 50; criollos in, 49; effects of, 12; influences on, 70; *pardos* in, 50
Independent Electoral Front (FEI): formed, 21
Independent Moral Movement, 164
Independent Venezuelan Association, 160
Indian Commission, 69
Indians (*see also under individual peoples*), 49; in colonial hierarchy, 7; conversion of, to Christianity, 69; cultures of, 63; destruction of, 63; education of, 69; geographical distribution of, 48; as percentage of population, 7, 63; population of, 48; religion of, 66, 67-68, 70; social structure among, 61; tribute from, 50
indigo: under *encomienda* system, 82
indocumentados, 55, 169; number of, 189
Industrial Bank of Venezuela (BIV), 116
industrial development: autonomous entities under, 33; under Caldera, 29; in Ciudad Guayana, 33-34; government programs in, 153; under Pérez, 33; oil profits used for, 51; semiautonomous entities under, 33
industrial infrastructure, 33
industrialization, 67
Industria Venezolana de Aluminio C.A. (Venalum), 106
industry (*see also under individual industries*): credit subsidies for, 126; electricity consumed by, 103-4; expansion of, 82; financing for, 117; geographical distribution of, 45; lobby, 160; local, 24; subsidies for, 24
Infantería de Marina. *See* Marine Infantry
inflation, 86; attempts to decrease, xxiii; under Herrera, 36; increases in, 15, 155; in 1980s, 88
infrastructure development, 13, 82; under Leoni, 28; under Pérez, 131
INP. *See* National Port Institute
Instituto de Estudios Superiores de Administración (IESA). *See* Graduate Institute of Public Administration
Instituto Nacional Agrario (INA). *See* National Agrarian Institute
Instituto Nacional de Puertos (INP). *See* National Port Institute
Instituto Postal Telegráfico (Ipostel). *See* Postal and Telegraph Institute
Instituto Venezolano de Petroquímicas (IVP). *See* Venezuelan Petrochemical Institute
Instituto Venezolano de Seguro Social (IVSS). *See* Venezuelan Social Security Institute
Interamericana de Alúmina (Interalumina), 105-6; production, 106
Inter-American Development Bank (IDB), 31, 131
interest groups, 155-62; armed forces as, 155-56
interest rates, 85-86; liberalized, 118; policies, 116, 117; subsidized, 118
International Monetary Fund (IMF); loans from, 84, 128, 131
investment: foreign, 127, 128; private, 125

Ipostel. *See* Postal and Telegraph Institute
iron: export of, 81, 110; industry, xxii, 106, 112; mines, 34; production, 108-10; reserves, 108
irrigation, 92-93, 96
Italian News Agency (ANSA), 166
Italy: coal exported to, 110; imports from, 124
IVP. *See* Venezuelan Petrochemical Institute
IVSS. *See* Venezuelan Social Security Institute

Jamaica, 10
Japan: exports to, 126; iron exported to, 110
Japanese Export-Import Bank, 128
Jews, 67
Joint General Staff, 197
judges, 147; corrupt, 206; powers of, 147; salaries of, 147; selection of, 147; shortage of, 209; system of appointing, 209
Judicial Council, 209
judiciary, 145-47; court structure, 146-47; *fuero militar* (military privilege), 147; judicial districts, 146; military tribunals, 147; organization of, 145; status of, 145
junta of 1958, 23

Kobe Steel Company, 108

labor: government support for, 24; laws, 87; movement, 136; relations, 88
labor force, 86-89; in agriculture, 87, 89; in commerce, 87; in construction, 114; formal sector, 86-88; in the government, 87; informal sector, 89; in manufacturing, 87, 111, 112; in mining, 87; number of workers in, 86, 89; as percentage of population, 87; in the petroleum industry, 87; rights of workers in, 87; in service industry, 87; women in, 42, 87
labor unions, 87-88; harassed by Pérez administration, 21; influence of political parties on, xxii; newspapers of, 166; number of workers in, 87; organization of, 17; outlawed, 17; as political interest group, 160, 165; protests by, xxiv; Roman Catholic, 161; teachers', 71
La Crítica, 166
LAFTA. *See* Latin American Free Trade Association
Lago de Maracaibo, 3, 4, 42, 48
Lagoven, 98
La Guaira, 6; AIDS in, 75; port, 122
land concentration, 91
land reform (*see also* agrarian reform), 27, 83; benefits of, 91; failure rate in, 91; under junta of 1958, 20, 91
land tenure, 91
land use, 91-92
La Patria Boba. *See* First Republic
Lara state, 48
La Religión, 165
Larrazábal, Wolfgang, 23, 29, 181-82
Latin American Economic System (SELA), 31-32, 126
Latin American Free Trade Association (LAFTA), 126
Latin American Integration Association, 168
LAV. *See* Venezuelan Airmail Line
law enforcement agencies, 208-9
Law of Unjustified Dismissals (1974), 32
Law on Immigration and Settlement (1936), 53-54
leather: export of, 7
Legion of Merit, 22
legislation, 144-45; initiation of, 144; cooperation in producing, 154
legislature, 143-45; elections, 143, 145; under 1961 constitution, 25, 143; party caucus in, 143
León, Juan Francisco de, 8
Leoni administration, 28, 182; cabinet in, 142; foreign policy under, 168-69
Leoni, Raúl, 16, 27, 136, 167; attempted coup against, 156
Levine, Daniel H., 26
Liberals, 12, 13
Lieuwen, Edwin, 14
Línea Aeropostal Venezolana (LAV). *See* Venezuelan Airmail Line
Lionza, María: cult of, 69-70
literacy: programs, 194; rate, xxi, 72, 155
livestock industries, 95; beef, 95; cattle, 41, 81, 95; pork, 92, 95; poultry, 92, 95; subsidies, 95
llaneros: in independence movement, 10; under Second Republic, 10
Llovera Páez, Luis Felipe, 21

López administration (1935–41): economic modernization under, 17; political expression under, 17
López Contreras, Eleazar, 17, 179
lower class, xxv, 62; church assistance to, 62; composition of, 41, 62; education for, 72
lumber industry, 33
Lusinchi, Jaime, xxviii, 37
Lusinchi administration, 84; agriculture under, 89–90; austerity measures under, 155; foreign debt under, 155

Macagua hydroelectric generation plants, 104
Machado, Gustavo, 136
Madrid Hurtado, Miguel de la, 185
Maiquetía International Airport, 122
manufacturing, 111–14; categories of, 112; domestic, 111; expansion of, 111; export of products, 113; inefficiency in, 111; labor force in, 87, 111, 112; nationalization of, 111; as percentage of gross domestic product, 111; structure of, 112
Maracaibo: AIDS in, 75; Guajiro people in, 66; illegal immigrants in, 55; migration to, 51; military region, 197; newspapers in, 166; population of, 53; port, 122; schools in, 74
Maracaibo Basin, 6
Maracaibo lowlands, 42; oil reserves in, 100; percentage of population living in, 52
Maraven, 99
March Resources Limited, 111
Marine Infantry, 182
marketing boards, 94
Martial Court, 210
MAS. *See* Movement Toward Socialism
mass media, 165–67; news agencies, 166; newspapers, 67, 165–66; shut down by Pérez, 21, 181; as source of information, 167
matériel: domestic production of, 196; importation of, 196; oil revenues for, 179; procurement of, 179
mayors, 151
Medina administration, 18
Medina Agarita, Isaías, 18, 162, 179; overthrown, 18–19
Meneven, 99
MEP. *See* People's Electoral Movement
Mérida de Maracaibo Province, 6
Mérida state, 48; migration from, 53; schools in, 74
Meridiano, 166
mestizos, 48, 49; as percentage of population, 63; social status of, 64
Metalmeg steel plant, 108
Metropolitan Police Force of Caracas, 209
Metropolitan Urban Commission, 55
Mexican Revolution (1910), 16
Mexico: in Contadora Group, 170, 184–85; in San José Accord, 184; under Spanish rule, 5
middle class, 59–61; beginning of, 15; composition of, 41, 59–60; education in, 60, 72; ethnic makeup of, 59–60; permeability of, 60; political activities of, xxvii, 60, 161–62; professions of, 60; social background of, 59–60; and social justice ethic, 60–61; women in, 59, 60, 67
Midwestern University, 74
military: capabilities, 192; doctrine, 192; manpower, 194–95; problems, 192; security posture, 184; training, of foreign troops, 179; tribunals, 210
Military Academy: enrollment in, 180; established, 179
Military Aviation School, 201
military personnel: benefits, 195; pay, 195; retirement, 195
militia system, 177–78, 179
Minas Carbón, 110
mining industry, 83, 104–11, 131; government role in, 104; labor force in, 87; profits, 105
ministers, 141–42
Ministry of Agriculture and Livestock, 90, 96
Ministry of Education: social justice goals of, 60
Ministry of Energy and Mines, 103
Ministry of Finance, 85, 130
Ministry of Foreign Affairs, 193
Ministry of Health and Social Welfare, 76; social justice goals of, 60
Ministry of Interior, 208
Ministry of Justice, 208, 210; church's operating expenses paid by, 68; courts of special jurisdiction under, 146–47; Indian Commission of, 69
Ministry of Labor, 87

Ministry of National Defense, 193, 196; Superior Board of, 197
Ministry of Public Education, 71
Ministry of Transport and Communications, 123, 166
Ministry of Urban Development, 114
MIR. *See* Movement of the Revolutionary Left
Miranda, Francisco de, xxi, 8, 178; army commanded by, 9; background of, 8; death of, 9; desire of, for independence, 8; surrender by, to Monteverde, 9
missionaries, 6, 69
Monagas, José Gregorio, 12
Monagas, José Tadeo, 12
Monagas administration (1846-58), 12; ousted, 13
monetary policy, 85-86; revisions of, 85
Monteverde, Domingo, 9
mountains, 42-45
Mount Roraima, 189
Movement of the Revolutionary Left (MIR), 26, 35, 152, 208; congressional representatives arrested, 26; outlawed, 26; students in, 161
Movement Toward Socialism (MAS), 30, 31, 35, 152, 154, 163
Movimiento al Socialismo (MAS). *See* Movement Toward Socialism
Movimiento de la Izquierda Revolucionaria (MIR). *See* Movement of the Revolutionary Left
Movimiento Electoral del Pueblo (MEP). *See* People's Electoral Movement
municipalities, 149-51

Naricual coal mine, 110
National Agrarian Institute (INA), 56, 91, 158
National Agricultural and Livestock Research Fund, 96
National Armed Forces (FAN), xxii, 183; Laws and Regulations of, 194
National Democratic Front (FND), 28, 29
National Democratic Party (PDN), 17, 162; legalized, 18
National Drug Commission, 206
National Electricity Company (CADAFE), 103
National Fishing Enterprise, 97
National Guard. *See* Armed Forces of Cooperation
National Housing Institute, 114
National Institute of Female Orientation, 210
National Intelligence Service, 197
nationalism, 11-12, 64
nationalization, 3-4, 34, 83, 98, 111, 149, 106, 153
National Opinion (Opina), 154, 163
National Opposition Union (UNO), 131
National Pedagogic Institute, 71
National Plan, Fifth, 33, 34
National Port Institute (INP), 121, 122
National Savings and Loan Bank (Banap), 118
National Securities Commission, 116
National Security and Defense Council, 197
National Security Police (SN), 21, 181
National Students Union, 161
National University of Carabobo, 71
National University of Zulia, 71
Naval Academy, 200
Naval Armament Training Center, 200
Naval Infantry Training Center, 200
Naval Police School, 200
Naval Postgraduate School, 200
Naval Superior War College, 200
Naval Training Center, 200
navy, 192, 199-200; administration of, 200; aviation, 200; insignia, 202, 203, 204, 205; matériel, 200; under Pérez, 181; personnel, 199-200; ranks, 202; reorganized, 180; training, 200; uniforms, 202
New Alternative, 164
New Democratic Generation, 154, 164
New Granada (*see also* Colombia), 10, 11, 188
New National Ideal doctrine, 22
newspapers, 165-66; censored, 166; corruption exposed by, 166; impact of, 67
Nicaragua, 170; oil debt canceled, 170; relations with, 170-71; United Nations peacekeeping mission in, 170
Nueva Generación Democrática. *See* New Democratic Generation, 154
nurses, 75
Nynas, 101

OAS. *See* Organization of American States

Office of Integrated Educational Planning, 158
Office of the President, 83
officers: cliquishness among, 179-80; commissioned, 194; mutual aid fund for, 179; noncommissioned, 194; training, 199; training abroad, 179
Officers Club, 181
Oficina Central de Coordinación y Planificación (Cordiplan). *See* Central Office of Coordination and Planning
oil (*see also* petroleum): discovery of, xxi, 98; diversification from, 126; effect of, on class system, 41-42; effect of, on import patterns, 124; exploration, 17, 51, 58, 99-100, 136, 172; export of, 81, 82, 97, 101, 124, 125, 182, 186; and gross domestic product, xxiii-xxiv; impact of, on military, 177; impact of, on society, 51, 182; income from, 34, 177, 186; price of, 4, 36, 77; production of, 81; refining, 100, 101, 172; reserves, 81, 97, 100, 187; strategic importance of, 187; subsidies, 184
oil boom, 82; effect of, on economy, 83-84, 128, 136; effect of, on society, xxi
oil industry, 15, 98, 177; corruption in, 98; impact of, on society, 53; as military mission, 183; nationalized, 83, 98, 149; problems in, xxviii; revenues used to purchase matériel, 179; taxes on, 20, 82
oil workers, 82; strike by, 17
Ojeda, Alfonso de, 4
OPEC. *See* Organization of the Petroleum Exporting Countries
Opina. *See* National Opinion
Opinión Nacional (Opina). *See* National Opinion
Organic Law of Education (1980), 72
Organización Venezolana (Orve). *See* Venezuelan Organization
Organization of American States (OAS), 175; Cuba expelled from, 26; embargo of Haiti under, xxv; membership in, 167
Organization of the Petroleum Exporting Countries (OPEC), 27; control of exports by, 126; membership in, 83, 155, 167, 172; and price of crude oil, 4
Organization of the Petroleum Exporting Countries Fund, 130
orimulsión, 100
Orinoco Asphalt (Bitúmenes del Orinoco), 100
Orinoco Delta, 45; agriculture in, 56; oil reserves in, 100; rainfall in, 46
Orinoco plains, 45
Orinoco Steelworks (Sidor) (*see also* steel industry), 33; debt of, 108; nationalized, 106; profit of, 108
Ortega, Daniel, 170
Orve (Organización Venezolana). *See* Venezuelan Organization

Pact of Punto Fijo, 24, 23
Páez, José Antonio, 10, 50, 61, 178; nationalism under, 11-12; as president, 12, 135
Páez administration (1830-46), 12
Panama: in Contadora Group, 170, 184-85; relations with, 169; slave labor in, 5
Panorama, 166
pardos, 7, 49; in independence movement, 50, 139
Partido Comunista Venezolano (PCV). *See* Venezuelan Communist Party
Partido Democrático Nacional (PDN). *See* National Democratic Party
Partido Democrático Venezolano (PDV). *See* Venezuelan Democratic Party
Partido Republicano Progresista (PRP). *See* Progressive Republican Party
Party of the Venezuelan Revolution, 164
Patriotic Junta, 161; demonstrations by, 23; organized, 22
Patriotic Military Union (UPM), 18-19, 180
patronage, 81, 159
Paz Galarraga, Jesús Angel, 28, 30
PCV. *See* Venezuelan Communist Party
PDN. *See* National Democratic Party
PDV. *See* Venezuelan Democratic Party
PDVSA. *See* Venezuelan Petroleum Corporation
pearls, 4, 81
peasant leagues, 61, 164-65
peasants, 61-62; composition of, 61; political activities of, 61; settlement patterns of, 61; urban migration by, 62
People's Advance, 164
People's Electoral Movement (MEP), 28, 30, 35, 164

Península de la Guajira, 188; Guajiro people in, 66
Península de Paria, 4
peninsulares, 7, 49
Pequiven. *See* Venezuelan Petrochemicals
Pérez, Carlos Andrés, 30, 31, 76; attempted assassination of, xxviii; campaign promises of, 149; election of, 138, 141
Pérez administration, first (1974–79), 31; economic reform under, xxii, 81; employment programs under, 32–33; Fifth National Plan of, 33, 34; foreign investment under, 171–72; oil windfall under, 31; spending by, 35; subsidies under, 32–33; support by, of Sandinistas, 185
Pérez administration, second (1989–): agriculture under, 90; attempted coup of, xxii–xxiii, xxv; austerity measures under, 155; corruption in, xxv, xxvii; economic reform under, xxii, xxiii, xxvi, xxvii, 81, 84, 90; foreign affairs under, xxv; foreign investment under, 171–72; industrial investment under, 113; measures by, against drug trafficking, 206; newer industries under, 113; protests against, xxvi, 159; reaction of, to protests, xxvii, 159; research and development under, 113; social welfare under, xxiii; structural adjustments under, 84, 90
Pérez Alfonso, Juan Pablo, 27
Pérez Jiménez, Marcos, 19, 21; as dictator, 21; Independent Electoral Front organized by, 21; opposition to, 22–23; Patriotic Military Union founded by, 180; resignation of, 23; United States support for, 22
Pérez Jiménez dictatorship, xxi, 181; corruption in, 68; education under, 71; immigration under, 54, 160; military under, xxii, 181; mining under, 106; ostentatious construction projects of, 22; overthrow of, 68, 148, 156, 181; protests against, 161; rights repressed under, 21, 163; social services ignored by, 22
Peru: battles for liberation from Spain, 11; imports from, 125; military training in, 179; relations with, 169; under Spanish rule, 5
Petkoff, Teodoro, 164
petrochemicals, xxii, 102–3; complexes, 102–3; export of, 125; production of, 102
Petróleos de Venezuela, S.A. (PDVSA). *See* Venezuelan Petroleum Corporation
petroleum (*see also* oil), 97–101; deposits, 42, 48; discovery of, 6; influence of, on politics, 4; influence of, on society, 15; as principal export, 3; production, 82; products, 100; revenues, 85; role of, in economy, 97
petroleum industry, 81, 83; under Caldera, 29; control of, 3, 29; corruption in, 102; growth of, 16; illegal immigrants working in, 55; labor force in, 87; lobby, 160; military responsibilities in, 193; nationalization of, 3–4, 34, 153; as percentage of gross domestic product, 97; taxes on, 85
Petroquímicas de Venezuela (Pequiven). *See* Venezuelan Petrochemicals
Piar, Manuel, 10
Piñerua Ordaz, Luis, 35
Polar brewery, 113
Police Academy, 209
police forces: local, 208, 209; national, 208
Policía Técnica y Judicial (PTJ). *See* Technical and Judicial Police
political parties, 144, 162–64; influence of, xxii; legalized, 19; newspapers of, 166; outreach by, to lower class, 62; radical, 203
political uprisings: anti-Gómez, 16; anti-Guzmán, 13; anti-Pérez, xxvii, 23, 154, 207; government reaction to, xxvii; military responsibilities in, 194
Polytechnic University of the Armed Forces, 199
Popular Unity, 30, 31
population, 48–53, 182; age distribution of, 53; in Caracas, 41, 45; geographical distribution of, 42, 45, 51–52; Indians as percentage of, 7; Indian tribes, 48; in 1990, 51; in urban areas, 41, 52; workers as percentage of, 87
population statistics: accuracy of, 52; birth rate, 52; death rate, 52, 75; density, 41; fertility rate, 52; growth rate, 52; infant mortality rate, 52–53, 75; life expectancy, 53, 75, 155; mortality rates, 52
port facilities: construction of, 13, 51; oil

profits used for, 51
Portuguesa state, 92, 93
Postal and Telegraph Institute (Ipostel), 123
poverty, xxi, 33
precious metals, 81
president (*see also* executive): armed forces under, 196; under constitution of 1961, 25, 138, 140-43; former, as senator for life, 138, 145; limitations on, 141; ministerial responsibility of, 141; powers of, 138, 141, 144; terms of office, 138
press. *See* mass media
price controls, 86
Prieto, Luis B., 28
prison: conditions, 210; kinds of, 210; population, 210
prison system, 210-12; conditional liberty in, 211; military responsibilities in, 193, 210; problems in, 211
privatization, 158, 159
professions: in elite class, 59; in middle class, 59-60; of women, 59, 60
Progressive Republican Party (PRP), 162
Protection Law for Mortgage Owners (1989), 118
Protestant churches: outreach by, to lower class, 62; power of, 67
Protocol of Port-of-Spain, 190
Pro-Venezuela, 160
PRP. *See* Progressive Republican Party
PTJ. *See* Technical and Judicial Police
public administration, 147-49
Public Administration Committee, 148
public policy, 164-65
public sector: employment in, xxii; privatization of, 142-43; production, 125
public spending, xxiii
public works, 13, 15; oil profits used for, 51
Puerto Cabello, 122
Puerto Ordaz, 105, 121-22

racial: mixture, 63, 64; tension, 77
Radical Cause, 164
radio: educational programming on, 71; impact of, 67; receivers, number of, 167
Radio Caracas Television, 167
Radio Nacional, 167
Rafael Urdaneta University, 74
railroads, 121; construction of, 13, 36
Ramo Verde School, 202
Ranchers' and Livestock Association, 160
ranchos, 26, 30, 56, 114; attempts to gain title to, 62; residents of, xxv
Rangel, José Vicente, 30
Ravard, Rafael Alfonso, 34, 37
Reagan, Ronald, 187
Reagan administration, 187
Real Compañía Guipuzcoana de Caracas. *See* Caracas Company
Recadi. *See* Currency Exchange Office
Red Flag (BR), 208
Régimen de Cambio de Dinero (Recadi). *See* Currency Exchange Office
regionalism, 64, 67
religion (*see also under individual sects*), 67-70; freedom of, 68; Indian, 69; role of women in, 69; syncretic, 69; traditional, 67-68
Renault, 112
Republican National Union (UNR), 162
Reuters, 166
Revolutionary Action Group, 164
Ricardos, Felipe, 8
Río Apure, 46
Río Caroní, 48, 103
Río Orinoco, 6, 45, 46
Río Orinoco Delta: exploration of, 4
Ríos, Antonio, xxvii
Río Unare Basin, 6
roads, 118-21; construction of, 13, 51, 131; highway system, 51, 121, 131; military responsibilities in, 193; network size, 121
Roman Catholic Church: attitudes toward, 68; expenses of, paid by government, 68; labor organization, 161; outreach by, to lower class, 62; political activities of, 24, 156-58; relations of, with Democratic Action, 68; relations of, with government, 69; role of, in education, 20, 69, 70, 71; schools, 69; television station of, 167; under *trienio,* 68; weakness of, 67
Roman Catholics: adherence of, to traditional beliefs, 68, 69; elite as, 59; Indians as, 49, 66, 68; political affiliations of, 19-20
Root, Elihu, 14
Rousseau, Jean-Jacques, 70
rural areas: defined, 53; health care in,

75–76; income in, 87; life in, 61; population in, 53; schools in, 71
Russian Revolution (1917), 16

Salesian missionaries, 69
San Antonio de Táchira meeting, 188
San Cristóbal military region, 197
Sandinista National Liberation Front (FSLN), 131, 170, 185; arms supplied to, 185
San Fernando military region, 197
San Isidro iron mine, 108
sanitation, 131
San José Accord, 101, 126, 131, 184
Santander, Francisco dc Paula, 11
Santiago de León de Caracas, 6
savings and loan associations, 118
School of the Americas (Fort Benning), 199
schools (*see also* education): enrollments in, 74; private, 60, 72; public, 71, 72; Roman Catholic, 69
Second Republic, 10
Securidad Nacional (SN). *See* National Security Police
security, internal, xxiii, 203–8; border security problems, 203–6; drug trafficking, 203; threats to, 203
security zones, 193
SELA. *See* Latin American Economic System
sembrar el petróleo. *See* sowing the oil
Senate (*see also* Congress), 18, 143, 154
service industry, 81; labor force in, 87; lobby, 160
Shell Oil, 99
shipbuilding industry, 33
Siderúrgica del Orinoco (Sidor). *See* Orinoco Steelworks
Sidor. *See* Orinoco Steelworks
Simón Bolívar United World Agriculture Institute, 96
Singapore Aerospace Industries, 201
Sistema Económico Latinoamericano (SELA). *See* Latin American Economic System
Sivensa steel mill, 108
slave raiding, 4–5
slavery, 63–64, 82; abolished, 12, 50
slaves, 49; in colonial hierarchy, 7; demand for, 7
slave trade, 7
SN. *See* National Security Police
Social Christian Party (COPEI), xxii, 149, 163, 164; co-optation of military by, 156; in elections, 21, 23, 29, 31, 35, 151, 152, 154; foreign relations under, 172; founded, 19–20, 156, 161, 162; interparty cooperation of, 24; leaders exiled, 21; role of middle class in, 162; role of Roman Catholic Church in, 20, 68, 69, 156; social justice goals of, 60 153, 155
social infrastructure, 12; program for developing, 17–18
Socialist League, 164
social policies, 82
social reform, 83; government commitment to, 153
social security, 77–78; laws, introduced, 18; system, 85
social structure: of barrios, 62; ethnic groups in, 66; fluidity of, 66; of Guajiro people, 49, 66; Indian, 61, 63; organization of, 64
social welfare, 70–78; under Caldera, 29; impact of, 67; organizations, private, 77; under Pérez, xxiii; program, 76; role of church in, 156
society: colonial, 7; impact of coffee on, 50, 82; impact of oil on, xxi, 15, 51, 53, 82
Somoza Debayle, Anastasio, 170, 184
South America: European exploration of, 4
Soviet Union: relations with, 29, 172
sowing the oil, 27, 82, 111, 121, 128, 153
Spain: American colonies of, 3; coal exported to, 110; conquest of Americas by, 63, 81; immigrants from, 49
Spaniards: social status of, 64
Spanish language: spoken by Indians, 66
"Spirit of the 23rd of January," 24, 25
Staff College, 199
standard of living, xxi
state-owned enterprises, 85; creation of, 158; debt incurred by, 158
states: autonomy of, 139; dependence of, 139; powers of, 139, 150
steamship company, 33
steel: export of, 81, 125; production of, 143
steel industry (*see also* Orinoco Steelworks), xxii, 33, 36, 81, 106, 112; competition in, 108; exports, 108; investment

in, 130; military responsibilities in, 193; nationalized, 83, 106; production, 108; subsidies, 108
stock market (*see also* Caracas Stock Exchange): fluctuations in, xxviii
strategic setting, 182–86
strikes, general: of 1936, 17; of 1957, 23; of 1989, 88; of 1992, xxiv
strikes, labor, 17
structural adjustment program, 86, 92; electricity under, 104; imports under, 125; public reaction to, 130
student demonstrations: by Generation of 1928, 161; anti-Gómez, 16, 136; anti-Guzmán, 13; anti-Pérez, xxiv, xxvii, 207
students: leftist, 25–26, 162, 203
Suárez Flanerich, Germán, 21, 181
Suárez González, Adolfo, 170
subsidies, 84; curtailment of, 126; for dairy industry, 95; elimination of, xxiii; for farmers, 96; for food, 25; for health care, 25; for housing, 25; for interest rates, 118; for local industry, 24; for steel industry, 108
Sucre, 74
suffrage (*see also* voting): universal, instituted, 19
Superintendency of Banks, 116
Superintendency of Foreign Investment, 130, 142
Superintendency of Insurance, 116
Supreme Court of Justice, 144, 145–46, 210; chambers of, 145; corruption in, 206; members of, 145
Supreme Electoral Council (CSE), 151
Switzerland: investment by, 128

Táchira state, 14, 15, 16, 48; illegal immigrants in, 55; migration from, 53
tariffs, 124, 125
TASS, 166
teachers, 71, 72
Technical and Judicial Police (PTJ), 208
telecommunications, 122–23
telegraph network: construction of, 13
telephone company, 122
television: educational programming on, 71; impact of, 67; sets, number of, 167; stations, 167
Televisora Nacional, 167
textile industry, 33
Third Republic, 10–11; established, 10
Third World: foreign investment under, 171–72; outreach to, 186
timber industry, 97
Timoto-Cuica people, 5, 48
tobacco: as cash crop, 94; under *encomienda* system, 82; as export crop, 50, 94
Tocoma hydroelectric complex, 104
tourism, 123–24; foreign tourists, 124; investment in, 130; tourist arrivals, 123
Toyota, 112
Trade Act (1974), 32
Traffic Police, 209
transportation, 118–22; air, 122; in Caracas, 45; impact of, 67; infrastructure development, 13; land, 118–21; network, 45; rapid-rail, 56; water, 121–22
trienio junta (1945–48), 160, 162, 165, 177, 180; church-state relations under, 68; defense budget under, 180; dismantled, 21; teachers' unions under, 71
Trinidad, 4
Trinidad and Tobago, 190; oil exploration in, 100
Trujillo Molina, Rafael Leónidas, 26, 169
Trujillo state, 48; migration from, 53

Últimas Noticias, 166
UN. *See* United Nations
unemployment; in 1980s, 87, 155; in 1990s, xxiv
Unidad Popular. *See* Popular Unity
Unified Police Command, 208
Unión Nacional Opositora (UNO). *See* National Opposition Union
Unión Nacional Republicana (UNR). *See* Republican National Union
Unión Patriótica Militar (UPM). *See* Patriotic Military Union
Unión Republicana Democrática (URD). *See* Democratic Republican Union
United Nations (UN), 173; border dispute submitted to, 191; membership in, 168; peacekeeping mission in Nicaragua, 170
United Nations Food and Agriculture Organization, 75
United Nations Special Fund, 130
United Press International (UPI), 166
United States: agreement with, to restrict money laundering, 206; citizens living in Venezuela, 53; coal exported to, 110;

debt owed to, 171; education in, 74; exports to, 126; financial aid from, 130; import policies, 171; imports from, 124; influence of, on education system, 72; intervention in Grenada, 184; investment by, 128; iron exported to, 110; matériel from, 187; military mission to Venezuela, 180; military training in, 179, 186; oil exported to, 98–99, 101; relations with, 32, 171, 186–87; strategic relations with, 186–87; support of Pérez by, 22; trade with, 124; voluntary restraint agreement with, 108
United States Steel Corporation, 106
United States Treasury, 129
United Vanguard, 164
United Workers' Confederation of Venezuela, 161
Universidad Centro-Occidental. *See* Midwestern University
Universidad de Oriente. *See* Eastern University
universities (*see also under individual universities*), 74; enrollment in, 74; government interference in, 71; student protests in, 161; women in, 42, 67; women's studies programs in, 67
University of the Andes, 74
Unocal, 101
UNR. *See* Republican National Union
UPI. *See* United Press International
UPM. *See* Patriotic Military Union
upper class. *See* elite class
urban areas (*see also* urban migration): defined, 53; income in, 87; oil profits used to modernize, 51; population, 41, 53
urbanization: impact of, 67
urban migration, 52, 53, 66, 69, 114; attempts to reverse, 56; influence of, on agriculture, 92; by peasants, 62
URD. *See* Democratic Republican Union
Uslar Pietri, Arturo, 28

Valencia: concentration of population in, 52; population of, 53; schools in, 71, 74
Vallenilla Lanz, Laureano, 14
Vargas, Julio, 19, 180
Veba Oil Company, 101
Venalum. *See* Industria Venezolana de Aluminio C.A.
Venevisión, 167
Venezolana Internacional de Aviación S.A. (VIASA). *See* Venezuela International Airways
Venezuela International Airways (VIASA), 122
Venezuelan Airmail Line (LAV), 122
Venezuelan Chamber of the Broadcasting Industry, 167
Venezuelan Children's Council (CVN), 58
Venezuelan Communist Party (PCV), 17, 26, 30, 35, 152, 163–64; congressional representatives arrested, 26; legalized, 20, 30; outlawed, 26
Venezuelan Confederation of Labor, 21
Venezuelan Corporation of Guayana (CVG), 33, 83, 104; joint ventures of, 104–5
Venezuelan Democratic Party (PDV), 18
Venezuelan Development Corporation (CVF), 24, 158
Venezuelan Emergent Right, 163
Venezuelan Investment Fund (FIV), 31, 83, 85, 106, 131; plans to dissolve, 143; role of, 143
Venezuelan Military Industries Company (CAVIM), 196
Venezuelan Organization (Orve), 17, 162
Venezuelan Petrochemical Institute (IVP), 102
Venezuelan Petrochemicals (Pequiven), 102
Venezuelan Petroleum Corporation (CVP), 27, 34, 98
Venezuelan Petroleum Corporation (PDVSA), xxii, 34, 81, 85, 97, 142, 158; Citgo purchased by, 130; creation of, 98; exploration by, 99–100; government involvement in, 37; politicization of, 37; problems in, xxviii; subsidiaries of, 98–99, 100, 110
Venezuelan Shipping Company, 122
Venezuelan Social Security Institute (IVSS), 76
Venezuelan Student Federation (FEV), 17, 161
Venezuelan Television Network, 167
Venezuelan Tourism Corporation, 123
Vespucci, Amerigo, 4
VIASA. *See* Venezuela International Airways
vice president, 138
Viceroyalty of New Granada, 6
Victorious Front, 29

Villalba, Jóvito, 16, 17, 136, 162, 163; and Democratic Republican Union, 20, 30; in 1952 elections, 21
Voluntary Dividend for the Community, 77
Voluntary Restraint Agreement (VRA), 108
voting, 138, 151

wages: minimum, 87; real, decline in, 15
water: transport, 121-22; treatment, 131
Wells Aluminum, 106
West Germany. *See* Federal Republic of Germany
women: in elite class, 59; in labor force, 42; in middle class, 59, 60, 67; in military, 194-95; opportunities for, 67; in politics, 67; professions of, 75; and religion, 69; roles of, 67, 69; suffrage for, 19; in universities, 42, 67
women's studies programs, 67
Workers' Bank, 115
working class, 62
World Bank, 116; aid from, 128, 131
World War II, 18

Zulia coal and steel complex, 36
Zulia state, 48; coal deposits in, 110; illegal immigrants in, 55; petrochemical complex in, 103; schools in, 71
Zulia University, 74

Published Country Studies

(Area Handbook Series)

550-65	Afghanistan
550-98	Albania
550-44	Algeria
550-59	Angola
550-73	Argentina
550-169	Australia
550-176	Austria
550-175	Bangladesh
550-170	Belgium
550-66	Bolivia
550-20	Brazil
550-168	Bulgaria
550-61	Burma
550-50	Cambodia
550-166	Cameroon
550-159	Chad
550-77	Chile
550-60	China
550-26	Colombia
550-33	Commonwealth Caribbean, Islands of the
550-91	Congo
550-90	Costa Rica
550-69	Côte d'Ivoire (Ivory Coast)
550-152	Cuba
550-22	Cyprus
550-158	Czechoslovakia
550-36	Dominican Republic and Haiti
550-52	Ecuador
550-43	Egypt
550-150	El Salvador
550-28	Ethiopia
550-167	Finland
550-155	Germany, East
550-173	Germany, Fed. Rep. of
550-153	Ghana
550-87	Greece
550-78	Guatemala
550-174	Guinea
550-82	Guyana and Belize
550-151	Honduras
550-165	Hungary
550-21	India
550-154	Indian Ocean
550-39	Indonesia
550-68	Iran
550-31	Iraq
550-25	Israel
550-182	Italy
550-30	Japan
550-34	Jordan
550-56	Kenya
550-81	Korea, North
550-41	Korea, South
550-58	Laos
550-24	Lebanon
550-38	Liberia
550-85	Libya
550-172	Malawi
550-45	Malaysia
550-161	Mauritania
550-79	Mexico
550-76	Mongolia
550-49	Morocco
550-64	Mozambique
550-35	Nepal and Bhutan
550-88	Nicaragua
550-157	Nigeria
550-94	Oceania
550-48	Pakistan
550-46	Panama

550-156 Paraguay
550-185 Persian Gulf States
550-42 Peru
550-72 Philippines
550-162 Poland

550-181 Portugal
550-160 Romania
550-37 Rwanda and Burundi
550-51 Saudi Arabia
550-70 Senegal

550-180 Sierra Leone
550-184 Singapore
550-86 Somalia
550-93 South Africa
550-95 Soviet Union

550-179 Spain
550-96 Sri Lanka
550-27 Sudan
550-47 Syria
550-62 Tanzania

550-53 Thailand
550-89 Tunisia
550-80 Turkey
550-74 Uganda
550-97 Uruguay

550-71 Venezuela
550-32 Vietnam
550-183 Yemens, The
550-99 Yugoslavia
550-67 Zaire

550-75 Zambia
550-171 Zimbabwe